AF538951

TEACHING SOCIAL STUDIES SUCCESSFULLY

TEACHING SOCIAL STUDIES SUCCESSFULLY

PROF. MARLOW EDIGER
Division of Education
Truman State University
Kirksville, Missouri
United States of America

DR. DIGUMARTI BHASKARA RAO
R.V.R. College of Education
D-4 3,S. V. N. Colony
Guntur-522006
Andhra Pradesh, India

DISCOVERY PUBLISHING HOUSE
NEW DELHI

Edition - 2015

ISBN: 978-81-7141-596-0

Teaching Social Studies Successfully

Published by:

DISCOVERY PUBLISHING HOUSE PVT. LTD.
4383/4B, Ansari Road, Darya Ganj
New Delhi-110 002 (India)
Phone: +91-11-23279245, 43596064-65
Fax: +91-11-23253475
E-mail: discoverypublishinghouse@gmail.com
sales@discoverypublishinggroup.com
web: www.discoverypublishinggroup.com

Printed at:
Infinity Imaging Systems Delhi

PREFACE

One of the important tasks of social studies is to help its clientele develop an insight into human relationships, social values and attitudes, to enable them to appreciate the rich human cultural heritage, to make them understand the web of relationships that develop between and among people and those that develop between people and their environment, and to prepare them for effective citizenship through human experience. Its content is drawn from several social sciences such as psychology, anthropology, geography, economics, political science, history and sociology but is not determined by the discipline of any one of these. Rather, the content and organisation of social studies derive directly from the purposes for which it is taught; those purposes include an understanding of human relationships, knowledge of environment, dedication to the basic principles and values of the society in which it is taught, and a commitment to participate in the processes through which that society is maintained and improved.

This meant for preservice and inservice teachers of social studies contains a scope and sequence that will assist each teacher to provide for every pupil to achieve as optimally as possible. The content of the book integrates well with content from science, mathematics, reading literature and language arts. This book will be useful much to those who wish to teach social studies innovatively.

Prof. Marlow Ediger
Dr. D. Bhaskara Rao

CONTENTS

1

Objectives in Teaching Social Studies

The social studies teacher needs to choose carefully those objectives that pupils are to achieve. The learning opportunities are to be aligned with the stated objectives, leaving leeway for pupils' questions and comments about course content. Sequence appropriate for pupils needs to be in the offing. Quality evaluation procedures need to be used so that it can be ascertained what pupils have achieved and learned. Optimal achievement is a must!

The social studies teacher needs to start in planning the social studies curriculum with a statement of carefully selected objectives. It is vital to choose meticulously each objective that pupils are to achieve. This will determine what pupils are to learn as a result of teaching. The social studies teacher should emphasise knowledge, skills, and attitudinal objectives. Too frequently, knowledge objectives predominate in teaching. However, quality skills and attitudes are equally salient to stress in ongoing lessons and units of study. We will begin by discussing knowledge objectives for pupils to achieve. Here, broad guidelines will be given in the selection of subject matter. Subject matter chosen should be important now and, if possible, in the future, although the future is impossible to predict. It needs to be relevant for pupils to use in solving problems in lessons and units being pursued. Subject matter needs to be important and not trivial.

Too frequently, what is trivial is taught and this wastes much of the pupil's and the teacher's time. To state important objectives, it might be wise to plan with other teachers so that ideas may be shared in terms of what is important to teach in the social studies. College/university level textbooks may be consulted to obtain ideas on vital subject matter in history, geography, political science, anthropology, sociology, and economics, as the subject matter relates directly to what is being taught. College level textbooks, written in history and the social sciences, are written by specialists in their respective fields of academic knowledge. The content from these college/university texts may be presented, using a variety of learning activities, on the understanding level of pupils being taught. The learner is the focal point of instruction. It is he/she that must do the learning and is to benefit from instruction (Ediger), 1997).

Objectives for pupils to achieve must be carefully selected, not haphasardly nor carelessly. There is so much content to teach that it behooves the social studies teacher to select relevant, vital objectives for pupil attainment.

Objectives to emphasise in teaching social studies need to stress important facts, concepts, and generalisations for learner acquisition. Examples of facts to teach pupils might include the following:

1. Nebachudnezer was ruler of Babylon when capturing Jerusalem in 586 BC.
2. Mohammed, born in 570 AD, was founder of the Moslem religion.

Facts tend not be disputed and are objective. As time goes on, additional evidence may be found to change what is now considered factual. Concepts, a second kind of subject matter, consist of one word or a phrase, but not a complete sentence as is true of facts. The following are examples of concepts: king, patriarch, Balfour Declaration, Dome of the Rock, temple, Menorah, crescent, Hajj, pilgrimage, and parliament. Generalisations, a third division of knowledge, consists of a relationship of concepts to make a broader statement, such as in the following:

1. The *Hajj* should be performed at least once in a person's lifetime, according to *devout Moslems*.

2. The *Menorah* is a *large candlestick* consisting of *seven candles.*
3. There are *Five Pillars of Islam.*
4. The *Rabbi* is a *Jewish religious leader.*
5. The *Muzzein*, from a *minaret*, calls *devout Moslems to prayer* five times a day.

In each of the above named generalisations, the concepts are underlined. In addition to knowledge objectives, the social studies teacher also needs to choose skills for learners to attain. Skills emphasise putting knowledge to use or to apply what has been learned. Important skills stresses pupil's achieving critical and creative thinking, as well as problem solving abilities. Critical thinking stress the skill to separate facts from opinions, reality from fantasy, and accurate from inaccurate content. Further skills emphasise detecting bias, avoiding band wagon approaches, the everybody does it approach, as well as the straining at a gnat swallowing a camel pursuit (Ediger, 1988).

Going back to critical thinking skills, the following are examples:

1. How do religious beliefs of Islam differ from that of Judaism?
2. Analyse and tell about each of the Five Pillars of Islam.
3. What are the differences in thinking between the Arabs and the Jews pertaining to the ownership of the Holy Land?

Creative thinking, as a skill, emphasises pupil's developing unique, novel ideas. Originality is of utmost importance for the learner when engaging in creative thinking. Among others, the following stress creative thinking:

1. Which religious beliefs are common to both Islam and Judaism?
2. How do each of the Five Pillars of Islam fit together to make a whole?
3. What can be done to stress negotiations between opposing sides in the Middle East dispute?

Skills in problem solving might stress the following:

1. What caused the Balfour Declaration to fall in satisfying both the Arabs and the Jews?
2. What were the underlying reasons for issuing the Balfour Declaration?
3. How is the Balfour Declaration involved in today's problems between Arabs and Jews?

Problem solving involves the use of many reference sources to seek an answer. Considerable time is needed for problem solving endeavours. Pupils may work individually or collaboratively in attempting to secure answers to the identified problems. It is best if the social studies teacher motivates pupils to choose the problems. With problems identified, there are dilemmas in attempting to achieve answers. Problem solution does not emphasise memorising information nor lectures given by the social studies teacher, but rather the problems are open ended and require deliberation and much thought to solve.

A third kind of objective for pupils to achieve are attitudinal goals. Attitudinal goals are long term in their attainment, but they are very vital. Quality attitudes assists pupils to achieve knowledge and skills objectives more thoroughly. Good attitudes towards the self and toward others are needed so that pupils individually and collaboratively may do better in school and in society. We have spoken to student teachers and cooperating teachers whom we have supervised in the schools about which attitudinal goals are vital for pupils to attain. There is much agreement here, but these teachers do state how difficult it is for some pupils to learn good attitudes. Which attitudinal objectives then should social studies teachers then emphasise in teaching pupils?

1. becoming involved in learning in ongoing lessons and units of study.
2. taking interest in learning about the social sciences.
3. wanting to achieve at a more optimal level.
4. applying what has been learned to a new situation in the school curriculum as well as in the societal arena.

5. wishing to attain worthwhile facts, concepts, and generalisations in the social studies.
6. being accepting of others in a caring environment.
7. working harmoniously with others in a committee or collaborative setting.
8. identifying problems to solve in ongoing lessons and units of study.
9. assisting others to do well in school.
10. feelings of wanting to compete assigned work successfully.

Choosing objectives for each lesson and unit of study in the social studies is a vital part of planning that should not be minimised. The stated objectives then become a plan or blueprint for teaching what the teacher desires pupils to learn.

CRITERIA FOR SELECTING OBJECTIVES

The objectives chosen for pupils to achieve in the social studies need to be attainable. They should not frustrate pupils in learning nor should they be too easy whereby boredom in learning occurs. Pupils need to feel challenge and yet be successful learners. The objectives need to be clearly stated so that the teacher and pupils understand what is contained therein. Teachers need direction in teaching and pupils need to understand meaningfully what they are to learn. There should be rational balance among knowledge, skills, and attitudinal ends. One category of objectives is not adequate to emphasise in a quality programme of social studies instruction. Objectives need to be arranged so that pupils individually experience appropriate sequence in learning. Quality sequence or order of emphasising objectives in teaching social studies assists pupils to attain more optimally. Each objective needs to be chosen carefully so that relevance and significance are inherent. Trivia needs to be omitted. Learning opportunities need to be selected which align with the stated objectives and yet there is ample room for pupils to raise questions in ongoing lessons and units of study. Teachers need to be certain that each pupil possesses the prerequisites to achieve vital objectives. Readiness and scaffolding are two important concepts in providing background information in order that pupils are successful in achieving each objective of instruction. Evaluation of achievement needs to be aligned in relationship to the stated objectives. Diverse procedures need to be used in the evaluation process so that individual differences and needs are met among learners.

A first question that needs to be asked about the social studies curriculum stresses, 'Which objectives should pupils achieve?' These objectives need to be ordered so that each pupil may be successful in learning. Pupils need guidance to perceive purpose and reasons for achieving these objectives. A second question pertains to the selection of learning activities to achieve the stated objectives in social studies. Here is where alignment of learning opportunities and objectives for pupil attainment is vital. Another salient question emphasises the organisation of the social studies curriculum. Should there be the separate subjects, the correlated, the fused, or the integrated curriculum. Then to, we need to appraise pupils to notice if the objectives have been attained. Evaluation techniques need to be used which will satisfy pupils and the teacher that the chosen objective have been realised by the former. Thus, a variety of evaluation techniques need to be used to appraise pupil progress.

MULTICULTURAL EDUCATION

There are pupils in our school that come from multiple cultures. We have very strong feelings in emphasising a multicultural social studies curriculum. Here the objectives need to emphasise, strongly, the following:

1. acceptance of all, regardless of race, creed or color.
2. ample time spent on contributions of African Americans, Asian Americans, Mexican Americans, and Native Americans in an integrated social studies curriculum.
3. rich experiences for pupils pertaining to the language, art, music, foods, clothing, religious beliefs, homes, dance, and values in diversity of study of multiple cultures.
4. time to interact positively with pupils of diverse cultures collaboratively in ongoing lessons as well as during leisure.

5. journal writing pertaining to what was learned pertaining to minorities.
6. pupil/teacher planning involving questions that learners would like to locate information on, within committee endeavours.
7. free time for pupils to self select library books to read on minority individuals and groups.
8. surfing the internet for information on minorities.
9. doing a project with purpose, plans, caring out the plans, and evaluation procedures performed collaboratively or individually.
10. resource people such as native Vietnamese, Cambodians, as well as Spanish speaking individuals from Central America and Mexico, coming to the classroom to speak and show objects from their respective cultures.

One item that is very important to emphasise in teaching about minority groups is to avoid teaching about their holidays largely or only. Why? This may not give a true picture of the minority group being studied. The sensational then should not be taught in isolation from other major customs and values of diverse minority groups. Biases need to be avoided in the curriculum. To frequently, the all or nothing approach is emphasised in teaching about a minority group. Thus, all dress in sombreros or none. Glamorising a group also needs to be avoided; each group has problems that need identification and solutions found. Pupils and the teacher need to realise that minority groups have a significance and importance of their very own.

Teachers today must strive to understand the different frames of reference brought to class by their students. There is a need to continue to avoid the problems that can arise from the misunderstandings that develop as cultures interact in the schools today. As teachers develop a deeper knowledge of the elements of culture and life orientation of the diverse groups they teach, they can serve as role models for the students. In addition, they can promote more accepting attitudes among the diverse cultures represented in the schools and communities, greatly impacting the need for peaceful and harmonious living in today's multicultural, global society (Morales-Jones, 1998).

MULTIPLE INTELLIGENCES AND OBJECTIVES OF INSTRUCTION

Rather recently, the Multiple Intelligences movement has received much emphasis. Gardner (1993) has received considerable attention for his advocacy of Multiple Intelligences. He has identified the following intelligences:

1. verbal/linguistic which includes reading and writing skills. Most tests in their taking require these two skills. Standardized tests such as norm referenced tests include achievement tests, most IQ tests, the ACT and the SAT, personality tests, and stated mandated tests, among others.
2. logical/mathematical.
3. visual/spatial which is heavily emphasised in geometry, art, and architecture.
4. musical.
5. bodily/kinesthetic which is stressed much in endeavours including physical education, dance, athletics, and calisthenics.
6. interpersonal intelligences such as achieving much in group endeavours and in leadership tasks.
7. intrapersonal indicates high achievement on an individual basis.
8. scientific intelligence which reveals itself in achieving well in objectivity and in nature and the natural environment.

Implications for the above intelligences in the evaluation process are the following:

1. most tests emphasise reading and writing. When taking tests, this favours those individuals who excel in verbal/linguistic intelligence.
2. there are seven other intelligences listed above in which individuals may excel in the evaluation process.

3. learning activities in the curriculum should emphasise each of the seven intelligences so that each individual learner may indicate how well he/she can do in ongoing lessons and units of study.

These eight intelligences may well serve as objectives in the social studies, some being emphasised more than the others due to uniqueness of content in the social sciences. Verbal/linguistic intelligence may be stressed in reading, writing, and speaking objectives in the social studies. Reading to obtain main ideas, facts, concepts, and generalisations may become salient objectives in the social studies. Writing journal entries, poems, reports, letters, biographies and autobiographies are major forms of writing to become objectives for pupils to attain in the social studies. Speaking activities involve discussions, oral reports, dramatic activities, debates, impromptu speaking, creative and formal dramatisations, oral reading, and reader's theatre.

Gardner's second intelligence, namely logical/mathematical may be stressed in objectives in social studies such as indicating how long ago an event occurred in an ongoing lesson; the determination of the area of a nation or state; location of regions, nations, and states by using degrees of latitude and longitude; measurement of distances between two points on a map or globe; and the study of the Egyptian system of numeration in a unit on The Middle East. Logical thinking may be stressed as objectives in critical and creative thought as well as in problem solving.

Gardner's third intelligence listed above, namely visual/spatial may become an objective in the social studies for pupil attainment through guiding the latter to do art work such as murals, dioramas, pencil sketching, water color products, and the making of models as well as construction work pertaining to what is being studied in an ongoing unit of study.

Gardner's musical intelligence may be emphasised in songs sung, music written, instruments played, and other forms of musical experiences as related to what is being studied by pupils in social studies. Body/kinesthetic objectives for pupils in the social studies may be reflected in objectives such as dances of various nations and cultures, games played, and creative expression to musical recordings of diverse nations and regions.

Interpersonal intelligence may be emphasised in committee and collaborative endeavours relating to identified problems needing solutions as identified by pupils with teacher guidance in the social studies. Intrapersonal intelligence stresses pupils achieving well in individual endeavours.

Science and scientific intelligence may be stressed heavily in historical units of study whereby pupils study the contributions of scientists and science in historical sequence.

The theory of Multiple Intelligences then advocates using the talents of pupils in pursuing objectives in ongoing lessons and units of study. Also, pupils should certainly be able and permitted to reveal learnings obtained through the Multiple Intelligences psychology. Thus, a pupil strong in body/kinesthetic intelligence should indicate what has been learned in social studies through physical movement and motion. This provides challenges to the teacher to be alert and knowledgeable about how the different intelligences may be used by pupils to reveal. What has been learned in the social studies.

OBJECTIVES EMPHASISING HIGH STANDARDS

There are numerous educators who favour stressing high academic standards for all pupils. The criticism has been that too frequently the teacher has held pupils to low levels of achievement, especially minority pupils. Those advocating high standards for all pupils believe that, too often, the minority child has been held to low standards with rote learning and memorisation of the easy and the trivial. Rather, all pupils need to achieve complex objectives. Also, the teacher needs to have high expectations for these learners. Thus, there is no reason for any child to be lagging behind others. Challenging objectives, learning opportunities, and evaluation procedures should be the lot of all pupils in ongoing lessons and units of study.

According to Ann Freel (1988), what can be done to close the achievement gap among pupils?

1. Set high standards. Develop clear, high goals for what students should know and be able to do. Give everyone—teachers, parents, students—samples of student work that meet the standards so they know what is expected.

2. Ensure that all students secure a challenging curriculum. Eliminate watered down courses. Make certain that all students have a curriculum and assignments aligned with the high standards.
3. Make sure all children have expert teachers. Invest heavily in professional development and ensure that teacher expertise is fairly distributed. Teachers who have expertise in their subjects and know how to teach that content will help students reach higher levels of achievement.
4. Keep your own 'educational watch.' Monitor progress constantly. Teachers, parents, and students must have regular information about how students are doing so that midcourse corrections can be made—and results can be rewarded. The data should be presented publicly, because every community needs good, honest information about how its young are faring in school.

A perennial question pertains to how high the goals should be for pupil achievement. Can they be set too high so that many pupils are left out of being successful in the social studies.

CORE KNOWLEDGE IN THE CURRICULUM

Core knowledge has been emphasised by other educators but possibly in a different way than what E.D. Hirsch stresses presently. Thus in the past, in particular, 'teach the basics' in the curriculum has been advocated. The basics have never been identified but due stress the following, according to its advocates:

1. subject matter, emphasised as objectives, that is important and essential.
2. frills and fads are to be eliminated; only the content that is relevant should be in evidence as being taught to pupils.
3. the subject matter is necessary for more complex ideas to be taught sequentially.
4. lax discipline is to be shunned so that teachers may teach and pupils may learn.

5. pupil/teacher planning of the curriculum is not be emphasised, nor are the interests of pupils to be considered as dominating the curriculum.
6. a separate subject, not a correlated nor fused integrated curriculum, is to be in evidence.

As another educator emphasising vital subject matter be taught to pupils, Jerome Bruner (1963) in the 1960s and 1970s advocated structural ideas be identified by academic specialists in their respective areas of speciality. He advocated the following:

1. key or structural ideas would be available to teachers who might implement these major ideas as objectives for pupil attainment.
2. a spiral curriculum would be necessary so that pupils might achieve each structural idea in depth increasingly so, as they progress through the different levels of schooling.
3. pupils were to achieve these key ideas inductively.
4. methods of inquiry used were those of the academician in his/her area of academic speciality. Thus in units on history, the pupil would use methods of acquiring structural ideas as the Ph.D. historian does (Ediger, 1995).

Structural ideas then become objective for pupils to achieve in a spiral curriculum. The objectives come from the academician who specialises in an academic area, directly related to the objectives pupils are to attain.

Presently, E.D. Hirsch (1998) advocates Core Knowledge for all pupils as they achieve in sequence on diverse grade levels. In an interview, he stated that Core Knowledge is an intelligent and specific content sequence that occupies about 50 per cent of the whole curriculum. Where it has been used, it has worked dramatically well for all dimensions of educational improvement. Teachers, seeing this, have decided to adopt it. Its importance lies not in its particular consensus-built content, but simply in the fact that it is well thought out and specific sequence. There is no magic in it. Well thought out alternatives would do as well. The principle can be stated forthrightly. You cannot have an excellent and fair school without a grade-by grade core which makes all students ready to learn in the next grade. This is a necessary condition for good schooling. But it is not a sufficient condition. Good, sensitive teaching, good leadership, morale, and tone—many other things are important—but without a grade-by-grade core you cannot achieve excellence and fairness. E.D. Hirsch is well known for his book Cultural Literacy: What Every American Needs to Know (Houghton-Mifflin, 1987). His more recent book is entitled The Schools We Need and Why We Don't Have Them (Doubleday, 1996).

For objectives of instruction, Hirsch would emphasise the following:

1. a core body of knowledge that each pupil needs to learn as he/she progresses through the public school years;
2. the body of knowledge is carefully defined and identified;
3. the knowledge is ordered as pupils are promoted to each grade level;
4. the body of knowledge is necessary for pupils to learn in order to understand what is being studied;
5. prior knowledge acquired assists pupils in attaching meaning to the new core knowledge to be learned.

From the above, advocates stress core knowledge as objectives for pupils to attain. Knowledge objectives then become paramount in the curriculum. The advocates of the basics, the structure if knowledge, and Core Knowledge philosophy desire subject matter objectives to be paramount in the curriculum. In comparison, Howard Gardner (1993) advocates multiple intelligences in teaching pertaining to how pupils learn in the different academic areas as well as pupils revealing what has been learned, such as through verbal/linguistic, logical/mathematical, visual/spatial, musical, body/kinesthetic, intrapersonal, and objective/scientific approaches.

REFERENCES

Bhaskara Rao, Digumarti, ed. (1996). *Encyclopaedia of Education For All*, 5 Volumes. New Delhi, India: APH Publishing Corporation.

Bruner, Jerome (1963), *The Process of Education*. Cambridge, Massachusetts: Harvard University Press, 33.

Ediger, Marlow (1997), *Social Studies Curriculum in the Elementary School*. Fourth Edition. Kirksville, Missouri: Simpson Publishing Company, 185-187.

Ediger, Marlow (1998), *The Holy Land*. Kirksville, Missouri: Simpson Publishing Company, 53-59. I

Ediger, Marlow (1988), *The Elementary Curriculum*, Second Edition. Kirksville, Missouri: Simpson Publishing Company, 99-100.

Ediger, Marlow (1995), *Philosophy in Curriculum Development*. Kirksville, Missouri: Simpson Publishing Company, 94-96.

Ediger, Marlow and Digumarti Bhaskara Rao (1996), *Science Curriculum*. New Delhi, India: Discovery Publishing House.

Freel, Ann (1998), 'Urban Achievement in Urban Schools: What Makes the Difference?' *Education Digest*, September, 64 (1), 22. Condensed and taken from *City Schools* in an interview with Kati Haycock.

Gardner, Howard (1993), *Multiple Intelligences: The Theory in Practice*. New York: The Basic Books.

Hirsch, E.d., 'An Interview with E.D. Hirsch, 'by Burton Melancon and Michael F.Shaughnessy, (1988), *The Oklahoma Reader*, 34 (1), 12.

Morales-Jones, Carmen A. (1998), 'Understanding Hispanic Cultures; From Tolerance to Acceptance,' *The Delta Kappa Gamma Bulletin*. 64 (4), 17.

Veena Kumari, B. and Digumarti Bhaskara Rao (2000). *Psycho-Social Correlates of Achievement*. New Delhi, India: Discovery Publishing House.

2

SCOPE AND SEQUENCE IN THE SOCIAL STUDIES

Scope and sequence are two concepts that need constant appraisal in the social studies. Too frequently, the curriculum is not evaluated often enough in terms of research results and desired standards, or in terms of rational thought. Pupils need to experience quality in each social studies lesson and unit of study. Thus, the objectives need to be studied carefully to ascertain their quality as well as develop the best scope possible in ongoing lessons and units of study. Do the objectives cover a breadth of content, skills, and attitudes that provide for adequate growth of pupils in the social studies. Equally important is to consider the sequence of learning opportunities for pupils. The following question also needs to be answered, 'Does the social studies curriculum provide for experiences which harmonise with child growth and development characteristics?' The two concepts of scope and sequence will be elaborated on in that order (Ediger, 1998, 139-144).

SCOPE IN TERMS OF ORGANISING THE SOCIAL STUDIES

How should the social studies curriculum be organised? A separate subject approach might be used. Here, a single academic discipline provides most of the subject matter for a social studies unit. Thus, for example, history might be stressed largely in stating objectives for pupils to achieve. We use the word 'largely' since it would be very difficult to stress the academic discipline of history only, in teaching a unit in the social studies. Why? Historical events took place in a specific region or area. For example, when teaching a unit on World War Two, the happenings occurred in identifiable areas, such as the 'D Day' invasion of France, or the 'Battle of the Bulge' in the southern border of Belgium. Thus, geography needs to be brought into the unit of study. With the use of maps and globes, the areas where World War Two took place may be located (Ediger, 1988, 97).

A step which relates subject matter increasingly so is the correlated curriculum. Here, two or three academic disciplines are taught as being related, not as separate entities. In the unit on World War Two referred to above, the history of those incidences will be taught along with geography in terms of the places of events occurring (Ediger, 1990, 31-36). Culture, or anthropology and sociology may become an integral part of the unit. Certainly, the home front during World War Two had a definite culture with its songs and music, such as 'Don't Sit Under the Apple Tree,' or 'Praise the Lord and Pass the Ammunition.'

A further approach in organising the social studies curriculum stresses the fused curriculum. Here, pupils might experience all the social sciences as being related, namely history, geography, anthropology, sociology, economics, and political science. For the latter two academic disciplines, pupils might study the economic situation during World War Two such as the kinds of jobs available during the time and the Gross National Product (GNP) during these war years. Political science may stress laws, rules, and regulations during World War Two, including rationing of certain goods and services.

One step beyond that of the fused curriculum is the integrated approach. Here, academic disciplines tend more and more to lose their boundaries and borders. In addition to the fused curriculum disciplines, mathematics, science, physical education, and the language arts might be included. Very frequently with the integrated curriculum, problem solving is emphasised. Academic disciplines needed depend upon the problem that is identified and to be solved in an ongoing unit of study. Thus, pupils with teacher guidance identify a problem. The problem is clearly stated and adequately delimited. Next, information is gathered in answer to the problem. The result is an hypothesis. The hypothesis is tested in a lifelike situation, not using a paper/pencil test. If the hypothesis stands up during the test, it is accepted. If not, the tentative hypothesis is rejected or modified.

The scope of the social studies might then emphasise the separate subjects, the correlated, the fused, or the integrated curriculum (Ediger, 1995, 163-165).

SCOPE IN THE SOCIAL STUDIES

What should be the breadth of subject matter taught in the social studies? Even within a unit, what would equal quality in terms of scope in teaching and learning? This a problem that social studies teachers and supervisors need to study, analyse, and come up with a viable solution. For example, if pupils are studying a unit on the Middle East area of the world, which nations should be included to provide for excellence in the concept of *scope* in the curriculum?

There are numerous nations in the Middle East. How many might pupils study in depth? Thus, the following nations in the Middle East might become a part of that unit: Lebanon, Jordan, Syria, Israel, Palestine, Egypt, Qatar, United Arab Emirates, Turkey, Iran, Iraq, Libya, among others. Numerous nations are represented here. Choices need to be made if depth teaching is to be stressed throughout the unit of study. Sometimes, a teacher may stress *depth* teaching for selected countries and *survey approaches* for others, due to time limitations in unit teaching. After all, there are numerous units of study to be taught in one school year and throughout the public school years. Survey approaches are not as viable and recommendable as compared to depth teaching (Ediger, 1995, 29-31).

Another problem in determining scope has to do with which areas of the social sciences should be stressed in each unit of study. If five nations are selected for teaching about the Middle East, for example, how many social science disciplines should be taught? The following academic areas might then be included in ascertaining the scope of the social studies:

1. history with a study of relevant events of the past of the nations being considered;
2. geography with essential land forms and climate being included in a social studies unit;
3. political science with emphasis placed upon governmental systems of countries being studied;
4. economics with a study of goods and services or gross national product produced in a given year or series of years;
5. culture with its customs, languages spoken, manners, music, dances, architecture, foods, archaeological, and other human inventions.

When depth teaching each of the above named social science disciplines together with the selected nation(s) to be taught provides increased problems in determining scope in the social studies. A teacher who has strengths in the following areas may even wish to add.

1. psychology with its emphasis upon the study of individual human behaviour.
2. social psychology and its stress upon the influence of institutions in society upon human behaviour (Ediger, 1995, 25-26).

Too frequently, state departments of education emphasise the inclusion of history and geography in testing pupils in terms of state mandated achievement in the social studies. We feel stressing these two social science academic disciplines only, gives pupils a rather narrow view of human beings and their motivation in life. When including additional social science disciplines, pupils increase their knowledge of human beings in the societal arena.

Scope in the social studies curriculum has been defined, too, in terms of human activities on the planet earth. Thus, the objectives pupils are to achieve might stress the following (Ediger, 1997):

1. human relationships in relating effectively to others;
2. individual endeavours that need to be satisfied and fulfilled;

3. civic responsibility in organisations developed to provide for effective rule and order in a society;
4. ethics in defining proper relationships among and with others;
5. vocational roles that satisfy economic and personal needs of human beings;
6. family responsibilities in the social domain;
7. emphasising healthful living among societal members;
8. knowledge, skills, and attitudes necessary for problem solving in a democracy.

Thus, for example, in having pupils achieve objective number one above, the social studies teacher needs to have pupils learn to work collaboratively within committee settings. There need to be definite criteria which pupils need to meet to fulfill human relationship objectives and responsibilities. These include respecting and accepting others, becoming a caring person, assisting others to achieve well, as well as developing a desire to work well with others and toward optimal progress and achievement.

Objective number two above stresses developing interests in avocations and hobbies, finding ultimately that the world of work is satisfying, engaging in constructive and not destructive personal behaviour, and experiencing life and living worthwhile rewarding.

In continuing with the rest of the above named objectives, objective number three pertaining to civic responsibilities stresses pupils learning to live by the laws of the land, be they local, state, or federal levels of government. Pupils should also think of needed changes to be made in society and work towards making these changes in an orderly manner. Pupils need to believe in fulfilling citizenship rights whereby they take a future active part in elections, think of running for elective offices, help to keep the environment free from misuse and pollution, and assist those needing help in everyday tasks in life.

Objective number four pertaining to ethics emphasises dealing honestly and truthfully with others, caring for the welfare of people in society, and being a morally, responsible individual.

Objective number five pertaining to vocational roles stresses studying and finding work that benefits the self and others in the societal arena, earning an income which buys needed goods and services, working together harmoniously with others in school and at the future work place, and improving situations in the school and in the societal setting.

Objective number six emphasises family responsibilities whereby the pupil is a contributing member to the family, fulfills his/her obligations in the family, and gives as well as receives love from family members.

Objective number seven stresses healthful living emphasising a clean environment, protection from diseases for the self as well as for others, eating nutritious meals, receiving proper medical and dental care, as well as working toward optimal mental health.

CRITERIA FOR SELECTING THE SCOPE OF THE CURRICULUM

There are numerous criteria for choosing the scope of the curriculum. The scope needs to have adequate breadth and yetdepth teaching is possible pertaining to each objective of instruction. If the scope is too narrow, pupils may not learn what is necessary in any academic discipline to truly understand the relationship of subject matter involved. Should the scope be too broad, a watered down curriculum may be in the offing. Survey teaching may then be emphasised whereby pupils do not have ample opportunities to understand and attach meaning to ongoing activities and experiences. It is indeed a problem to identify a middle ground between too wide or too narrow a scope in the curriculum (Ediger, 1995, 23-28).

We would suggest that teachers, administrators, supervisors, and university professors in their academic areas of speciality get together and harmoniously develop an appropriate scope in the curriculum, Bruner (1961) advocated the involvement of academicians in selecting subject matter for pupils to achieve. This is a very viable recommendation to make. He also advocated that pupils learn to work as the academician does in his/her academic area of specialisation. Thus, the historian would be involved in selecting key ideas for pupils to achieve in history, or the geographer would be involved in choosing structural content for pupils to achieve in geography. The methods of the historian, for example, would also be identified and used by pupils. Thus, pupils would lean to use primary and secondary data sources to evaluate and use in problem solving. This sounds like a complex task in securing input from academicians, but it is certainly important. Pupils might then acquire major ideas, instead of trivia, in social studies units of study. It is always important for public school personnel to be involved in appraising subject matter taught to perceive if the content selected is vital, relevant, purposeful, and significant for learners. Evaluating the scope of the curriculum is even more important. There is much subject matter to be taught in the social studies. There are many skills that need to be acquired by learners. Time is of utmost importance in teaching what is relevant. Thus, the scope of the curriculum needs careful scrutiny and identification. The breadth of content to be taught may become too broad and the subject matter and skills therein may not be taught in depth. And yet, the scope needs to be broad enough so that social studies content and abilities become adequate to truly understood the people being studied. Erroneous ideas come about when what is taught is so narrow in scope. Perhaps, stereotyping of human beings is then an end result. We strongly recommend that each social studies unit have content and skills covering history, geography, economics, political science, sociology, and anthropology.

If it is not possible to secure the services of academicians in choosing structural ideas and the scope of the social studies, we recommend the following:

1. teachers, supervisors, and administrators study and evaluate what should be taught in terms of knowledge and skills;
2. grade level teachers periodically meet together to identify vital content and skills for each unit of study;
3. workshops and other inservice meetings be held so that collaboratively vital objectives may be determined;
4. faculty meetings zero in on identifying salient scope in the curriculum. From a faculty meeting, teachers may meet in committees to choose what is important to teach in determining scope in the curriculum;

5. academicians in their respective areas of speciality be invited as resource personnel at inservice programmes to improve the social studies Curriculum;
6. teachers study and read content from college/university level textbooks in the social sciences to select vital content and skills for pupil acquisition in elementary school social studies;
7. professional meetings should be attended by teachers, at the state and national levels of social studies, to learn more about scope and the general social studies curriculum;
8. a learning community consisting of teachers, supervisors, administrators, and parents set up to study the scope of the curriculum;
9. a professional library of educational journals be available to teachers to study the diverse elements of the curriculum;
10. research studies made to ascertain what other school systems and states are doing to determine the social studies curriculum.

A good school is a busy school accomplishing, achieving, growing, and developing in curriculum improvement. The status quo is not satisfactory and needs to be evaluated critically and creatively within the framework of problem solving to come up with better objectives, learning opportunities, and appraise techniques for pupils.

EXPECTATIONS OF EXCELLENCE

The National Council for the Social Studies (NCSS, USA, 1994) came up with a detailed study of standards in teaching social studies that are voluntary for teachers to follow in teaching pupils. Their ten thematic strands in the social studies which might well provide quality scope are the following (Italics mine):

1. **Culture**. *Here, pupils might study common characteristics of different cultures. They may also study belief systems, cultural change, and language*

systems of diverse cultures with their affects upon human beings.

2. **Time, continuity, and change.** *Acquiring relevant events of the past as well as reconstruction of the past are goals for pupils to achieve. Pupils should attempt to understand and attach meaning to earlier significant periods of time. Change is a key concept for pupils to realise when studying vital happenings history.*

3. **People, places, and environments.** *Here, pupils are to study the significance of geography in their own personal lives as well as places removed from the local, state, and national arenas to include the world in its diverse manifestations. Concepts such as land forms, region, latitude, longitude, parallels, meridians, and changes that occur in the environments are important for pupils to attach meaning to and come up with viable spatial views.*

4. **Individual development and identity.** *Thus, a study of psychology and sociology become important for pupils. Learning is a continuous process and is ongoing, be it in formal or informal educational programmes. Individuals must have personal needs met such as physiological, safety and security, participation through belonging to groups and memberships in social organisations, acknowledgment of special capabilities possessed, and knowledge needs for application and for recreation.*

5. **Individuals, groups, and organisations.** *Learners need to have adequate knowledge, skills, and abilities pertaining to institutions as they affect human behaviour. The family, religious organisations, economic institutions, and civic/social organisations do impinge upon the thinking and thoughts of each person. Pupils should certainly understand in depth how numerous organisations affect their personal behaviour formally and informally. This brings into the social studies the academic disciplines of sociology and anthropology, in particular.*

6. **Power, authority, and government.** *Pupils need to study in depth how political institutions affect human behaviour. Political science or a study of local state, and federal governments become salient. Here, pupils need to understand the concept of power. Any level of government can be highly powerful and have its affects on human beings in a direct and indirect way. The role of government and the role of human rights need to be understood and evaluated by pupils. Making changes and the procedures to do so is highly important for pupils to understand. Majority versus minority wants are important to consider in any power structure of government. Governments need to change as time elapses to be current and meet human needs.*
7. **Production, distribution, and consumption.** *These are salient concepts for pupils to understand meaningfully and make application of these abstractions. The study of economics needs to be integrated into the social studies. In society, there are farmers, businesses, companies, and corporations that produce goods and services. All people in society are consumers of goods and services. Problems arise in society pertaining to which and how many goods and services to produce as well as who is to consume these goods and services. The gaps between rich and or may be great indeed whereby lavish life styles may be compared with those of very needy people.*
8. **Science, technology, and society.** *These areas certainly do make for rapid changes in society. Automation in factories and businesses, wide use of computer technology in an information age, as well as modern means of transportation/communication have transformed and modified the entire world in being brought closer together in terms of interactions. Pupils need to study science and technology in an integrated social studies curriculum whereby the benefits of science and technology are available to all in society and not a favoured few or select group.*

9. **Global connections.** *The areas of a quality environment. Health care, human rights, inter dependencies, as well as political and social differences among peoples need to be studied by pupils with the intent of working towards human rights for all on the planet earth. The areas of geography, sociology, anthropology, and science become important contributors in the social studies curriculum.*

10. **Civic ideals and practices.** *Pupils need to learn about and be involved as an active participant in society as well as implement tenets of being a good citizen. Pupils should be concerned about making a positive difference for all peoples, as members in the societal arenas.*

The above ten named areas then might well comprise a quality scope or breadth of what is to be studied by learners in a quality social studies curriculum. Faculty need to study and analyse the scope of the present social studies curriculum with the intent of moving toward a revised concept of scope or what should be taught. This is to be done to provide the best social studies curriculum possible for pupils.

MULTIPLE INTELLIGENCES THEORY

Howard Gardner (1993) emphasises in multiple intelligences theory (MIT) that pupils should use their strengths in learning in different curriculum areas. Regardless of the unit being taught, pupils should have their needs met with learning in terms of intelligences possessed. Dr., Gardner identified the following intelligences, (italics mine):

1. **verbal linguistic**. *Here, pupils may experience reading and writing activities in the social studies.*

2. **logical/mathematical.** *As needed, pupils need to experience learning opportunities in mathematics and logical thought in ongoing social studies lessons and units of study. For example, the history oft he Egyptian System of Numeration might well be brought into a unit on The Middle East (Ediger, 1998).*

3. **visual/spatial.** *Pupils may do art projects and construction activities that are directly related to what is being taught in the social studies (Ediger, Journal of instructional Psychology, 1997, 190).*

4. **musical.** *There are numerous compositions in music pertaining to any historical period of time, such as, 'Mine Eyes have Seen the Glory of the Coming of the lord,' written during the Civil War years of 1861-1865 (Ediger, 1996, 242-246).*

5. **body/kinesthetic.** *pupils learn much by participating in folk dances that are stressed in the related ongoing unit of study. When I supervised student teachers in the public schools, one committee of pupils devised a folk dance pertaining to the fiords of Norway, in a unit on the Scandinavian Countries of Europe.*

6. **interpersonal.** *Here, pupils like to work in committees and group/collaborative endeavours. These pupils achieve more so in group as compared to individual endeavours. Their intelligence indicates being highly capable in collaborative work in the social studies. Thus, there should be many opportunities to engage in committee work such as constructing objects and items related to the current unit.*

7. **intrapersonal intelligence.** *Pupils in this category achieve more optimally when working individually as compared to committee endeavours. Here, pupils may engage in individual activities that could be the same/similar as mentioned above for these who like interpersonal educational experiences.*

LOGICAL SEQUENCE IN THE SOCIAL STUDIES

Sequence pertains to the order of objectives to be achieved by pupils and to the order of learning opportunities for pupils to achieve these objectives. It is very important for the social studies teacher to provide the best possible sequence for learners in teaching and learning situations. One approach is to stress a logical approach. Here, the teacher chooses which objectives pupils should achieve in a particular order. Logically, the teacher evaluates each objective to ascertain if the order for pupils to achieve the stated objectives moves from the easiest to those increasingly more complex. The teacher is the judge. As the unit progresses, the teacher may notice if he/she is providing the best logical sequence based upon how well pupils are learning. With formative evaluation, the teacher within the unit being taught appraises if changes need to be made in sequential learnings for pupils, based on learner success in each ordered activity (Ediger, 1997, 20-25).

There are selected computerised programmes which contain programmed items, arranged logically in ascending order of complexity. For example, pupils in a software programme, read a few sentences from a frame on the monitor, respond to a question covering content read. The learner obtains feedback on the monitor if he/she responded correctly. Generally, the response typed in by the pupil in answer to a question is multiple choice in format. Sometimes, if a pupil responded incorrectly he/she is given a second chance to respond correctly. If correct originally, the pupil is rewarded, perhaps, with a smile face on the monitor. If incorrect, the pupil involved is provided the correct answer. In either case, the pupil is then ready for the next sequential item in linear programming. Usually, the programmes follow a read, respond, and check procedure over and over again on the monitor. The programmer may write these items with a sequence whereby pupils respond correctly ninety-five per cent accuracy rate. Thus, if the steps are to great between two items, an additional item amy be added. Pilot studies are made to take out weak sequences as written by programmers. With programmed learning, results of pupils are given in numerical terms, such as per cent correct, percentile ranking, or standard deviation indicators (Ediger, 1996, 123-124).

State mandated objectives written in behavioural terms may also contain a logical sequence. The behaviourally stated objectives are written very precisely and in measurable terms. Either a pupil does/does not attain an objective as a result of instruction. The learning opportunities, chosen by the teacher, need to assist pupils to achieve each objective in sequence. Generally, the learning opportunities are chosen by the teacher. Criterion referenced tests (CRT), also a part of the state mandated objectives, measure how well pupils do in achieving the stated objectives. The CRT is aligned with the objectives. A logical sequence is in evidence since the teacher may order the objectives as well as the learning opportunities for pupils to achieve each objectives. Pupils are given these state mandated CRTs at designated intervals such as grades two, six, and ten. What pupils did not achieve may be diagnosed and remedied. numerical figures again are provided as to how well pupils did, such as per cent correct, percentiles, or standard deviations.

Behaviourism as a psychology of learning stresses the use of precise objectives, written in measurable terms. The pupils either does/does not achieve any single objective as a result of instruction. The learning opportunities are aligned with the objectives so that pupils may achieve each objective in teaching and learning stituations. Also, the testing approach and procedures, generally multiple choice items, are formally aligned with the objectives. Validity is then involved with the testing done, which matches closely with the stated objectives. With machine scoring, reliability should be high. If a pupil is then tested again through test/retest, alternative forms, or split/half, his/her reliability should be quite consistent numerically. There are exceptions to this statement. If a pupil is tired, hungry, ill, or upset emotionally, he/she may not test consistently from one setting to the next in testing situations.

With behaviourism, sequence in learning resides within the logical thinking of the programmer or teacher. Should state madated objectives have a definite recommended seqence, then the order of objectives arragement resides within the state department of education whose supervision selected the ends for pupils achievement (Ediger, 1996, 41-42).

PSYCHOLOGICAL SEQUENCE IN THE SOCIAL STUDIES

A psychological sequence stresses the importance of rather heavy pupil involvement in choosing the order of objectives as well as learning opportunities to achieve each objective. Several procedures may be mentioned here. One approach is to use learning stations. These may be developed with pupil/teacher planning. The following stations, as an example, may have been planned for an ongoing unit of study:

1. divers kinds of art activities;
2. different materials available for reading content;

3. musical experiences;
4. drama and dramatic learning opportunities;
5. a food making centre;
6. a folk dance/movement station;
7. an audio-visual centre;
8. a material objects place for viewing and learning.

A task card may be located at each centre or station to provide suggestions for pupil learning. The learner may then choose which sequential tasks to work on from the task cards at the different centres. The selections made may be either individual or collaborative endeavours. Sequence resides within the pupils, not the teacher nor in textbooks.

A different approach in stressing a psychological social studies curriculum is to emphasise a contract system. Here, the pupil with teacher guidance develps a contact of learning activities to be completed by a certain agreed upon date and signed by both the learner and the involved teacher. Thus as an example, the pupil may work out a contract such as the following to complete individually or within a committee:

1. read pages 35-60 in the basal textbook and wrtie ten main ideas covering the content read;
2. make a model relief map of the geographical setting;
3. read and summarize a self selected library book that relates to the content in the basal, number one above;
4. develop a mural of three important concepts in the ongoing unit of study;
5. write a formal dramatics presentation to be performed in a group within the classroom setting.

With the above named contract, the pupils sequences the experiences in a psychological manner. Generally, humanism, as a psychology of learning, stresses a child centered curriculum whereby the learner is heavily actively planning and choosing what to learn in an ordered way. Humanists tend to emphasise the following:

1. the learner being active in selecting objectives, learning opportunities, and appraisal procedures;
2. the teacher encourages, assists, and helps individuals and committees to make optimal progress;
3. the child is to do the learning not an outside source such as the teacher, state departments of education with their state mandated objectives and criterion reference tests, nor from content involving commercially purchased instructional materials, unless these are personal choices of the pupil;
4. sequence or order in learning must come from the one who is to do the learning;
5. a variety of learning opportunities need to be in the offing so that choices may truly be made, from among alternatives (Ediger, 1997, 20-26).

Conclusion

Scope is an important concept which needs adequate attention in the social studies curriculum. Scope needs to be evaluated in terms of how to organise the curriculum, the involved academic disciplines to be included, and inclusion of human activties that permeate society. Definite criteria need to be used to appraise each procedure in determining scope. The National Council for the Social Studies in 1994 came out with an excellent set of ten concepts whereby the scope of the social studies may be ascertained. Multiple intelligances theory has also much to contribute in determining scope.

Sequence may be implemented through a teacher centered approach. The teacher then logically orders the objectives and learning activties for pupils in the social studies. In contrast, a psychological sequence is learner entered whereby there is considerable input from pupils in selecting objectives and learning activities int he social studies.

Scope and sequence need to be evaluated constinuously to implement a quality social studies curriculum which assists each pupil to achieve optimally.

REFERENCE

Bhaskara Rao, Digumarti, C. Sridevi and K. Vijaya (1995), *Achievement in Social Studies*. New Delhi, India: Discovery Publishing House.

Bruner, Jerome (1961), *The Process of Education*. Cambridge, Massachusetts: Harvard University Press.

Ediger, Marlow (1998), 'Block of time in Teaching the Social Studies,' *College Student Journal,* 25 (2), 139-144.

Ediger, Marlow (1988), *The Elementary Curriculum,* Second Edition, Kirksville, Missouri: Simpson Publishing Company, 97.

Ediger, Marlow (1990), 'Maps and globes in the social studies in the elementary school,' *Geografia w Szkole,* 43 (217), 31-36, published in Poland.

Ediger, Marlow (1995), *Philosophy in Curriculum Development.* Kirksville, Missouri: Simpson Publishing Company, 163-165.

Ediger, Marlow (1995), 'The School Principal and Curricular Concerns,' *Education Magazine,'* Qatar National Commission for Education, nr. 114, 29-31, published in the Middle East.

Ediger, Marlow (1995), 'School Administration as Decision Making,' *Education Magazine*, Qatar National Commission for Education, nr. 115, 25-26.

Ediger, Marlow (1995), 'Leadership in Curriculum Development,' *Education Magazine*, Qatar National Commission for Education, nr. 113, 23-28.

Ediger, Marlow (1997), 'Portfolios, the Pupil, and the Teacher,' *Education Magazine*, Qatar National Commission for Education, nr. 120, 20-26.

Ediger, Marlow (1996), *Essays in School Administration* Kirksville, Missouri: Simpson Publishing Company, 126-135.

Ediger, Marlow (1997), *Social Studies Curriculum in the Elementary School*, Fourth Edition. Kirksville, Missouri: Simpson Pubilshing Company, 41-67.

Ediger, Marlow (1998), *Teaching Mathematics in the Elementary* School, Kirksville, Missouri: Simpson Publishing Company, 216-245.

Ediger, Marlow (1997), 'Social Studies and the Middle School Student,' *Journal of Instructional Psychology*, 24(3), 190.

Ediger, Marlow (1996), Elementary Education, Kirksille, Missouri: Simpson Publishing Company, 242-246.

Ediger, Marlow (1996), 'The Principal and the Curriculum,' *The Progress of Education,* 70(6), 123-124, published in India.

Ediger Marlow (1997), *The Modern Elementary School.* Kirksville, Missouri: Simpson Publishing, 20-25.

Ediger, Marlow (1996), Technology in the School Curriculum,' *Journal of Research in Educational Media,* 3(4), 41-42, published in India.

Ediger, Marlow and D. Bhaskara has (2000), *Teaching Mathematics Successfully,* New Delhi, India: Discovery Publishing House.

Gardner, Howard (1993), *Multiple Intelligences: Theory into Practice,* New York: Basic Books.

NCSS (1994). *Expectations of Excellence—Curriculum Standards for Social Studies.* Developed by the Task Force for the National Council for the Social Studies and approved by the NCSS Board of Directors, 1994. Washington, DC. NCSS.

3

TRENDS AND ISSUES IN THE SOCIAL STUDIES

Social studies teachers and supervisors need to study recent innovations in the teaching of social studies and compare these with what is presently being emphasised in the local curriculum. Before any changes are made, teachers and supervisors need to analyse, synthesise, and appraise any given trend. A study of trends in teaching social studies may come from the following data sources: educational journals and publications from professional organisations: teacher education textbooks; workshops; attendance at local, state, and national meetings for educators; and discussions within the framework of a community of learners.

From these data sources, what might emerge as relevant trends in teaching social studies?

AN INTEGRATED SOCIAL STUDIES CURRICULUM

Social studies educators are advocating that content in the social studies needs to represent a unified curriculum. Separate academic disciplines such as history and geography should not be stressed in ongoing lessons and units of study. Rather, teachers need to plan that diverse academic disciplines should be related so that pupils perceive knowledge as being an integrated whole.

In teaching thematic units in social studies, the teacher may emphasise the following in an integrated curriculum.

1. history with its content on relevant events of the past.
2. geography with stress placed on concepts such as location, place, human-environment, movement, and regions.
3. political science with emphasis on studies of diverse forms of government, be it federal, state, or local.
4. economics with its study of different economic systems on the planet earth. Studies also include the Gross National Product (GNP) of a nation. The GNP includes all the goods and services produced by any nation in a certain interval of time, such as one year.
5. sociology with its primary emphasis being upon pupils studying roles, norms, economic status, and human organisations, in general.
6. anthropology with its stress placed upon a study of culture, including the religious beliefs, values, art, architecture, music, drama, and dance of a given subculture of nation.

Additional academic disciplines that might become a part of social studies include mathematics. For example, in a unit on ancient Egypt, pupils might study the Egyptian system of numeration. Science might become a part of social studies thematic units when the history of transportation is studied by pupils. Thus in studying the invention of the steamboat by Robert fulton in 1806, learners should understand the scientific principles involved in what steam power is and how it can be harnessed for water transportation. These are merely examples of how mathematics and science might well become a relevant part of an integrated social studies unit of instruction. Teachers developing thematic units should allow guildelines such as the following in thinking about the degree that diverse academic disciplines should be integrated:

1. does it serve a useful purpose without 'forcing' integration of content for its own sake?

2. will it guide pupils to understand subject matter better pertaining to the unit being studied in social sutides?
3. does it prevent from weakening the social science discipliens that provide content for teaching social studies?
4. will it provide for quality sequence in teaching social studies?
5. might too many academic disciplies be brought in to a thematic social studies unit so that the social studies looses its identity?

The emphasis should be upon quality in a social studies unit, not content integration merely to have it be so. The social science disciplines should predominate in ongoing social studies lessons and units of study. Additional academic discipines merely enrich or guide pupils to perceive relationship of necessary ideas in a thematic unit. What pupils have gained in subject matter knowledge in the social studies should be used in school and society. Ediger (1996) wrote:

Too frequently, school and society are separated from each other. This results in the social studies becoming qutie abstract for pupils. Learners might then acquire much abstract knowledge in terms of facts, concepts, and generalisations, but meaning here is minimised. For learners to be ablve to use what has been acquired, they need to have numerous opportunities to apply what has been achieved. Application should be made in the real world of society so that two separate realms, school versus society, do not exist . . .

Pupils should have ample opportunities to perceive the relationship of the school curriculum and the community. The two should be integrated, not separate entities. Too frequently, pupils fail to see how the social studies can become useful and functional.

GUILDELINES FOR TEACHERS IN TEACHING SOCIAL STUDIES

Social studies teachers need to have appropriate guidelines to use in developing and implementing thematic units of study. Each guideline followed needs to stress what educational psychologists recommend in the instructional endeavour.

A. Teachers Need to Teach in a Manner which Captures Learner Interest

We have noticed dull units taught by student teachers and cooperating teachers who we supervised in the schools. There are many things these teachers might do to change from drab social studies teaching to that which captures learner interest. We have observed comparable units taught in two different classrooms, one being very interesting to pupils while the other classroom experiences boredom. What makes the differences between these teachers? Teachers who make for boredom in the classroom fail to provide a variety of learning opportunities, do not provide for diverse levels of achievement, are impersonal in their teaching, do not assist pupils to feel they belong and develop feelings of belonging, indicate a lack of caring and empathy for learners, and show favouritism to selected pupils. These traits need identification and changes made from what is to what should be in teaching elementary school social studies.

What do good social studies teachers do that is opposite of the ineffective once? We have observed the following contextual traits of excellent school social studies teachers:

1. strive hard to secure and maintain interests of each pupil in ongoing lessons and units of study;
2. use different teaching strategies and materials of instruction to engage learners actively in the instructional process;
3. accept all pupils as having worth and value in the curriculum;
4. care for the achievement and welfare of each learner;
5. are responsible persons who prepare well for teaching each day and are able to implement quality instruction;
6. have a good knowledge of social studies curriculum development;
7. participate actively in diverse kinds of inservice education activities;
8. learn from other teachers involving a community of learners, such as in the teacher's lounge, before

school, after school, and other suitable times during the day and week;

9. possess positive altitudes toward inservice education in its numerous forms;
10. appraises the self to determine areas of teaching social studies that need strengthening.

With the above enumerated items, the quality social studies teachers works in the direction of securing and maintaining pupil interest in the social studies. If pupils already possess interest in pursuing a specific social studied unit, the teahcer needs to assist pupils to build on these interests so that more optimal achievement may result. Eisner (1985) wrote:

The admonition to build o the child's interest is often made as a corrective for educational programmes that neglect them as sources of curriculum aims and content. Traditional educational programmes are developed out of principles that identify educational value within particular subject matters or disciplines. Becoming educated means learning how to use the ideas within these disciplines. This approach has two educational devastating consequences. first, it is often irrelevant to the child. Second, it fails to cultivate the child's idiosyncrasy by providing few opportunities that are of particular importance to the child.

B. Teachers Need to Provide Meaningful Learning Experiences for all Pupils

Meaning theory stresses pupils understanding what has been learned. Thus pupils can say or write in their very own words that which has been learned. If pupils understand facts, concepts, generalisations, and mian ideas, they are able comprehend subject matter being studied.

We have observed teachers who teach highly factual materials to pupils. Thus pupil memorise many names, dates and places in social studies units of instruction. Seemingly, these memorised names, dates and places are soon forgotten. One has only to discuss with pupils that which was memorsied to notice that a rapid rate of forgetting occurs. However, the pupils that experienced meaning in ongoing lessons and units of study are able to retain for a much longer period of time content achieved in the social studies. It seems as if all people desire to remember better what was learned. We truly believe if individuals made a point to understnad what was taught, they would have a much better retention rate. Each person should monitor along the way if subject matter acquired is understood in a meaningful way. The receiver of information, either inductively or deductively, must evaluate the self to ascertain if content is being understood.

C. Teachers Need to Guide Pupils to Perceive Reasons for Learning

The Pupil may establish these purposes. Thus the learner has questions and problems identified which need solutions. The purpose for learning here is to obtain answers for these questions and problems. Reasons for study and achievement are an end result.

If pupils do not identify purposes, the teacher needs to state relevant questions and problems. Pupils then need to be stimulated to accept these purposes. It can be done. We have observed numerous teachers who guide pupils to accept predetermined questions and problems. A good videotape, properly introduced, provides readiness and acceptance for studying a new unit of study. Sometimes the readiness or background information factors are crucial for pupils to perceive purpose in learning. If pupils do not possess this knowledge to benefit from the new thematic unit, they might well fail to grasp purpose for studying the new unit of study.

The teacher may state or present reasons to pupils for studying the oncoming unit. These reasons need to be given clearly and concisely. Audiovisual materials may be used along with each reason. The reasons for studying the new unit and the scenes from the video-tape should harmonise and relate to each other. Under these conditions, we have found, pupils accept what the teacher has provided as reasons for studying the new unit. Along the way, as the unit progresses in being taught, the teacher needs to provide additional reasons or review the reasons previously provided. The social studies teacher may observe which pupils possess reasons and which do not for pursuing, achieving, and growing.

Informal observations by the teacher can provide valuable feedback to the teachers as to the degree that learners are actively engaged in learning. Pupil purpose is a valuable concept to emphasise in teaching and learning situations. We truly believe that pupils fail to learn as well as they should due to a low purpose level. The teacher may do a good job of emphasising these purposes so that pupils truly learn much. Stating the objectives, previous to instruction for a unit or daily lesson can do much to guide pupils to perceive purpose in learning.

Having pupils perceive purpose inductively is more difficult to implement as compared to deductive procedures whereby the teacher states why a unit or lesson are important to the pupil. However, we have observed numerous teachers who do a good job of having pupils perceive purpose inductively. Here, the social studies teacher raises questions for pupils to answer as to why a unit or lesson is important to pursue. Quality questions, stated with clarity and with the use of visual materials, can generate purposes from pupils for learning. Energy levels rise when pupils perceive purpose for learning. Enthusiasm begets purpose for learning. Reasons are then accepted for data gathering and problem solving.

There are educators, largely behaviourists, who believe strongly in pupils receiving awards for achieving well in social studies. To besure, there are pupils who achieve more if awards are given for learning as compared to depending upon intrinsic motivation whereby learning is its own reward. if awards are provide for achieving, the following guidelines should be followed by teachers:

1. announce to pupils prior to instruction what specifically needs to be learned to achieve the award;
2. state the objective in measurable terms so that there will be no misunderstanding if a pupil has not achieved satisfactorily to achieve the reward;
3. give the award immediately after a pupil has achieved at the satisfactory announced level. If tokens are to be given upon satisfactorily completing an assignment, this should be announced prior to instruction. These tokens may then be exchanged for a prize at a more suitable time;

4. display, indicate, or show to pupils what the prizes are for satisfactory achievement. By seeing the prizes, a pupil might be motivated to work hard and achieve;
5. keep your word on which prizes will be given. if an alternate prize to be given, due to running out of certain awards, an announcement needs to be made prior to instruction.

D. Pupils Need to Experience Success in Social Studies

We believe that pupils need to be as successful as possible in the social studies. Failure comes about in everyday life without planning for it. So, let us plan for pupil success in each unit and lesson. The self concept of the learner goes downhill with experiences involving falure. Successive failures means that a pupil does not feel he/she can achieve success in learning. Thus to raise pupil achievement, success on the part of learners individually needs to be in the offing. The teacher then needs to select objective which are new but attainable and challenging. Individual differences in terms of abilities, interests, and talents need to be considered. Learners are different from each other in many ways including achievement in the social studies. The present achievement level of each pupil needs to be considered with care so that success in learning might be an end result. Pupils individually and in committees may achieve objectives at diverse levels of complexity. Objectives individually or collaboratively may be achieved by learners at different rates of speed. The teacher's goal here is to have each pupil learn as much as possible. Success in goals attainment should be an end result.

E. Pupil Application of What Has Been Learned

Ample opportunities need to be in the offing whereby pupils make application of previsouly acquired learnings. Problem solving is a good, practical way to use knowledge. Thus with problem selection, pupils need to gather data or information for its solution. In finding and using the information, pupils make use of what is and has been learned. The answer to the problem or question if an hypothesis and needs testing in new situations. The testing of the hypothesis also involves using what has been learned. An hypothesis needs to be as accurate as possible; thus testing in a practical situation makes for application of knowledge as well as skills achievement.

We believe problems can be selected by the teacher and/ or by pupils whereby the latter may be successful in securing solutions and testing each possible solution. Problems can be of different levels of complexity as well as arrangements in their solutions made to provide for individual differences among learners. We believe the self concept to be very important of each learner and successful learning aids in achieving better feelings about the self.

Pupils as well as adults tend to feel embarrassed if situations involving failure are met, especially with others watching. The teacher has the delicate task of choosing what is not too difficult for pupils to attempt to achieve. Frustration and feelings of failture might well be an end result if the objectives of instruction are too complex. The opposite end of the continuum stresses goals that are excessively easy for pupil attainment. The latter situations might well make for feelings of boredom. Thus objctives should be achievable in social studies for pupils as well as be challenging, but not frustrating nor boring. A teacher has to realise that there are pupils who truly do excel in what is very complex to learn; effort and motivation are there to achieve. We believe, however, that for most pupils the teacher should find tasks that are not too difficult nor too easy for pupils to achieve. We need to have high reasonable expectations for learner achievement with challenging goals of instruction. We place emphasis upon the word 'reasonable' so that success in learning is an end result.

F. Balance Among Objectives

We believe that pupils need to experience three kinds of objectives such as knowledge, skills, and attitudinal goals. Why? We believe these three kinds of objectives interact and are not separate from each other. Quality attitudes, for example, assist pupils to achieve more knowledge and skills objectives. Many of our student teachers and cooperating teachers we supervised in the schools have said again and again that good attitudes take care of many weaknesses in learning. Those pupils who desire to learn and work hard at achievement due to positive attitudes, we believe, might well be winners in life. To be sure not all of success in life has to do with effort, people can be plain lucky and be at the right place at the right time. However, all things being equal, if one can imagine that, sheer effort should make the difference if one learner tries hard and the other doesn't. We have had student teachers and cooperating teachers show written work and art products from pupils that were not talented and gifted in the social studies and yet with sheer effort came up with excellent work! There have been written and art projects completed by the more talented and gifted and yet the work, it would appear, could have indicated much higher quality. Developing quality attitudes within learners is a high priority objective, good attitudes do improve the level of knowledge and skills objectives pupils achieve. Throughout the history of education, there have been educators who strongly recommended that attitudinal objectives receive paramount importance in teaching. Ediger (1995) wrote the following:

There have been numerous educators who have advocated affective/attitudinal ends as being more vital for pupils to achieve as compard to cognitive objectives.

Erasmus (1466-1536) advocated making learnings as interesting as possible for learners. He also believed that the act of learning cannot be hastened or hurried; the teacher may have to wait for students to reach a certain stage of development before selected learnings can be acquired... .

Michael de Montaigne (1533-1592)... believed that feelings possessed by individuals determine their deeds and acts. Thus, a person has feelings before he/she acts... .

Jean Jacque Rousseau (1712-1778) advocated raising and developing the child in harmony with tenets in nature. Rousseau believed the conscience of an individual to be the best guide in decision-making procedures... .

Friedrich Froebel (1782-1852) believed that the world of kindergarten pupils be related directly to taking care of plants. The teacher needs to provide a stimulating environment for pupils... . Pupils and plants unfold in their development if properly nourished.

Present/recent day educators who believed strongly in affective education include the following:

1. John Holt. Holt advocated that pupils should have ample opportunities to choose learning activities. Teachers should not use levers of fear and threat in getting pupils to conform to the former's desires....
2. Carl Rogers and Arthur Combs. Both educators differentiated between the concepts 'learning' as compared to 'teaching,' e.g. pupils learn but cannot be taught. Pupils then need adequate chances to select objectives and learning activities....
3. Sidney Simon. Simon has done much work involving values clarification strategies. The teacher then needs to assist pupils to think and understand indepth values adhered to presently... .

We find it interesting that two athors wrote about pupils evaluating the quality of teaching emphasised in a classroom setting: Barclay and Benilli (1995-1996) stressed using a questionnaire whereby primary and intermediate grade pupils evaluated teachers using the following evaluating device:

Considering the Bottom-Up Perspective on Quality

1. Do I usually feel welcome, rather than captured?
2. Do I feel that I belong rather than being one of the crowd?
3. Do I usually fell accepted, understood and protected, rather than scolded or neglected by adults?
4. Am I usually accepted, rather than isolated or rejected by the majority of my peers?
5. Am I usually addressed seriously and respectfully, rather than as "precious" or "cute"?
6. Do I find most activities enaging, absorbing, and challenging, rather than just amusing, fun, and entertaining?
7. Do I find most experiences interesting, rather than frivolous or boring.

8. Do I find most activities meaningful, rather than mindless or trivial?
9. Do I find most experiences satisfying, rather than frustrating and confusing?
10. Am I usually glad to be here, rather than eager to leave?

When evaluating the above listed criteria for evaluating teachers, it is qutie obvious that a child centered curriculum would be stressed. The focal point is the learner, not subject matter nor externally devised content objectives for pupils to achieve.

In addition to affective/attitudinal objectives, learners also need to achieve knowledge ends. Knowledge objectives pertain to vital facts that pupils need to master. These facts should be important, not trivia, and might be achieved in problem solving activities, such as in securing answers to problems and questions. Concepts are vital to attain. Concepts are represented by a single word or a phrase. Important concepts to achieve in geography include 'meridians, parallels, degrees, latitude, longitude, equator, Tropic of Cancer, and Tropic of Capricorn.' Inside of each concept are many vital facts. Thus the concept Tropic of Capricorn contains the following facts, among others:

1. it is located 23.5 degrees south of the equator.
2. it is a parallel to the equator running east to west, or west to east direction.
3. the sun is most nearly overhead on this imaginary line at noon on December 21 or 22.

Generalisations are another important facet of knowledge objectives. Generalisations emphasise a relationship of concepts. Generalisations are stated as declarative sentences, but are broadly stated, not as isolated facts. We will mention a few generalisations as an example within a unit of study or within a lesson for pupils to achieve.

1. Important beliefs in Islam include praying five times daily facing Mecca in Saudi Arabia, giving alms, saying the confessional, making a pilgrimage to Mecca at least once during one's lifetime, and fasting during

Ramadan. Within this generalisation are the following concepts: 'facing Mecca when praying,' 'alms,' 'confessional,' 'making the pilgrimage,' and 'fasting during Ramadan'. These concepts are related to form a generalisation. Each concept has certain facts. Thus the concept 'praying five times a day facing Mecca' has the following facts:

1. Mecca is the birth place of Mohammed.
2. Mecca is the holiest city of Islam followed by Medina, the place of Mohammed's entombment.
3. The Koran, the holy book of Islam, commands that individuals of the faith pray five times a day facing Mecca.

Knowledge objectives then determine what pupils are to learn in terms of subject matter in the social studies. Perhaps, the oldest kind or type of objectives stressed in teaching have been knowledge or cognitive ends. Ediger (1995) wrote the following:

There are well known educators of the past who placed high priority upon knowledge of cognitive objectives as compared to attitudinal or affective ends. Puritans of Colonial New England (1630-1776) sequentially emphaised memorisation of content pertaining to individual letters of the alphabet, selected syllables and words, the shorter Westminster Catechism, and portions of the Bible. Rote learning of content in these situations emphasised the lowest level of cognition. Ultimately pupils with teacher direction learned to read the Bible and other religious literature... in the curriculum.

Joseph Lancaster (1778-1838) introduced the Monitorial System of Instruction into the United States. The major methods of instruction emphasised by Lancaster was memorisation of content by pupils... .

With the introduction of Pestalozzi's methods of learning, memorisation of content was greatly deemphasised. Johann Heinrich Pestalozzi (1746-1827) stressed the importance of using concrete materials to stimulate pupil thinking. Thus in speaking activities, real objects and items provided a focal point for study... .

Johann Friedrich Herbart's (1776-1841) methods of instruction were generally based on cognitive learnings... . Herbart believed the mind to be like a blank sheet at birth. The teacher then needed to provide learnings which might imprint upon the minds of involved learners. Literature and history, in particular, might provide appropriate content on a relatively blank sheet mind... .

Additional educator from the history of education who advocated cognitive ends for individuals to achieve included the following:

1. Socrates, in ancient Athens, emphasised a questioning approach (Socratic method) to lead participating individuals to clarify their thinking pertaining to abstract concepts... such as justice, cooperation, and courage.... .
2. Plato (427-347) belied that what is perceived in this world is inferior compared to what exists in heaven. Thus, a table, chair, or person, in the here and now, is imperfect, as compared to the ideal chair or person in heaven. High level cognitive objectives need achieving when thinking of and applying universal ideals of justice, courage temperance, and wisdom. Forms and universality of ideas were ultimate reality to Plato.

In each of the above named educators, use of the mind or intellect came first in terms of objectives stressed in teaching such as memorisation of content; subject matter including history and literature, as Herbart emphasised came first in the curriculum, imprinting themselves upon the minds of initial blank sheets; and reasoning/thinking to apprise one's own thinking or to obtain knowledge of the Forms of Plato. It took time before higher levels of cognition were stressed in the curriculum such as John Dewey's problem solving procedures stressed in the early 1900s and still popular today. There have been additions, of course, to Dewey's problem solving procedures *Democracy and Education*. Among others, these additions include Jerome Bruner and his inductive methods of pupil learning and learners achieving key, structural ideas from the major academic disciplines (Bruner, 1960). Both John Dewey and Jerome Bruner emphasised inductive learning in the curriculum.

All educatros today stress using problem solving, critical and creative thinking in the curriculum. We recommend these three goals as being at the heart of the social studies. Numerous coples of mandated objectives for pupil achievement from different states in the United States emphasise problem solving being at the centre of objectives for pupils to achieve. Critical and creative thinking are also mentioned frequently in these state mandated objectives. We believe critical thought and creative thinking as being directly related to problem solving endeavours. Thus, problem solving, critical and creative thinking are of utmost importance in teaching social studies today. They are also important in everyday life in which individuals continually identify relevant personal and social problems with attempts made at arriving with needed solutions.

In addition to attitudinal/affective objectives and knowledge goals for learner acquisition, there are also skills ends to emphasise to the social studies. There will be overlapping here between knowledge and skills objectives. The following are vital skills for pupils to achieve that were already discussed above;

1. Problem solving with its flexible with its flexible steps of choosing a vital problem, gathering information from a variety of sources in answer to the problem, develop an hypothesis or tentative answer to the problem, check the hypothesis in a lifelike situation if possible, and revise the hypothesis if necessary.
2. Critical thinking with its emphasis upon pupils learning to separate fact from opinion, reality from fantasy, as well as accurate form inaccurate statements. Learners should also be able to detect bias and slogans in content written or spoken.
3. Creative thought with its focal point upon pupils developing original unique content as well as originality in thinking in the social studies.

There are additional skills that pupils need to develop, including the following:

1. Reading information from maps and globes.
2. Developing and reading content from different kinds of charts, tables, graphs, and figures.

3. Reading in a meaningful manner subject matter from basal texts, library books, pamphlets, magazines, and encyclopaedia articles as they relate to ongoing lessons and units or study in social studies.
4. Listening carefullly and comprehending subject matter from diverse autio-visual aids such as vidoeo tapes, video disks, and CD ROMS.
5. Using technology skillfully such as word processors, E-mail, Internet and World Wide Web, and the electronic bulletin board, among others.
6. Listening critically and creatively to oral reports, discussions, seminars, tapes and audio-visual content, explanations, directions, and lectures.
7. Developing communication skills in giving book reports, providing directions, making introductions, impromptu speaking, reporting results from problem solving, stating research findings, demonstrating how to do something, and explaining a completed project to others in the social studies.

Tener (1995-1996) listed the following ways for pupils to develop skills in critical thinking:

* Outlining
* Graphing
* Summarising
* Interpreting
* Relating
* Classifying
* Researching
* Evaluating
* Identifying fact or opinion
* Generalising
* Drawing parallels
* Self-correcting

* Applying criteria
* Hypothesising

The social studies teacher then needs to have appropriate methodology to guide pupils to engage in higher levels of cognition including critical thinking. In school and in society, it is so important that individuals be able to think and to think through different situations. One can memorise facts but not be able to critically appraise them nor be able to make use of these factual items. Pupils need to go beyond mastery of facts and do something with factual items learned and that is to thing about them and make use of what has been learned.

There have been debates among educators about a subject centered versus an activity centered curriculum in the school setting. Ediger (1995) wrote the following:

These two curriculum types appear to be at opposite ends of the curriculum. With a subject centered curriculum, abstract content is emphasised in teaching and learning. Mental achievement becomes a major goal. With activity centered curricula, pupils construct, make, do, and are actively involved in ongoing lessons and units of study. Pupils, however, may learn much subject matter through an activtiy centered curricula. The products then are an inherent part part of content learned.

...A late leading subject matter advocate in curriculum development was William Chandler Bagley (1874-1946). Bagley opposed teaching

1. Subject matter which does not contain precise, specific, and exact content. Content consisting of opinions and subjective ideas was definitely not advocated as being a part of the school curriculum.
2. subject matter which tends to change as to its exactness. Content needs to be stable in its corectness and not subject to conitnuous modification and change.
3. frills and fads inthe curriculum. Dr. Bagley advocated that essential common learnings be taught rather than stressing an activity centered curriculum. Activity centered methods are time consuming and do not emphasise that which is basic for all to learn.

...At about the same time, William Heard Kilpatrick (1871-1964), also late professor at Columbia University in New York City and an advocate of an activity centered curriculum, was opposed to the following:

1. pupils learning subject matter outside the framework of learner purposes.
2. pupils being passive recipients in the classroom. rather, learners should be actively involved in choosing objectives, activities and experiences, as well as evaluation procedures.
3. A teacher determined curriculum containing essential learnings for all pupils. Dr. Kilpatrick did not believe that essential subject matter could be identified in the school curriculum.

From the above opposing points of view, we obtain a basic point of view as compared to an open-ended phillosophy in teaching pupils. There are educators who believe in teaching the basics to pupils. It is difficult to say what these basics are. However in general, one can say there is essential subject matter that all should learn. This point of view is expressed by the general education philosophy of teaching.

The activity centered educators looked more at the interests and purposes of pupils whereby learners are rather heavily involved in determining objectives, learning opportunities, and evaluation procedures. The basics appear today in state mandated objectives for pupils to achieve, outcomes based education, and those advocating setting high standards for all pupils to achieve, including passing a statewide tests to graduate from high school. There is much stress here upon identifying what pupils should know and be able to do upon high school graduation. The activity centered educators believe in pupil interest in curriculum development propelling learners to achieve more optimally, rather than having subject matter dictated that must be mastered.

The social studies teacher needs to stress balance among knowledge, skills, and attitudinal objectives for pupils to achieve in each unit of study in the social studies. One category of objectives for pupils to achieve is not adequate in a modern programme of social studies. The three categories of objectives interact and cannot be separated entirely from each other in teaching and learning situations. Thus, for example, the teacher does want to have pupils use (skills objectives) what has been learned in terms of subject matter content (knowledge objectives). Hopefully with use of knowledge by pupils of content acquired, positive attitudes towards the social studies will be a relevant end result.

TRENDS IN SOCIETY AND THE SOCIAL STUDIES

The academic disciplines do not provide all the content necessary for pupils to be productive citizens in society. But they do provide major structural ideas in developing the social studies curriculum.

Teachers of social studies need to stay abreast of news happenings locally, statewide, nationally, and internationally. They also need to stress a good current events programme in teaching and learning situations for pupils. News reports and careful observation of happenings in society by pupils with teacher guidance might well provide excellent content, in part, of ongoing lessons and units to study in the social studies. Which trends are relevant in society for pupils to study?

A. Ample Learnings Pertaining to Minority Groups

Minority groups in society have felt they are not getting a fair shake in the economic and social world. African Americans, Mexican Americans, Asian Americans, and Native Americans, among others, have felt discrimination in education, housing, and job opportunities. Many times the feeling is that these minority groups are the last ones hired and the first ones fired when layoffs occur. Minority salaries and wages ware much lower, all things being equal, as compared to others in society. Very frequently, minorities live in low income, unsafe, slum areas. Their opportunities to succeed in life are indeed limited.

Feelings of conservatism in society emphasises federal budget cutting for food stamps, education, housing subsidies, welfare costs, and backing for affirmative action. These budget cuts hurt poor people and those least able to succeed in society. What truly is bad in society is when budget cutters cut on money available for heating fuel when weather and temperature readings are very low. A wealthy society such as the United States should have no difficulty in paying for needs of unfortunate people.

We believe the following implications for the social studies are relevant for the first societal trend:

1. an adequate number of units need to emphasise study of minorty groups in society. Objectives for these units should sterss understanding accepting, and caring for people of minority group persuasion.
2. Learning activities to achieve objectives should stress problems, difficulties, and achievements of minorities in society.
3. Evaluation procedures to ascertain pupil achievement need to emphasise contextual appraisal using a variety of procedures and approaches.

B. Change in Society

Societal trend number two emphasises the concept of 'change' in society. It appears that change is all around us. The natural and social environment are continually changing. Thus new technology is continually coming to us with computers, the internet, E-mail, the electronic bulletin board, CD ROMS, and video-disks, among others. The school curriculum has an obligation to consider and evaluate technology in society and its possible use in the school curriculum. The following implications are an end result:

1. School facutly need to study and evaluate the worth of each technological change to notice its worth in improving the curriculum. Technology used by pupils with teacher guidance should assist the former to achieve vital objectives in the social studies.
2. Inservice education should be in the offing to guide teachers and administrators in learning needed skills in technology use. These acquired skills should be used in teaching and learning situations.
3. Surveys should be conducted to determine what needs to be emphasised in the workshop setting to assist teachers to use technology in a manner which guides more optimal learner progress.

Teachers and administrators need to study changes in the societal arena to notice what is good, enduring, and has value in curriculum development.

C. Mobility in Society

Trend number three pertains to pupil mobility in society. With pupils changing schools and school districts rather frequently, it behooves social studies teachers to provide for a mobile pupil population. Quality sequence in learning may be lacking for selected pupils. Thus a pupil leaves school a having, for example, studied the beginning of a social studies unit on Argentina and Brazil. The pupil moves to another district and the teacher is ending a unit on New Zealand and Asutralia. The sequence here leaves much to be desired. What are the implications for these kinds of situations?

1. Teachers need to determine what a receiving pupil has studied previously in social studies. A planned social studies curriculum should be implemented whereby the pupil might sequentially make up objectives which he/she is lacking in pursuing the receiving school's curriculum.
2. The new pupil should be assisted in getting to know classmates so that feelings of belong may be an end result.
3. Acceptance and friendliness should be experienced by the new pupil in school. Finding out about the new pupils' talents and skills are necessary so that esteem needs of the learner may be met.

D. The Natural Environment

Trend number four in society indicates a need to preserve the natural environment as being of vital importance. We cannot continue to deplete land, water, and air resources. Good land is necessary to produce an adequate supply of food and fibre for human consumption. Without a well nourished population, there cannot be optimal achievement in school and at the work place. It takes energy from human beings to be productive in supplying goods and services to the general population. Feeling well physiologically is a must for all people. Living in poverty definitely means lower pupil achievement in school as well as less productivity in society in the world of work. Thus quality, clean farm land, uncontaminated, is needed to produce what is needed for human consumption by individuals in the societal arena. The heavy use of pesticides and herbicides has made for concerns on the part of environmentalists. Then too, with dumping of trash, debris, and waste products has made for land not being used properly. Acres and acres of good farm land is given to depositing of junk and discarded items.

Clean air and water is necessary for human survival. Unless we have clean air and water, the human race might not be able to survive. We read much about contaminated water supplies from chemicals and animal body wastes. More concern will have to be shown pertaining to our air and wtaer resources. Human productivity is based on a clean environment free from harmful pollutants.

The rate of plant depletion, including forests, makes for fewer sources that can minimise harmful levels of carbon-di-oxide. The automobile has been a major polluter in society. The levels of pollutants from cars have been cut down due to federal and state regulations; there is still too much of pollution of the natural environment. Now is the time to monitor the environment carefully and work in the direction of cleaning up what needs to be discarded in a safe, non-polluting way. Much care needs to be given in selecting sites for economic development. The better farm land should be spared and hilly land used instead. With economic development too much emphasis is placed upon expediency rater than thoughtful consideration as to what will happen to the air we breathe and the water we drink. There are definite implications here for developing the curriculum.

1. An adequate number of social studies units should deal with relevant objectives, quality learning opportunities, and appropriate evaluation procedures pertaining to caring for the environment.
2. Information in these thematic units should be accurate and important for pupils to aquire. The unit must capture pupil interest, purpose, and meaning.
3. In planning and implementing these units of study, educators as well as specialists pertaining to environmental problems should work collaboratively.

USING LEISURE TIME WISELY

Pupils presently as well as adults have spare time available from their daily endeavours. How will this time be used? It can be used wisely to relax and enrich the person. Leisure time may also be used in a destructive manner whereby it causes anxiety and feelings of boredom. Leisure time can be very rewarding if used wisely in a manner to develop the self to grow, develop, and achieve. Learning should be lifelong and enriching. How might the teacher educate pupils presently, so that learning will be lifelong and leisure time will be used wisely?

1. Have quality library books available at an interest centre directly related to ongoing lessons and unit in the social studies.
2. Introduce selected books to pupils to encourage reading.
3. Develop a bulletin board display of library books which will guide pupils in wanting to read.
4. Tell stories that relate to the library books at the interest centre. As this is done, hold up the related library book for all to see.
5. Select library books on diverse reading levels for the interest centre so that pupils individually may choose a book to read on his/her reading level. Assist pupils when needed in reading a library book.

Reading quality literature is a very good leisure type activity. Discussions can follow pertaining to what has been read. I have noticed too where pupils share their leisure time experiences in school such as engaging at home in stamp collecting, coin collecting, pencils and pens with advertisements being collected, as well as rocks, postcards, and match books being collected, among other items, to show how spare time may be used profitably. Pupils are unique in what they are interested in and what is shared should be respected and accepted by listeners. Interest of pupils need to be cultivated, recognised, and shared. There are adults in the community who are also willing to come to the school setting to share their hobbies and interests. Now is the time to cultivate good habits of lifelong learning and develop hobbies and interests among pupils. As time goes on, individulas might then develop new interests or continue with those developed in the lementary school years. A pattern or model will have been presented in the elementary years whereby pupils might continue with interests and hobbies as adults. Each person desires to have esteem needs met. Personal interests and hobbies possessed provide opportunities for being recognised for achievement and progress.

We believe, too, that pupils who receive recognition for having personal hobbies and interests will also wish to receive attention for academic excellence presently and jobs/occupations pursued as time goes on. All pupils should be successful in school so that recognition for each learner is possible.

To make full use of hobbies and interests of pupils as they are shared in school, learners might write related journal entries, experience charts, and diary items. Social studies units may also be taught on hobbies and interests of pupils. Ample time must be given to share with classmates and other learners what is being pursued in terms of hobbies and interests.

RIVALRY AMONG AND WITHIN NATIONS

There is strife and wars among nations and within nations. Wars take their toll of human life and property. People are left homeless and in poverty due to wars. Jobs and industries are destroyed and people are left homeless, in many cases. Relief agencies rush in and attempt to minimise the suffering. It is difficult to predict where the next catastrophe will take place. There is dissatisfaction within a nation pertaining to the type of government experienced as well as economic opportunities being too limited to meet needs of people. What implications are there for pupils in the social studies curriculum involving situations such as these.

1. Pupils need to study social studies units and current events items that deal with wars and the consequences of war.
2. Pupils need to pursue items of study involving what can be done to alleviate suffering and harm from wards and their after effects.
3. Pupils need to learn causes of war and their effects.

4. Pupils need to realise the negative in war endeavours and not glory in its undertaking.
5. Pupils need to appreciate efforts made toward peaceful resolutions of conflict and strife whereby justice and harmony result.

To achieve the above enumerated items pertaining to strife and war, pupils should use a variety of reading, audio-visual, and technological learning oppotunities to attain relevant objectives. A quality current events programme using diverse newspapers, and news magazines, together with stimulating discussions should assist pupils in creative and critical thinking as well as problem solving. Herrera (1996) wrote the following:

Schools today must prepare students to become productive members of an increasingly diverse society. Multicultural education programmes will enable students to understand and appreciate their own culture and the cultures of ethnic groups. But, more important, multicultural education provides the opportunity for minority students to interact with the dominant culture in an environment that is safe and trustworthy and is respectful of each individual. A successful multicultural programme will encourage teachers to examine their prejudices and their expectations of ethnic minority students. As teachers learn to focus on the educational needs of these students and the diversity they bring to the classroom, their preparation and delivery of the curriculum will ensure student success.

Conclusion

There are many ingredients that go into developing a quality social studies curriculum. Thus the teacher needs to obtain the 7interests of pupils in teaching and learning situations. He/she should teach in a manner which guides pupils to understand and attach meaning to ongoing lessons and units of study. Pupils need to be stimulated to perceive purpose in learning. Success for pupils in learning is a must. Three kinds of objectives need to be stressed in the social studies; these are knowledge, skills, and attitudinal objectives. Rational balance among objectives needs to be implemented so that learners perceive these ends as being interactive and not separate entities.

Societal trends that are relevant and need careful consideration in curriculum development including the following:

1. Respect for and teaching about minority groups.
2. Change in society and its curricular implications.
3. Mobility of population in the societal arena.
4. Preserving the natural environment.
5. Wise use of leisure of leisure time.

References

Barclay, Kathy (1995-1996), 'Evaluating Teaching Quality, *Childhood Education*, Vol. 72, No. 2, page 92.

Bhaskara Rao, Digumarti, ed. (1998), *Reforming School Education.* New Delhi, India: Discovery Publishing House.

Bruner, Jerome (1960), *The Process of Education.* Cambridge, Massachusetts: Harvard University Press.

Dewey, John (1916), *Democracy and Education.* New York: The Macmillan Company.

Ediger, Marlow (1995), 'Cognitive Versus Affective Objectives,' *The Progress of Education*, Vol. 69, No. 9, pages 172-174, Published in India.

Ediger, Marlow (1996), 'Social Studies: Integrating School and Society, *Journal of Instructional Psychology*, Vol.23, No.2, pages 121-125.

Ediger, Marlow, (1995), 'Subject Centered Versus An Activity Centered Curriculum,' *Education,* Vol.116, No.2, pages 268-271.

Eisner, Elliot W. (1985), *The Educational Imagination,* Second Edition. New York: The Macmillan Company, page 70.

Herrera, Sharon (1996), 'Multicultural Education: Meeting the Needs of Ethnic Minority Students, *The Delta Kappa Gamma Bulletin,* Vol.63 No. 1,24.

Tener, Norton (1995-1996), Information is Not Knowledge', *Childhood Education,* Vol.72, No.2, page 100.

Vijaya Bharathi, D. and Digumarti Bhaskara Rao (2000), *Educational Philosophies of Swami Vivekanand and John Dewey*, New Delhi, India: APH Publishing House.

4

Learning Opportunities in the Social Studies

The social studies teacher needs to choose learning opportunities so that pupils may achieve vital objectives. Care must be given in the selection of these activities so that optimal pupil learning might be an end result. Learning opportunities in and of themselves will not necessarily assist pupils to achieve more optimally. Each activity needs to be mingled with appropriate methodology so that objectives may be attained by learners. Pupils individually differ from each other in many ways. Thus it behooves the teacher to select that which harmonises with the developmental level of the learner as well as what harmonises with his/her style of learning. Pupils differ in capacity to learn. They differ in interests possessed. Selected pupils achieve better in social studies as compared to others in the classroom setting, what is important to the teacher is that each pupil is guided to learn as much in social studies as possible. We believe strongly that teachers need to ask themselves the following questions pertaining to learning opportunity selection when teaching pupils in social studies:

1. Will new interest be developed in the social studies lesson or unit being pursued?
2. Will proper sequence be maintained in that pupils can

be successful learners when new learning opportunities are being emphasised?

3. Will pupils be motivated and possess an inward desire to learn?
4. Will individual differences be provided for that each pupil attaches meaning to what is being learned?
5. Will each pupil feel that purpose or reasons for learning are in evidence?
6. Will pupils be stimulated to ask questions and identify problems in ongoing lessons and units of study?
7. Will the unit possess feelings of relevance by pupils so that vital objectives are achieved?
8. Will pupils achieve desirable knowledge, skills, and attitudes in each thematic unit of study?
9. Will pupils be able to make use of what has been learned so that relevance in learning is an end result?
10. Will pupils be able to achieve well while working individually as well as in cooperating learning endeavours?

In providing for individual differences, Maxim (1983) wrote the following:

So it goes when ultraformal group instruction resides as the major mode of teaching social studies allotted twenty-five to forty minutes every other day. All the children work on the same subject at the same time using textbooks, workbooks, or...worksheets as the major learning activities. Very few teachers today rely on such a rigid routine of instruction, for most are trying to meet the children's individual differences. In effect, they believe that, as much as possible, social studies programmes should be carefully designed so that each child is given maximum opportunity to achieve each specific goal, basic to this belief is an awareness of individual differences among the children and an ability to choose instructional methodologies that have the greatest possibility of clearly communicating information to all of the children. Sometimes, though, the difference among children are so great, even within the walls of one classroom, that it often seems as if the only single thing held in common among a group of twenty-five youngsters their assignment to the same teacher. What are some of the ways youngsters differ from each other one another? A typical class of fourth graders might differ in these ways:

Self confidence, sex, achievement levels, enthusiasm, age, interests, motivation, weight, values orientation, social adjustment, race, intelligence levels, self-perception, height, ethnic backgrounds, behaviour, creativity, socio-economic class, life experiences, emotional factors, reading levels, physical health, learning modalities, and personality.

STRATEGIES FOR THEMATIC TEACHING IN THE SOCIAL STUDIES

To initiate a social studies unit means to develop learner interest in achieving. Interest is a powerful factor in learning. The attention of the learner is there when interest has been aroused. If pupils, for example, are to study a unit on Australia, it would be good for the teacher to prepare a quality bulletin board display. The display needs to have a caption such as 'Visiting Australia'. Four good illustrations with abstract wording underneath each has a tendency to encourage pupil interest. The teacher may then tell about these illustrations briefly. The following are provided as a model for illustrations on the bulletin board:

1. A sheep station in Australia.
2. Desert life in the interior of Australia.
3. Modern urban life.
4. Natives such as the aborigines.

An additional learning activity to initiate the unit might be a video tape that all pupils may view on Australia. Here, pupils might identify questions and problems to solve pertaining to what was viewed. Resources to use to secure answers and develop hypotheses might also be discussed in sequence. Committees for cooperative learning may be operationalised so that problem solving might be stressed in collaborative endeavours.

A resource person who has lived in Australia should be contacted to speak too pupils using audio-visual aids. The resource person needs to be informed as to what should be emphasised in the presentation. Questions might be raised by pupils to obtain necessary information pertaining to the video-tape presentation.

Related library books on an interest centre should be introduced by the teacher to pupils. The library books need to be on different reading levels for pupils. Learners need to be motivated individuals to secure and read sequential library books that relate to the ongoing unit of study.

Should additional activities be needed as initiating activities to launch the new unit, the teacher might try the following:

1. Have pupils tell what they know about Australia without duplicating on what others have said. For this brainstorming session, the teacher or a pupil may write on the chalkboard ideas that have been mentioned.
2. Have a bowl containing questions pertaining to Australia with each question on a small piece of paper. Sequential pupils at random pick a slip of paper from the bowl and read the question that is thereon. The involved learner answers the question if able to do so. If the answer is not forthcoming, the pupil may pass the paper on to another learner to answer the question. The game continues until a need exists to change to a different kind of learning opportunity. The teacher may tell from this activity what pupils know about Australia and what needs emphasis in terms of additional objectives. Pertaining to learning activities, Gange' (1985) wrote:

Instruction designed for effective learning may be delivered in a number of ways and may use a variety of media. The term *media*, when employed in an educational context, means whatever combination of things and systems of things used to deliver communications or other stimuli to the learner. Media do not design or formulate these communications, they simply deliver them. The content and scheduling of the communications delivered by media may be relatively simple matters, like a set of familiar quotations written on a chalkboard; or then may be quite complex, as in the case of feedback to the learner from a computer screen. The content and its scheduling have been created by an instructional designer, a teacher, a instructor. Delivery of what has been designed is the function of media or combination of media.

STRATEGIES FOR DEVELOPMENTAL ACTIVITIES

Once pupil interest and purpose has been developed with the use of initiating activities, the teacher needs to guide pupils to achieve with the ensuing development experiences. Here, the teacher has pupils develop facts, concepts, and generalisations in greater depth than was true in the initiating activities. Different learning opportunities need to be in evidence to guide pupils to think more fully in greater depth. Which experiences might then be emphasised?

COOPERATIVE LEARNING

In continuing with problems solving activities identified in the initiating experiences, additional problems may also be selected within the ongoing unit on Australia. These might include the following with background information coming from an audiovisual presentation:

a. Why does Australia have unique animals such as the duck-billed platypus, the koala bear, the kangaroo, the cassowary, the ostrich, among others?

b. How does the eucalyptus tree in Australia differ from other trees such as the oak tree and the walnut tree?

Learners may then work collaboratively to solve these problems using a variety of reference sources. There are relevant criteria which need to be followed for cooperative learning to function well. These criteria include staying on the topic and not digressing, respecting the thinking of others, developing feelings of belonging, being recognised for contributions made, giving each pupil a chance to participate fully in the discussion activity, and appraising the quality of ideas presented. Ediger (1986) wrote:

If a unit has been initiated properly, pupils may have been challenged in the asking of questions. Questions by pupils should also be raised during the developmental and culminating activities in ongoing units of study. Pupils can then be divided into committees in working towards solutions to problems.

Committees may be arranged on the basis of pupil interests. For example, a small group of pupils my want to develop a model Puritan village directly related to the unit being studied. Another group of pupils could form a committee with teacher assistance in getting data or information from a variety of sources on farming methods of the Puritans. A third committee of pupils may develop a relief map emphasising the New England area. A fourth committee of pupils can develop a frieze or mural on important events in the days of the Puritans. A fifth committee could dramatise important happenings in the Massachusetts Bay Colony. Each committee, no doubt, would find it necessary to locate more information as additional questions arise within the ongoing learning activities. Findings from the committees may be shared with the class as a whole.

Working on committees can be beneficial for pupils since they may select the topic or problems they would want to work on most. This should help in the development of positive attitudes toward learning within pupils. Shy pupils feel more relaxed in a small group as compared to the class as a whole. Pupils may select activities which make for feelings of success.

READING FROM THE BASAL TEXTBOOK

Here, pupils may read to secure information for problem solving. They might also read to extend knowledge such as reading to learn more about kangaroos and/or koala bears of Australia. Pupils may read to contrast information. Thus a previously obtained answer to a problem might be checked with information from the basal. The reading then is done to appraise the accuracy of information from other reference sources used in problem solving. Critical thinking is inherent and becomes important. Reading critically and creatively are vital for success in learning and in life. With creative thought, the pupil thinks of unique ways to solve a problem. Novel means of showing information acquired are also important. Eisner (1997) wrote the following:

Ours is a school system that gives pride of place in the skilled use of language and number, the venerable three r's. No one can cogently argue that the three r's are unimportant. Clearly, competency in their use is of primary importance. But even high levels of skill in their use are not enough to develop the variety of mental capacities that children possess. The three r's tap too little of what the mind can do. Where do we learn what the mind can do? We learn about its potentialities not only from psychologists who study the mind but also by looking at the culture—all cultures—because culture displays the forms humans have used to give expression to what they have imagined, understood, and felt. Each product humans create embodies the forms of thinking that led to its realisation, each one of them provides testimony to what human beings can achieve, each represents a silent but eloquent statement concerning scope and possibilities of the human mind, and each one comes into being through the use of one or more forms of representation.

If culture is, as I have suggested the most telling repository of human capacity, then I suggest we inspect the culture to discover what might be called 'cognitive artifacts' (the products of thought). that we understand what we can of the forms of thinking that led to each, and that we try in the process to grasp the kind of meaning that each provides. I am saying that it is the sciences and the arts—the architecture, the music, the mathematics, and the literature found in culture—that give us the clearest sense of what humans are capable of creating. Understanding these achievements can, and in my view ought to, provide a basis for making decisions about what we teach.

Eisner suggests that more emphasis be placed upon the arts in teaching pupils. He believes that pupils lack experiences in the arts and therefore have a difficult time expressing the self in creative forms. There are many ways and approaches for pupils to reveal what has been learned, and it is not all shown through the conventional means of writing words and mathematics symbols. Art, music, architecture, drama, dance, among others, are ways of showing what has been learned and achieved. Pupils who lack experiences in the arts also lack abilities to reveal in diverse ways what has be acquired. Reading activities then may provide information to pupils in problem solving and in portraying information.

In addition to reading to solve problems, to thinking creatively and critically, pupils might also read to secure vital facts. Reading to acquire facts is generally done at a relatively slow rate, especially if many facts are to be acquired at a given time. There are always essential facts to read and many of these facts might be used in the solving of problems. We place a heavy emphasis here upon reading vital facts, not any kind of factual information in an ongoing unit of study. For example, there are salient places and items that pupils should have knowledge about when studying another nation such as the names of capital cities, port cities, agricultural products grown and produced, and products manufactured. Understanding, not mere memorisation, by pupils of each vital fact is important. Textbook content may have excellent facts for pupils to learn.

Pupils should also learn to scan content read in social studies textbook. Not all content is read at the same rate of speed. Sometimes, a reader wishes to obtain a quick overview of selection to notice if it has needed content for problem solving for general interest in reading.

The pupil then scans the subject matter in the text to notice if the subject matter surveyed has wanted content. Not all words are read since this would take much time. Rather the essential ideas are noticed to determine if the entire selection should be read more carefully. Scanning is a valuable skills for all to learn. Throughout life, one glances over subject matter or objects to notice if further investigation is necessary.

Skimming of content is salient in riding to notice important facts that need to be learned. Here, entire selection need not be read for the purpose of securing relevant items such as when World War Two began and when it ended. Learners might also read to notice what the three major farm crops of a given region are through skimming. Again, not the entire selection needs to be read. The few items needed from reading can be acquired through skimming. It is a rather quick kind of reading to obtain highly precise information that clearly sticks out from other print such as dates or numerals or capital cities which have capital letters always, and not just when a sentence is begun.

Reading to follow directions is very valuable. In school and throughout life, a person reads directions so that proper completion of a project is possible. We have often wished we could read directions better and then do a project accurately. We hear others say the same thing. The way directions are written might make interpretation difficult. We would suggest pupils reading directions and then telling in their very own words what these directions mean. If pupils have problems with following directions, the teacher needs to determine why. The following might be causes:

1. the pupil has problems reading the abstract words.
2. the ideas are presented in a vague way.
3. the pupil may be able to read the words, but not comprehend the meaning.
4. the pupil is distracted from reading activities.
5. the pupil lacks background experiences in order that the directions may be understood.

The social studies teacher needs to diagnose and determine that needs to be done in terms of remedial work to overcome the learner's difficulties in all forms of reading experiences. Very often, pupils read directions to do an exercise on paper or to work within an activity centered curriculum.

Reading to determine causes and effects is a very important kind of reading. In historical units, there are causes for happenings that occur. Thus, pupils need to be able to state possible reasons for an event to have occurred. Individuals seemingly remember history better if causes are linked with the happenings as they are being studied. Pupils need to be assisted to identify why an event occurred. We believe this can be taught rather directly by having pupils discern possible reasons for any vital event that transpired in history.

Being a good reader has many advantages for individuals throughout life. Recreational reading then has its advantages. In one's spare time, reading good literature has its many pluses. With an ample supple of library books directly related to the social studies unit being studied, pupils individually may select a book to read for sheer enjoyment as well as to gather information for problem solving. A student teacher whom one of the authors supervised in the public schools used library books only for pupil reading in an ongoing social studies unit. No basal text was used. Pupils freely contributed ideas read from these books as the unit progressed. One could also use the basal text along with the library books in teaching social studies. We recommend both be used.

Pertaining to unit teaching, Skeel (1970) wrote:

Unit organisation has the advantage of offering the opportunity to meet individual needs. Children who have special interests or skills can be guided toward tasks that fulfill these needs. Research can be conducted in areas of a study that are of particular interest to individual children. Those of exceptional ability can engage in research in greater depth and can thus acquire skills beyond the normal level. Children who have talent in music, art, writing, or drama have an opportunity to use these skills.

Group activities can also contribute to the individual's development. For example, the child who has difficulty in getting along with other children who is assigned to a group activity of real interest... will, hopefully, acquire skills of cooperative behaviour. Equally important is the opportunity for the child with leadership ability to channel this energy into worthwhile activities. Shy children who would hesitate to enter into activities and discussions before the total group will often do so within small groups.

USING WORKBOOKS TO ACHIEVE OBJECTIVES

The use of workbooks in the social studies has been frowned upon by numerous educators. We think the issue is more of how these workbooks are used rather than being bad in and of themselves. We have observed student teachers and cooperating teachers whom we supervised in the public schools who made wise use of workbooks that go along with and are related to the basal text. The workbook pages here have been used to

1. review what has been taught previously.
2. enrich what pupils have learned.
3. branch out to new concepts and generalisations directly related to content taught.
4. solve problems identified for pupils.
5. develop inferences by learners.

We have also noticed that workbook exercises are inclined to include.

1. mundane and routine things for pupils to do.

2. irrelevant and insignificant items for learners to work on.
3. busy work for pupils.
4. unrelated activities.
5. materials of instruction which are too complex for a given set of children.

What then are selected solutions in making workbooks in social studies a vital experiences for pupils? Certainly, teachers needs to be certain that pupils have the needed background experiences to benefit from any workbook exercise. If pupils lack certain knowledge and skills, they will not do well nor attend effectively to ongoing tasks in the workbook. If pupils do not understand certain vocabulary terms in the workbook activity, these need clarification. Meaning and understanding need to be attached to the unknown. Then too, there will be pupils who need assistance to pronounce unknown words correctly. A common cause of failure to learn from reading is not knowing certain words in pronunciation or not being able to attach meaning to these words.

If a workbook activity is too complex, the teacher might be able to make it more sequential. Perhaps, the teacher may need to teach selected concepts and generalisations so that the new content is understandable and pupils can be successful learners in workbook activities. Not all items, of course, need to be worked on a workbook page, if there is a lack of perceived value therein. We have observed student teachers and cooperating teachers who have made it clear in parent/teacher conferences that not every item will be worked on successive pages in a workbook. These teachers then select what is relevant and vital for pupils to complete so that important objectives are achieved. Parents need to understand that leaving out selected activities form workbook pages is done for a purpose and that is to eliminate what is perceived to be unimportant.

USING SLIDES IN TEACHING

We like to take slides of places that have been visited. Very frequently, students in undergraduate and graduate classes use them in ongoing social studies units. We have known other college supervisors of student teachers as well as lay people who take many slides; many of these slides are shown at civic and religious organisations. Most of these would be very suitable to show to pupils in an ongoing unit of study. Here are things we like of well taken, clear slides for teaching purposes;

1. We can spend all the time in teaching we need on any one slide.
2. Pupils may raise any number of questions on a single slide. There is no hurry then on moving on to the next slide.
3. We can arrange the order or sequence in showing and discussing the slides. My narration may add to improving sequential content in the slides.
4. We can use slides to initiate, develop, and culminate a social studies thematic unit.
5. We can add or delete slides as time goes on in teaching and learning.

USING FILMSTRIPS IN TEACHING SOCIAL STUDIES

There are educators who say that using filmstrips in teaching social studies is outdated. We would hasten to add that it depends upon the content therein. There are selected materials in teaching that one can obtain in side or filmstrip form but not in a video-tape teaching aid. We have also noticed student teachers and cooperating teachers who use filmstrips in teaching that have good content to assist pupils to achieve objectives.

Filmstrips can be used much like slides to initiate, develop, and culminate a thematic unit in social studies. The sequence of frames on a filmstrip cannot be rearranged as is true of slides. However, the teacher may omit certain frames or rearrange the showing of selected frames through manipulation of filmstrip projector use. The frames stay as they were originally in the filmstrip.

If a teacher, for example, is teaching a unit on 'The Middle Ages', there will be frames in the filmstrip pertaining to a manor, knights, workers in a guild, peasants harvesting grain, castles, and homes of poor people. If a unit has the following objectives pertaining to 'The Middle Ages,' the filmstrip content might well shed light on these objectives of instruction:

1. describe orally what life on manor would be life.
2. write how a page and squire became a knight.
3. list in sequence the steps involved in becoming master in the guild.
4. develop a bulletin board display on how peasants harvested grain on a manor.
5. draw a picture of a castle surrounded by huts for peasants.

A variety of reference sources might be used here in addition to the filmstrip which, as described, has content pertaining to each objective.

USING VIDEO-TAPES IN TEACHING SOCIAL STUDIES

Video-tapes contain movement and motion which is not true of slides and filmstrips. Thus video-tape will possess more of realistic qualities in teaching and learning. If teacher is teaching about the crusades in a unit on 'The Holy Land,' the following geographical features may be observed in a video-tape:

1. The Sea of Galilee being approximately 600 feet below sea level.
2. The Jordan River carrying water for the Sea of Galilee to the Dead Sea.
3. Jericho being 800 feet below sea level and Mount Herman in the extreme north in the Holy Land being 16,000 feet above sea level.
4. East Jerusalem having a wall completed in 1142 AD.
5. The Plains of Esdraelen begin the breadbasket of the Holy Land.

These content items on the Video-tape may well match up with objectives including the following:

1. Pupils in cooperative learning will develop a relief map of the Holy Land.

2. Pupils will place vegetation as is contained in the Holy Land to surround the model Sea of Galilee, the Jordan River, the Dead Sea, and the Plains of Esdraelen.
3. Pupils will make a model of important sites for tourists near Ancient Jericho.
4. Learners will make a model of the wall around East Jerusalem using a large cardboard box, scissors, and tempera paint.
5. Pupils will collect and prepare information in giving an oral report on The Plains of Esdraelen, located directly south of Nazareth.

USING THE OVERHEAD PROJECTOR

The overhead projector has many advantages in use if the contents on the screen are clear. Pupils in a classroom need to be able to see the visual on the screen with clarity. The following may be presented visually, as examples, using transparencies and the overhead projector:

1. population figures of capital cities and nations as these are being compared in an ongoing unit of study.
2. line, bar, and circle graphs showing agricultural crops produced in different nations as well as within a nation.
3. scenes of farming, urban life, transportation, education, musical instruments, religious scenes such as in architecture, and written symbols.
4. a narrative chart that tells a story such as how water is pumped and treated in sequential steps.
5. drawings to show steps in a process such as making a food product.

Each of these learning opportunities in using transparencies and the overhead projector should relate directly to an important objective of instruction such as number one above with the objective—Using information projected on the screen, pupils will say orally how the population figures differ when comparing nations and capital cities studied in our present unit. This is not to say that learning opportunities must always relate directly to the stated objectives of the course or unit title. Objectives, carefully chosen, provide guidance and direction to the teacher in terms of what is salient and important to teach. Each objective needs to have passed tests in terms of being relevant and significant. Then too, there is room for pupils to make discoveries on the projected materials and items on the screen. A very important general objective is that pupils think creatively and critically in each unit of study in the social studies. When making discoveries, learners can be quite creative. In an open ended curriculum, opportunities must be provided for pupils to be creative.

USING COMPUTERS IN THE SOCIAL STUDIES

Computer use is increasing in importance each school year. If pupils are to keep up with trends in society, certainly they need to have many positive experiences presently in working with technology. For example, pupils need to experiences software and computers that meet the following criteria for each programme.

1. the programme must fit in sequentiaily in terms of what is being emphasised and taught.
2. the programme needs to be on the understanding level so that pupils attach meaning to ongoing experiences.
3. the programme needs to present new content that is achievable by learners and yet the subject matter does not duplicate with content which may be learned from other kinds of teaching materials.
4. the programme needs to be sequential for the engaged pupils.
5. the programme needs to provide for the needs of individual pupils.

Learners should be able to obtain needed information for problem solving activities from internet, World-wide Web, E-Mail, and software packages. Technology changes rapidly and learners need to keep abreast of important uses and subject matter contained in the information superhighway. In an information age, pupils have excellent opportunities to secure much content with rapid retrieval to solve problems. Information obtained needs to be appraised in terms of significance and saliency when solving problems. The information must relate directly to the problem. Higher levels of cognition are involved when learners appraise the mass amounts of information available from numerous reference sources. The level of application is important to stress when technology is used. Problem solving does stress applying knowledge obtained to solve vital problem areas.

There are disagreements among educators as to the extent modern technology should be emphasised in the curriculum. Noble (1996) wrote the following:

Educators need to understand the high tech moguls and marketeers, despite their government supporters , are scrambling to predict the future, are seduced by their high tech fantasies, and are locked in treacherous high stakes gambles. Education for them has typically been a sideshow, a proving ground, or a long shot investment. Their state-of-the-art technologies have not in the past been products with direct or immediate applications for education, nor will they be in the future. Further, their skewed predictions about education and technology are no better than our own.

Educators, therefore, need not keep abreast of every innovation for fear of losing ground or falling behind. Leave the experiments to the technophiles. The rest of us, unashamedly and with renewed integrity, should follow our own sense of sound educational practices, using proven technologies where applicable. There is no need to join the mad rush into the future or to gamble with our student's education.

Dwyer (1996) takes a different point of view in which he advocates heavy use of technology and not being left behind by writing the following:

The promise of technology is that it will greatly improve the efficiency and effectiveness of our institutions and evolve as an avenue for lifelong learning and universal communication. But along with that promise come inevitable problems: How will schools keep up with the pace of change? How will we ensure equitable access to everyone? How will we deal with information complexity and quantity? What about standards for quality? How do we protect the intellectual work of our writers, artists, scientists, and engineers? Where the curriculum do we help children to navigate this new world? How do we make the minimum number of mistakes that we will surely make as we open school doors to the exotic future?

...The serious questions about the use of technology in schools must be answered with care and forethought. In many instances they will only be answered through trial and error—we have not travelled that route before. But above all, they must be answered by all stakeholders in our children's futures, working in concert. Educators cannot leave these questions to others; they must be the salient voices; the designers of experiments, the risk takers, and the critics of results.

Technology, whether we like it or not, is changing the notion of who we are as citizens of that planet. We can pretend that this is not happening and hold onto the past as long as we can. Or, we can grab this opportunity to build a world of peace, prosperity, and understanding.

USING CD ROMS AND VIDEODISCS

The social studies teachers needs to engage in inservice education opportunities to fulfill needs in using diverse forms of technology in a professional manner. With inservice education, teachers in the field of instruction may learn to use technology in a—manner which assists each pupils to achieve as optimally as possible. Learners do possess diverse styles of learning and each style needs to be carefully considered when developing an instructional strategy in teaching the social studies. What might pupils obtain from interaction with CD ROMS and video-disks?

1. content pertaining to the solving of problems.
2. music of a specific culture or nation.
3. art products produced in a particular country.
4. scenes of architecture of different nations and cultures.
5. recipes for foods of diverse nations and groups.

The list actually can be endless in terms of what pupils might learn from the engagement with CD Roms and video-disks. Here is another source of information to use in extending pupil knowledge, in developing ideas in greater depth, and in integrating content.

EXCURSIONS IN THE SOCIAL STUDIES

To bring in more reality into teaching and learning situations, many teachers have pupils visit places to experience first hand that which is concrete and real. We have supervised student teachers and cooperating teachers who engaged in having pupils experience that which exists away from the school grounds and yet is practical and utilitarian for learners. We must mention here that we have also observed good excursions by pupils with teacher guidance right on the school grounds. Thus, an excursion locally had learners experience different forms of erosion such as gully and sheet erosion. The preventative measure was also shown such as planting grass to prevent soil erosion. Thus there can be a lot to experiences by pupils right on the school grounds.

Moving away from the school grounds, one of the authors have observed the following by pupils with teacher guidance:

1. a poultry farm whereby 15,000 laying hens in separate cages, each housing six layers, were observed in a unit on 'Egg Production on the Farm.'
2. pupils saw automation in which mash (feed) for the cage layers came down the troughs, every forty minutes.
3. water for the hens ran downhill in the troughs continuously. Laying hens need much water for egg production.
4. oyster shell, for the completion of the shells on eggs inside the laying hen, was automatically available for laying hens.
5. automatic packing of eggs in cases was also seen by pupils and teachers during the excursion.

Pupils observed scenes and listened carefully to lecture items and discussions during the excursion. After arriving back in the classroom, learners wrote journal entries on their observations. Additional activities whereby use was made of what was observed included the following:

1. making a 'movie set' and accompanying tape to describe each scene.

2. writing a short book by a committee pertaining to learnings that occurred during the excursion.
3. mailing a thank you letter to the operator of the laying houses for the opportunity to visit and ask questions.
4. developing a bulletin board display on the excursion.
5. giving an oral report by a committee on modern methods of egg production.
6. reading library books and other materials to develop a committee report which is shared with other committees.
7. completing a mural by a committee on egg production and distribution.
8. writing poems, prose, and narrative accounts on egg production.
9. doing a creative and a formal dramatics presentation on the care of cage layers in producing eggs.
10. summarising ideas from a video-tape pertaining to laying hens.

RECORDING LEARNER PRODUCTS AND PROCESSES

Pupils need to have ample opportunities to see/hear their work and their procedures taped in order to receive feedback. Thus pupils may see/hear the following on video-tape or cassette tape:

1. how a committee is functioning when working on a project.
2. how well a class is following guidelines in a discussion setting.
3. how effectively a child or committee is able to tell of what he/she has constructed in an ongoing unit of study.
4. how pupils's exhibited attitudes are assisting in achieving objectives.
5. how the quality of pupil products compare with previous endeavours.

Teachers need to keep records of previous pupil achievement and compare them with present achievement to notice progress. Each pupil needs to achieve as much as possible in social studies. Thus, it behooves the teacher to have data available to reveal how well a child is doing in different kinds of learning opportunities.

SNAPSHOTS AND THE SOCIAL STUDIES

Many pupils and teachers have cameras which take clear and excellent pictures. These pictures can be used wisely to indicate learner progress presently as well as in the future. They can be posted in the classroom to encourage pupil review of what was learned as well as show classmates what was achieved. We have seen pictures taken by pupils and teachers on the following learning opportunities.

1. a cooperative learning activity whereby pupils in the classroom made a model grain farm.
2. snapshots of pupils on an excursion to a farm producing soyabeans and corn.
3. pupils inventing and playing a game on farming in the Midwest.
4. a dramatic activity involving pupils dramatising life on a farm.
5. a frieze made by four pupils on a committee showing sequential scenes pertaining to soyabean and corn production.

Snapshots can be used to initiate a unit by having pupils study what last year's learners did in ongoing social studies units. They may be used to guide pupils to develop learnings in greater depth such as studying how soyabeans and corn are planted to make for optimal production. The snapshots might also be used to assist pupils to review that which had been learned previously.

An opaque projector may be used to enlarge each snapshot so that the class as a whole might be taught. An opaque projectors might not be new innovation, but it can be used wisely in teaching and learning.

In addition to enlarging snapshots using an opaque projector, we have also observed teachers using illustrations from diverse reference sources for enlargement on a classroom wall. In the unit on grain farming in the Midwest, one of the authors notice a student teacher and a cooperating teacher who showed the following illustrations using an opaque projector:

1. a twenty row corn planter planting corn.
2. a self-propelled combine cutting six rows of corn at one time.
3. a two ton truck unloading corn at a grain elevator.
4. a large tractor with a swivel in the middle disking farm land for seeding.
5. a self-propelled combine unloading grain from the augur while cutting six rows of corn at the same time.

Each snapshot and illustration may be discussed in depth with pupils involved. As much time as is needed may be spent on any one scene. An inductive or questioning approach might be used to assist pupils to achieve relevant generalisations. Deductive procedures might also be used whereby the teacher points out relevant factors on each snapshot or illustration to pupils in an interesting manner. The snapshots or illustrations should be shown with quality sequence involved. Important scenes need to be discussed. The irrelevant and the unimportant should be culled from any social studies unit. Major concepts and generalisations need to be stressed in teaching and learning situations.

USING PUPPETS

Pupils tend to enjoy making and using puppets in the social studies. We have observed in classrooms where pupils made the following kinds of puppets:

1. *Stick puppets.* Here a pupil drew a farm animal and pasted it on a tongue depressor stick.
2. *Sock puppets.* Learners in cooperative learning took socks and stitched on buttons for eyes as well as pieces of cloth for ears and a mouth. Additional facial features were sewn onto the sock as needed.

3. *Paper mache' puppets*. These kinds of puppets are probably the most difficult to make of all puppets. Strips of paper, approximately three inches by one inch, are soaked in flour and water. The wet strips are then pasted around some object, such as a sphere or ball. After the paper strips have dried, tempera paint may be used to locate the eyes nose, and mouth. Paper mache' may be used to make ears for the resulting face. There should be room for the hand at the base of the head or an inserted stick may serve the same purpose for holding the puppet.

A combination of these puppets may be made and used in a dramatic presentation pertaining to what is being studied in the social studies. How might the puppets be used? First, it does take careful planning and quality pupil interaction to make puppets. Neatness and accuracy of work is important in making puppets. Each person in cooperative learning involved in puppet making needs to have an important role in planning, making, and using the puppets.

Dramatisation parts needs to be distributed among participants. Each participant needs to have ample information in the part being played pertaining to an ongoing social studies unit. The dramatic presentation should capture observer attention, be clearly presented orally, have appropriate sequence, and be meaningful to listeners. A puppet may have the following role in a unit on farm animals:

1. a dairy cow grasing in the field.
2. a farmer mending farm fences.
3. a draft horse pulling a wagon.
4. a sheep following a fence row.
5. a dog watching over the farm.

The dramatic activity may be presented in the home classroom as well as to other learners in the school setting. Cooperative learning emphasises cooperation among pupils in harmonising actions to plan, make, and complete each puppet. Using the puppets in dramatic presentations emphasises further needs for cooperation among learners.

USING FLANNEL BOARDS IN THE SOCIAL STUDIES

A flannel board can be an excellent device to use in teaching pupils. Flannel boards are relatively easy to make. The teacher may take a piece of cardboard, approximately two feet by three feet in dimension. The cardboard, needs to be neatly enclosed with flannel. A light brown or yellow coloured flannel works best so that the cutouts thereon may show up well. The cutouts then should be darker in colour and made of felt so that they attached to the flannel while the teacher is teaching. We have also noticed teachers who put a piece of felt in back of a paper cutout which then sticks on well to the flannel board. What might be put onto the flannel board, either in felt or paper form? If, for example, a unit in social studies on 'Visiting the Zoo' is taught, the following may be placed on the flannel board:

1. several kangaroos in an enclosure.
2. a polar bear with its pupil made 'ice image' background.
3. a tiger and a lion, in separate cages, with several cubs.
4. a giraffe reaching toward leaves on a tree.
5. a refreshment stand for visitors.

When pupils raise questions pertaining to content on the flannel board, they may be assisted by the teacher to gather information in answer to the problem area. If a fact is needed to answer the question, the teacher may state the answer or help learners find the needed content. A problem area requires more effort in securing necessary subject matter. A variety of reference sources should be used to obtain data; these reference sources should be on the understanding levels of involved learners. Then too when reading is involved, learners need to be able to read with meaning and understanding. Necessary written work here needs to harmonise with the present developmental level of the involved pupil. The teacher should not expect what is impossible for learners tc attain, nor should the expectations be below what each learner can do and achieve. There is a delicate balance here for the social studies teacher. Optimal achievement is wanted from each pupil. There needs to be high expectations for each pupil to achieve, but not the impossible.

USING THE CHALKBOARD

The chalkboard is an old standby to use in teaching. Why? It is handy to use with the chalkboard in front of the room and available chalk on the tray. Each pupil needs to be able to see clearly what is written on the chalkboard. What might a teacher or pupil write on the chalkboard as a lesson or unit progress?

1. important facts, concepts, and generalisations being discussed.
2. directions for pupils to follow in completing an exercise from the text, workbook, work sheet, or other experience.
3. an outline of sequential ideas covered in a discussion.
4. a drawing of a salient part of a map being studied.
5. drawings of possible projects for pupils to choose from in an ongoing unit of study.

The chalkboard may be used as a learning activity along with other devices. There needs to be a purpose in teaching when teachers use the chalkboard. No material of instruction is used for the sake of doing so but rather to clarify, edify, and make meaningful. We believe a chalkboard my assist pupils to achieve more optimally. it is a tool for instruction, but should never be perceived as an end in and of itself.

Conclusion

The social studies teacher needs to use a variety of learning opportunities in teaching pupils. Pupils differ from each other in many ways; it behooves the teacher to provide for optimal achievement for each learner. Time that is wasted if learner achievement has to be made up for at a time when sequential progress should be in the offing. Some pupils learn best from concrete materials such as from objects, items, and excursions. Others learn best from semiconcerete materials such as audiovisual aids. Still others learn best from the abstract such as listening to and reading social studies content. Which procedures do pupils learn best from in a classroom? The teacher needs to make that decision based on knowledge pertaining to each pupil.

Learning opportunities are there to assist pupils to achieve carefully chosen objectives. These objectives must be relevant, important, and possess perceived worth to pupils. Knowledge, skills, and attitudinal goals must be in the offing in proper balance, among these categories of objectives. Learning opportunities need to guide the teacher and pupils in teaching and learning situations. Thus pupils need guidance to attain that which is worthwhile. Individual differences including present achievement levels and background information need adequate consideration. A variety of learning opportunities assist the teacher to select those that are of optimal benefit to pupils in goal attainment. There should be times when pupils may select what they wish to learn with a thematic unit. There are also times when there is more direct teaching by the teacher in critical and creative thinking as well as in problem solving. Certainly, with a variety of planned learning opportunities, the teacher has a better chance of providing for individual differences as compared to using a single media only or largely.

Teaching and learning procedures need to follow selected guidelines; Ediger (1994) listed the following:

1. *Meaningful lessons and units of study.* With meaning, pupils understand and comprehend that which was contained in ongoing learning opportunities.
2. *Interesting content and skills in the curriculum.* With interest, the pupil and the curriculum become one, not separate entities. Pupils attend and achieve from ongoing lessons and units of study.
3. *Purpose in learning.* With purpose for learning, pupils accept reasons for attaining relevant facts, concepts, and generalisations presented.
4. *Sequence in learning.* With quality sequence, pupils relate newly acquired content with that previously achieved. Previously attained content provides readiness for the new objectives to be achieved.
5. *Balance among objectives stressed.* Thus, knowledge, skills, and attitudes—three kinds of objecties need to be achieved by students. These objectives interact and are not in isoaltion form each other. For example, if pupils possess quality attitudes, they should achieve needed knowledge and skills more readily.

Teachers following the above named criteria for teaching should find pupils more engaged and actively involved in learning. Learners who perceive that personal needs are met in learning will find that achieving, growing, and developing are vital, necessary, and relevant. Teachers must determine ways of assisting pupil to attend and have an inward desire to learn.

References

Bhaskara Rao, Digumarti (2000). *Educational Psychology*. Guntur, India: Nagarjuna Publishers, (in Telugu language).

Ediger, Marlow (1993), 'A Grade Six Project in the Social Studies,' *Canadian Social Studies*, Summer Issue, pages 40-43.

Ediger, Marlow (1986). *Social Studies Curriculum in the Elementary School*, Third Edition. Kirksville, Missouri: Simpson Publishing, page 142.

Ediger, Marlow (1994), 'Early field Experiences in Teacher Education, *College Student Journal*, Vol. 28, pages 302-303.

Dwyer, David (1996), 'A Response to Douglas Noble, We're In This Together,' *Eduational Leadership*, Vol. 54, No. 3, page 26.

Eisner, Elliot W. (1997), 'Cognition and Representation' *Phi Delta Kappan*, Vol. 75, No. 8, page 350.

Gagne', Robert M. (1985). *The Conditions of Learning Theory of Instruction*. New York: Holt, Rinehart and Winston, page 282.

Marlow Ediger and D Bhaskara Rao (2000), *Teaching Mathematics Successfully*. New Delhi, India: Discovery Publishing House.

Maxim, George W. (1983). *Social Studies and the Elementary School Child*. Second Edition. Columbus, Ohio: Charles E. Merrill Publishing Company, pages 121 and 122.

Noble, Douglas D. (1996), 'Mad Rushes Into The Future: the Overselling of Educational Technology,' *Educational Leadership*, Vol. 54, No. 3, page 23.

Skeel, Dorothy J. (1970), *The Challenge of Teaching Social Studies in the Elementary School*. Pacific Palisades, California: Goodyear Publishing Company, Inc., page 65.

5

Pupil Learning in the Social Studies

Teachers of social studies need to have adequate subject matter background courses taken in the preservice years of university education. These courses include history, geography, political science, anthropology, sociology, and economics. It would be excellent if teachers also had ample coursework in philosophy, psychology, and world literature. Thus social studies teachers must have adequate subject matter background in the social sciences to teach the social studies well. In addition to subject matter knowledge, teachers also need to be able to help pupils understand, connect with, and achieve higher levels of cognition in different social studies units. Being a quality person in pedagogy is vital when assisting each learner to attain optimally (Ediger, 1998, ERIC—ED#424112).

THE TEACHER AND SUBJECT MATTER KNOWLEDGE

Each unit taught in social emphasises that the teacher have sufficient knowledge to do a good job of teaching. We will discuss each academic discipline in the social sciences and what this means for teachers who are or will be teaching the social studies.

All social studies teachers need to be students of history.

Almost every social studies unit taught brings in history as subject matter content. From kindergarten to the end of the high school years, the teacher will be teaching history. In some units of study in social studies, history largely will be stressed. In other units of study, the teaching of history may have more of a minor role. For each unit taught, the teacher needs to guide pupils to understand what history is. Thus in history, relevant ideas from the past need to be identified by the teacher and taught to learners. There is so much history to learn in any unit of study that it behooves the teacher to make careful choices as to what truly is salient. Trivia and irrelevant content need to be weeded out. History then deals with a study of time. When did the event occur in sequence in the time dimension?

A second social science discipline that needs to be emphasised is geography. Geography stresses the concept of *place*. Events such as in history occur within a specific place. There is a definite location involved here when discussing place. Maps and globes serve as models in locating geographical places. There are definite kinds of land forms, climate, soils, flora, fauna, and bodies of water within a geographical region. Within a geographical region, there are selected human endeavours. These endeavours include economic activities, different socio-economic levels involving a pattern, population forces, languages spoken, and religious beliefs adhered to. There is a relationship between the natural environment and human endeavours (Ediger, 1998, ERIC#ED424112).

Human technology is applied to the natural environment which modifies the latter. Problems then arise such as water and air pollution, as well as disposal of diverse kinds of waste products, toxic and nontoxic. Natural forces cause disasters such as hurricanes, floods, earthquakes, and volcanic eruptions, among others. Human beings also cause disasters such as water pollution, oil spills, soil erosion, and nuclear accidents. Values and ethics are involved when discussing how human beings should use the environment. Pupils need a thorough understanding of how human interaction with the environment can help or hinder the planet earth for human habitation (Ediger, 1997, ERIC#ED415448).

A third social science discipline that needs adequate attention in social studies units of study is political science. In political sciences, learners study the concept of *power*. Governments have the power to tax people as well as govern human behaviour to maintain quality health and conduct. Violations of laws can have a serious consequence depending upon the crime committed. For example, murder can be dealt with in society through life imprisonment of death sentences. Pupils need to experience an ample number of units dealing with local, state, and national levels. It is important to know the laws of the land (Ediger, 1998, ERIC—ED419943).

Sociology and anthropology will be dealt with together here. Both academic disciplines emphasise the concept of culture, among other things. We will briefly discuss the concept of culture. The language spoken in a given region stresses culture. In Arab nations of the world, Arabic will be the dominant language. In France, the French language is dominant. We learn the language that affects us in our environment. Ironical situations do occur whereby a son/daughter turns out completely different as compared to the parent or parents.

Pupils need to have ample opportunities to study the languages of other cultures studied in ongoing units of study. This may mean listening to records of languages used in the nations being studied. Learners may wish to learn to use simple survival words in that language such as saying hello, goodbye, how are you? a few representative food items, and the numbers to ten. They should learn about the values of a given culture such as Old Order Amish using horses and carriages for transportation. Pupils also need to study the architecture of a culture such as bedouins living in tents instead of permanent dwellings involving houses. The music and dances of specific culture can differ much from that of home base. In all knowledge, skills, and attitudinal objectives attained in an ongoing unit of study, learners must learn to appreciate and prize other cultures. It is salient for pupils with teacher guidance to plan and develop native dishes of food representative of the culture or nation(s) being studied. Art work of a given culture when studied can further enrich the lives of pupils. Each culture has unique processes and products of art work which gives a region its identity. Additional cultural ideas for learner acquisition include learning about the games and recreational endeavours of a given people. Not all cultures feel that basketball and football, as played in the United States, are leading spots endeavours. Games played and recreational endeavours pursued vary from culture to culture (Ediger, 1997, Chapter Eight).

The last social science discipline which generally comprises the social studies curriculum involves economies. How people earn a living and how they spend that income involves the study of economics. Means of earning a living can vary from area to area, city to city, and nation to nation. The items purchased from the income earned will also be different from place to place. There are certainly great differences in the kinds of goods and services purchased by human beings. The total amount of goods and services produced in a nation emphasises the gross national product (GNP).

GOALS TO ATTAIN IN THE SOCIAL STUDIES

Each goal for pupil attainment must be selected carefully. There are numerous goals which can be chosen for learner attainment that it behooves the teacher to emphasise relevant ends for the former. If a state mandates that certain objectives need to be achieved by pupils, a more centralised procedure is involved in the selection of goals. State departments of education then involve selected teachers and administrators in choosing these goals. If selected goals are developed on the district level, then the ends are chosen closer to home base as compared to the state level. Best it is if the teacher teaching his/her own pupils chooses goals for the latter to attain. The teacher by studying pupils is in the best position to know what their needs are in the social studies as well as what their interests are. Taking care of needs and interests in teaching-learning situations should assist learners to attain more optimally in the social studies. If too many needs and interests are not being fulfilled, much is lacking in the total school environment for pupils. An excessive number of goals then need fulfillment which are difficult to do. For example, pupils who do not eat breakfast at home can become very hungry by the time the noon meal is served unless the school serves a nutritious breakfast to children when they arrive in the morning. By taking care of physiological (food) needs, pupils can achieve at a more optimal rate when the academic areas are emphasised such as in the social studies. Also, if the temperature reading in the classroom is not appropriate, the pupil can not concentrate well on learning. There needs to be proper temperature reading in the classroom so that pupils can learn and achieve vital goals (Epstein, 1995).

Three kinds of objectives need to be selected for pupils attainment in the social studies. The first kind of objectives are knowledge. Thus which concepts, generalisations, and facts should pupils achieve in any social studies unit of study? Careful consideration of each objective should then be in the offing. If pupils are studying a unit on 'The Middle East,' teachers and supervisors may choose the following concepts for learner attainment: Immigrants, Balfour Declaration of 1917, Mac Mahon-Hussein correspondence, The Land of Palestine, Adolph Hitler and Nazi Germany 1933-1945, kibbutz, moshav, village, bedouin, Islam, Judaism, United Nations Resolution of 1947, 1948 Arab-Israeli War, refugees, boundaries, 1956 Suez canal dispute (war involving Israel, Britain, and France versus Egypt over the Suez canal), 1967 Six Day War (Israel versus Egypt, Syria, and Jordan), Black September, 1970 war between the Palestine Liberation Organisation and the nation of Jordan), 1973 Yom Kippur war involving Egypt and Syria versus Israel, Egypt and Israeli peace treaty of 1979, return of the Sinai Peninsula from Israel to Egypt, Persian gulf war in 1991 due to invasion of Kuwait by Iraq, signing of peace treaty between Israel and the Palestine Liberation Organisation in 1993, peace treaty between Israel and Jordan of 1994.

The above are listed as suggested concepts for teachers to teach in a unit on the Middle East. Concepts taught must be appraised in terms of importance in understanding the Middle East conflict. There is so much that needs to be taught that teachers need to select with great care that which learners are to acquire.

Equally salient is for the teacher to choose vital generalisations for pupils attainment in the social studies. In the unit on the Middle East, the teacher may wish to teach the following generalisations after selecting these with great care:

1. the Balfour Declaration of 1917 was promulgated by Great Britain toward the close of World War One. It promised the land of Palestine as a homeland to the Jews. The land of Palestine had been controlled by the Ottoman Turkish Empire since 1517. The MacMahon

Hussein correspondence of 1915 promised the same real estate to the native Arabs to become an independent nation.

2. Jewish immigrants then came from different nations into Palestine. The native Arab population feared for their land in Palestine when Jewish Immigration increased.
3. the rise of Adolph Hitler as Chancellor in Germany in 1933 emphasised persecution and repression of Jews in that nation. Thus Jewish migration to the Holy Land increased.
4. Jews had come to the land of Palestine in small numbers since 1882 and developed cooperatives called the kibbutz, a collective farm. Other Jews developed Moshavs to cooperatively market their farm products even though farms were owned individually.
5. Native Arabs in rural areas lived in villages whereas bedouins were nomads who herded their sheep and goats where the grass was sufficient. City dwellers were the third category of Arabs in the land of Palestine. Important cities here included Hebron, Bethlehem, Nablus (ancient Samaria), East Jerusalem, and Ramallah.
6. the major ideas or pillars of Islam are belief in one God with Mohammed as his prophet, prayer five times a day at designated times, pilgrimage to Mecca in Saudi Arabia and Ramadan, and belief in the Moslem creed.

The Dome of the Rock, a beautiful Mosque in East Jerusalem, is the place, according to devout believers, where Mohammed made his midnight ride to heaven and returned back to earth again. The Koran is the holy book of devout Moslems.

Judaism is based on the Torah, the first five books of the Old Testament. However, the entire Old Testament is important to devout Jews. The book of Esther is especially salient outside the frameworks of the Torah.

7. disagreements between Arabs and Jews became serious over Jewish immigration which resulted in serious skirmishes involving the two sides from 1920-1948. Both Jews and Arabs also opposed the British Mandate over Palestine which Great Britain had received form the league of Nations following world War One. The Jews had initially, of course, strongly favoured the Balfour Declaration of 1917. Violence among the three sides became futile in working out a solution.

8. The United Nations General assembly voted in 1947 to partition the land of Palestine into a Jewish state and an Arab state. The Jews who would receive 55 per cent of the land of Palestine accepted the United Nations resolution whereas the Arabs who would receive 45 per cent were strongly opposed. The Jewish state of Israel was declared in 1948 in their allotted area as proposed by the United Nations. The nation of Jordan invaded the West Bank and took that area of Palestine to become a part of the state of Jordan. The native Palestinians on the West Bank were now citizens of Jordan, located east of the Jordan River. Jordan then had 20 per cent of the land formerly called Palestine whereas Israel had 80 per cent. According to the United Nations resolution of 1947, Israel was to have 55 per cent whereas the native Palestinian Arabs were to have 45 per cent of what used to be Palestine. Also during the 1948 war, Egypt captured the Gaza Strip, a part of Palestine. Palestinians in the Gaza Strip were then occupied by Egypt. Approximately 700,000 Palestinian Arabs become refugees.

9. in 1956, Great Britain and France together invaded Egypt from the west so that the former could continue to maintain control over the Suez Canal. Israel invaded Egypt from the east and captured the Sinai Peninsula. The three invaders withdrew from their occupied territories under pressure from the United States. Egypt nationalised the Suez Canal which had formerly been controlled by Great Britain.

10. during the 1967 six day war, Israel captured the Gaza Strip and the Sinai Peninsula from Egypt, the Golan Heights from Syria, and the West Bank of the Jordan River from the nation of Jordan. More Palestinian Arab refugees resulted, totaling 2.5 million in number.
11. in 1970, the nation of Jordan drove out the Palestine Liberation Organisation (PLO) from their borders. The Palestine Liberation Organisation then was driven out of Jordan and into Lebanon.
12. in the 1973 Yom Kippur war, Egypt and Syria attempted to regain (from Israel) the Sinai Peninsula and the Golan Heights. The attempts failed due to a powerful Israeli army. The United States airlifted in supplies to Israel during the 1973 war. The stalemate with major skirmishes in the Middle East continued between Israel and the neighbouring Arab nations.
13. in 1977, President Anwar Sadat from Egypt made a trip to Israel to address the Israeli Knesset and announced readiness for a peace treaty. The treaty was signed in 1978 and Egypt received the Sinai Peninsula back. This also made possible United States aid in the amount of 1.8 billion dollars a year to Egypt whereas Israel annually receives $3 billion.
14. in 1990, Iraq invaded Kuwait, an oil rich nation. The United States, Britain, and France together with token forces from other nations heavily bombed Iraq. Iraq withdrew from Kuwait and the ruling Saba family again returned to govern Kuwait.
15. in 1993, Israel and the PLO signed a treaty in Washington D.C. The latter received the Gaza Strip and the city of Jericho as places for self rule. There are approximately 3 million Palestinian Arab refugees presently in Jordan, Lebanon, Syria, and Egypt. The Palestinians desire much to have an independent state or nation (Ediger, 1998, 57 pp).

A second category of objectives to stress is skills for pupil attainment. Pupils should increase abilities to read and write critically and creatively as well as solve relevant problems. Higher levels of cognition are then emphasised in teaching and learning situations.

A third set of objectives for learner attainment are attitudes. With quality attitudes, pupils have an inward desire to achieve more optimally in knowledge and skills. There should be an inherent desire to learn as much as possible in the present lesson and unit of study being emphasised in the social studies (See Hackman and Schmitt, 1997).

UNIT TEACHING IN THE SOCIAL STUDIES

Resource units in the social studies need to be developed carefully with much thought going in to each section. Titles for units should be relevant or the unit should not be taught. Teachers, supervisors, and administrators need to spend much time on careful selection of each unit of study. A Justification Section for teaching the unit of study is a must in the resource unit. A second section of the resource unit needs to emphasise the purpose or reasons for teaching the unit. What is it that pupils should get out of the unit that other units cannot provide? Each unit chosen should make its definite contributions. Each social studies unit has its uniqueness and originality, separate from others. This section of the resource unit should be well thought out since social studies units should not duplicate, but provide new challenging, attainable objectives for learner achievement.

A third section of the unit should stress the objectives section. Here the teacher or team of teachers need to write out knowledge objectives that pupils needs to attain. The knowledge objectives need to reflect careful thinking on the part of teachers, supervisors, and administrators as to what is deemed salient for learner attainment. The objectives section should also identify skills that pupils should achieve. These skills must be worthwhile and functional in the lives of children. Utilitarian skills must then be written down in the unit plan. Unimportant skills need to be eliminated. Flexible steps of problem solving are indeed worthwhile to stress. Reading for a variety of reasons should be emphasised by the teacher in teaching-learning situations. Analysing a situation before making a decision or choice is a useful end for learner attainment. Use of creative ideas in thinking is very valuable for all pupils. Thus synthesis of content is needed when gaps in knowledge and skills are noticed by learners. The attitudinal dimension of objectives are indeed salient. Quality attitudes by pupils assist in achieving better in knowledge and skills. To improve attitudes, learners must experience success, meaning, and interest in the social studies.

A fourth part of the resource unit stress learning opportunities. These learning opportunities need to engage pupils actively in ongoing activities. Active involvement is preferable to passive receivers of content. A strategy to implement in unit teaching is to have initiating activities. These activities introduce the new social studies unit to pupils. Initiating activities are a very salient part of the resource unit. If a unit is successfully implemented, the chances are learners will be more likely to be engaged in learning as compared to beginning activities that fail to secure learner attention. To initiate a social studies unit adequately, the teacher needs to have good bulletin board displays which pupils like to view and ask questions about. These questions can become a framework for discussions among learners and with the teacher. In addition to bulletin board displays containing pictures directly related to the new social studies unit, the teacher may also show and discuss with learners a video-tape. The contents in the video-tape provide background information for pupils so that the objectives of the new social studies unit might be attained more optimally. Objects on an interest center, introduced in a stimulating manner and examined by learners may further provide interesting experiences which should guide pupils in wanting to achieve more optimally (APA Task Force on Psychology of Education, 1993).

The teacher needs to determine how many initiating activities should be provided pupils so that the new social studies is launched in a motivating manner. Additional activities than those mentioned above may be used to initiate a new unit in the social studies.

After an adequate number of initiating activities have been used to launch the new unit, the teacher needs to think of and implement quality developmental experiences. The developmental activities stress teaching in depth, rather than using survey procedures of instruction. Depth teaching emphasises intensive learning by pupils of each fact, concept, and generalisation in the objectives section of the resource unit. For depth learning, the following activities are recommended, among others:

1. reading from the social studies textbook those selections that pertain directly to the unit being taught. Readiness for reading must be stressed.
2. making a mural of related content.
3. developing posters of content being studied.
4. constructing a model.
5. cooperating in doing an experience chart covering subject matter studied.
6. reading library books pertaining to the unit objectives.
7. viewing and discussing an audio-visual aid's illustrations and content.
8. dramatising subject matter read.
9. giving an oral report in class on a related topic. The report is evaluated in terms of quality standards.
10. discussing in a committee what was learned form a dramatic presentation.

The teacher needs to diagnose where pupils need more assistance to attach meaning to content learned. Continuous progress for each learner on an optimal basis is desired. Each pupil needs to be actively involved in ongoing learning opportunities.

An appropriate procedure must be used to end a social studies unit properly. It is sad when pupils lack interest in any social studies unit and are lethargic in the classroom. Culminating activities are used to end a unit in the social studies. To culminate a unit, the teacher needs to develop a strategy which guides learners to review and relate what has been studied and learned. The following activities, among others, work well as culminating experiences for pupils:

1. discussing what has been learned within the unit of study.
2. doing a creative or formal dramatics pertaining to previously acquired ideas.

3. writing a summary of content learned.
4. outlining main ideas attained in the unit.
5. engaging in research to acquire additional subject matter on a personal topic of interest.
6. evaluating each activity in the unit in terms of being helpful to learners.
7. writing creative prose and poetry on selected topics covered in the unit.
8. suggesting other relevant content to cover in the completed unit of study.
9. taking tests on the content covered in the unit of study.
10. going over the content in the preceding test results to determine what needs to be covered in terms of pupils learning.

PHILOSOPHY OF TEACHING SOCIAL STUDIES

The social studies teacher has several options from which to adopt one or more philosophies in teaching-learning situations. A problem solving procedure should be stressed in whole or part in ongoing lessons and units of study. Here, the teacher within context assists learners to identify a problem. The problem should be relevant and adequately delimited. Pupils individually or within a committee may develop an answer or hypothesis to the problem. The hypothesis is tentative and subject to testing in a lifelike situation. Data or information might then be gathered in testing the hypothesis. The original hypothesis can then be modified, if needed.

A second philosophy of teaching might stress a subject centered curriculum. Here, learners acquire facts, concepts, and generalisations outside the framework of problem solving. It might be very difficult for pupils to acquire needed subject matter, entirely inside of problem solving situations. Subject matter that is salient might then be taught in direct teaching. In direct teaching, this might pertain to meaningful explanations provided by the teacher. We would strongly recommend using inductive procedures also whereby learners respond to broad questions raised by the teacher. Pupils also need to ask questions and respond to each other's question. The questions may or may not involve problem solving experiences.

In the use of subject matter approaches in teaching social studies, pupils are to learn vital facts, concepts, and generalisations, Mental development of pupils is emphasised more so than physical or emotional achievement. Physical and emotional development, however, is relevant to the subject centered social studies teacher if learners succeed in acquiring abstract content.

A third philosophy of teaching stresses the use of measurably stated objectives. These precise ends are clearly stated so that there is rather clear agreement on their meaning. It is possible to measure, after instruction, if a pupil has or has not attained the relevant end. Prior to instruction, the teacher may announce to pupils what needs to be learned in order to be successful achievers. What is to be learned is stated precisely in the measurably stated objective to be emphasised in teaching pupils. Pupils. Pupils can then be rather certain what is to be attained.

A fourth philosophy of teaching to use in teaching social studies is to emphasise a learning stations approach. Here the teacher or pupils with teacher guidance may develop a series of stations containing concrete, semi-concrete, and abstract materials. The stations and materials relate to a single social studies unit title. Ateach station, there are task cards which provide pupils with possibilities for learning. Each pupil might then select which tasks to complete and which to omit. The pupil is the chooser. There are more tasks available than what can be completed by any one pupil. Each learner then may choose what to learn and what to omit. Pupil purpose is then involved in making each selection, be it individual or group endeavours. Tasks not possessing perceived purpose can beomitted by the pupil. Interest is definitely a deciding factor in pupil decision making when selecting which tasks to learn and which to omit.

Conclusion

It is important to choose objectives carefully so that pupils attain relevant ends. The teacher should attempt to emphasise vital knowledge, skills, and attitudinal objectives for learner attainment in each unit of study. Unit selection must emphasise that which can guide pupil achievement in areas that other units can not do. Important units in social studies must then be chosen for pupil engagement.

There are significant philosophies of teaching that the teacher may stress in teaching. The philosophy or philosphies chosen should harmonise with the pupils personal learnng style. Each pupil needs to attain as optimally as possible in the social studies.

References

APA Task Force on Psychology in Education (1993), The Learner Centered Psychological Principles: Guidelines for School Reform and Redesign. Washington D.C: American Psychological Association and the Mid-continent Regional Education Laboratory.

Bhaskara Rao, Digumarti (1999), *Teacher and Eduction.* New Delhi, India: Nagarjuna Publishers (in Telugu language).

Ediger, Marlow (1997), *Social Studies Curriculum in the Elementary School*, Fourth Edition, Kirksville, Missouri: Simpson Publishing Company, Chapter Eight.

Ediger, Marlow (1998), 'Teaching Science as Inquiry,' ERIC#ED424112.

Ediger, Marlow, (1998), 'The Curriculum: Academic or Utilitarian?' ERIC#ED419943.

Ediger, Marlow (1998), *The Holy Land.* Kriksville, Missouri: Simpson Publishing Company, 57 pp.

Ediger, Marlow (1997), 'Character Education and the Curriculum,' ERIC#ED415448.

Ediger, Marlow and D. Bhaskara Rao (2001), *Teaching Science Successfully.* New Delhi, India; Discovery Publishing House.

Epstein Joyce L. (1995), School/Family/Community Partnerships. *Phi Delta Kappan*, May Issue, 701-712.

Hackman, Donald G., and Donna M. Schmitt (1997), 'Strategies for Teaching in a Block-of-Time Schedule, *NASSP Bulletin*, 81 (588), 6.

6

READING IN THE SOCIAL STUDIES

Being able to read well is a must in the social studies as well as in other curriculum areas. Most social studies teachers stress a considerable amount of reading that pupils need to do in ongoing lessons and units of study. It is true that there are additional kinds of learning activities, and a variety of learning opportunities should be in the offing so that all pupils may learn as much as possible. Reading is one way and a good approach to learn in the social studies. There are certain ingredients in teaching that will assist pupils to improve reading skills in the social studies. Each pupil needs to be a successful learner. Improved self concepts develop as a result of achieving success in ongoing lessons and units of study. Pupils individually desire to be recognised for what has been done well. Certainly, reading in the social studies can offer pupils rich and satisfying experiences in learning. The talents of each pupil need to be recognised, reading being no exception. How might a successful programme of reading be emphasised for all pupils? (Ediger, 1997, 93-97).

READINESS FOR READING

A basic in reading content in the social studies is for pupils to experience adequate background information. A pupil cannot read and understand new subject matter unless prerequisites have been met. The social studies teacher, as a professional, helps pupils attach meaning to the new content to be read. He/she is aware of subject matter pupils should understand before they are to read to achieve new objectives.

There are numerous methods the teacher may use to provide guidance and assistance in establishing readiness within pupils for reading. For early primary grade pupils, the Big Book concept may be used. Here, the teacher discusses the illustration in the book pertaining to content within pupils. First, the teacher reads orally from the Big Book that has print large enough for all to see in the classroom. Learners look at the words as the teacher reads orally. Pupils then may recognise the new words in context as well as receive additional background information. Next, the pupils read together with the teacher in an oral manner. Pupils have additional opportunities here to recognise the new words as well as review the content read. Rereading aloud may occur, if desired or if needed. Using the Big Book approach, pupils need not divide their attention from reading the content as well as seeing the new words in print. Holism is then involved in reading social studies subject matter. Each phase in using the Big Book needs to be emphasised, such as the teacher discussing with pupils the illustrations therein, prior to the former reading it aloud with learners. Pupils then follow the sequential words in context as the oral reading progresses. Pupils reading aloud together with the teacher provides additional opportunities to recognise the new words as well as achieve background information. With a second cooperative oral reading, involving pupils with the teacher, there are additional chances to review the words in identification as well as the content read. Rereading provides further opportunities to polish reading skills and rehearse knowledge for the early primary grade pupils in the social studies (Ediger, 1998, 94-95).

The Big Book philosophy has merits for intermediate grade pupils who face problems in word recognition and comprehension when textbooks are used. Comprehension goes downhill as fewer and fewer words are identified in reading content. Prior to the reading aloud activity, pupils may discuss the illustrations in the text to obtain background information. A good reader may then read aloud to those who lack proficiency in securing ideas from reading. Each of the latter may follow along in his/her own social studies textbook as the subject matter is read aloud. Word recognition problems are minimised greatly as a good reader reads aloud to those who need assistance. Rereading might be emphasised as is necessary. Pupils may then be ready to discuss the subject matter read with others in the classroom setting.

Intermediate grade pupils may also be taught by the teacher using the following strategy to assist in providing readiness for reading:

1. discuss the content in the illustrations with pupils in the classroom.
2. print words that pupils will meet in the basal in neat manuscript style on the chalkboard, generally within context in a sentence. If a word processor is available with a large screen or monitor, the teacher may type in the new words into the computer for all pupils to see.
3. point to each word when pronounced orally with pupil involvement.
4. go over these words, such as in step three, several times until mastered by learners. Assist pupils to use each word in a meaningful sentence.
5. have questions or purposes for reading whereby learners need to read to obtain answers for each.
6. discuss answers and other content in a discussion, following the silent reading experience (Ediger, 1988, 21-22).

In these six flexible steps of instruction pertaining to readiness and the actual act of reading, a few pupils may experience a separation of the new words to be mastered that will appear in the text and are printed on the chalkboard with the subject matter to be read silently. However, this problem may be minimised as the reading activity progresses. The six steps of readiness for reading in the social studies listed above might also be used for oral reading. Certainly, selected pupils, as a whole, might well become successful in comprehension by using this procedure in teaching. Each pupil needs to achieve as optimally as possible in the social studies.

INDIVIDUALISED READING IN THE SOCIAL STUDIES

The social studies teacher needs to have numerous library books available for pupils to select from and read. Empowerment of pupils is important so that they feel more confident in learning and in achievement. If pupils can choose, from among alternatives, which library books to read sequentially, they, no doubt, will pick those which may be of most benefit personally. The library books need to be on different reading levels so each pupil may choose a challenging book to read. Learners individually should not feel frustrated with content that is too difficult, nor bored with those that are too easy. The library books for pupils to read should be on different topics, but relate directly to the social studies unit presently being taught. Thus, if a thematic unit on transportation is being taught, there need to be library books for pupils to choose from on the following topics:

1. history of transportation.
2. transportation in developing nations.
3. transportation as related to geography and geographical regions.
4. rules and laws pertaining to transportation.
5. vocations available in the field of transportation.
6. different forms of transportation available.
7. transportation and its relationship to communication.
8. transportation and the world of business.
9. problems in transportation.
10. safety and transportation.

With internet and the world wide web being available to an increasing number of schools, pupils may access necessary data using computers. The information sought needs to relate to the thematic unit being studied. Critical thinking should be stressed in that pupils separate the relevant from the irrelevant, the accurate from the inaccurate, and factual from that which is imaginary. Creative thinking is important in that learners might use content learned to write diverse forms of poetry and complete unique works of art as these relate to the thematic unit being studied. Problem solving also should receive adequate attention in teaching in that pupils individually or in committees identify a problem within the thematics social studies unit, secure information in developing an hypothesis/answer.

With individualised selection of library books related to the thematic unit being studied, pupils may contribute what has been read in discussions conducted within unit teaching framework. I have observed this approach to work well with no basal textbook used in teaching and learning. Pupils actively participate in the discussion when bringing in to the discussion subject matter read from the completed library book. There can be much enthusiasm here with diversity of content presented, but all being directly appropriate for the thematic unit being taught. A lively, purposeful discussion may be held in an atmosphere of respect.

The teacher needs to evaluate which pupils benefit much from individualised reading in the social studies and which benefit more from the basal. It is the pupil that needs to do the learning to achieve vital objectives in the social studies. Pupils then need to have a voice pertaining to which reading materials are most beneficial. With library books, a related cassette may play the recorded words and sentences as individual pupils, with reading problems, follow along, silently or orally. It is best to use a variety of reading materials so that pupils may check one source against the other, critically and creatively (Ediger, 1996, 229-233).

PHONICS AND THE SOCIAL STUDIES TEACHER

An important question in teaching social studies involves the degree to which the teacher needs to be a teacher of reading. We would say definitely that social studies teachers should be teachers of reading. Why? Pupils need to do much reading to secure information for each unit taught. There will be additional concrete and semi-concrete experiences that pupils will have in each unit of study. Reading is not the only avenue of learning, but it is a vital approach in information acquisition in school and in society (Ediger, 1988, 1-6).

When being a teacher for two years on the West Bank of the Jordan from 1952-1954 and also helping to distribute clothing to Palestinian refugees on the West and East Bank—both were the nation of Jordan at that time, I saw bedouins getting off the bus between Jerusalem and Jericho, walking along a path to their tentative community of tents and livestock. These nomads could not read or write. Nomadic life tends to be harsh where less than five inches of rain falls per year in a desert region. The grass soon withers and is gone in a region/area. Bedouins then move on to where the grass is more adequate for their camels, sheep, and goats (Ediger, 1988, 1-10). Now, the nation of Jordan is doing much to educate bedouin children. For example, in southern Jordan, bedouin children are bussed long distances to school. There is a new school for bedouin children and for others, near Aqaba in the southern tip of the nation of Jordan.

What we are saying is that people lose out on much when being completely or nearly illiterate. Not being able to read or write when so many jobs here and abroad require quality reading skills and abilities is a disaster. Then too, reading for enjoyment is vital for each person. We live in the country, five miles from the city of Kirksville. A neighbour located next to us cannot read or write. Not only are good jobs difficult to obtain without these skills, but enjoyment in life for leisure type activities are hindered without the ability to read well. Presently in the United States, an illiterate person appears to be one who reads below the tenth grade level. One can do much, much reading of different kinds of content on the tenth grade level of graded subject matter!

Social studies teachers then need to be quality teachers of reading so that pupils may obtain adequate subject matter and skills from the unit being taught. There are pupils who are hindered in reading due to a lack of phonics skills. Phonics should only be taught to pupils who cannot benefit from reading due to lacking word attack skills to unlock the unknown. Phonics should not be taught for the sake of teaching sound/symbol relationships, but a purpose is involved and that reason being to assist pupils to improve in reading comprehension in the social studies. If a pupil cannot recognise a word while reading, he/she should attempt to use context clues to identify that word. If context skills do not work, then attempting to associate a sound with an initial symbol in the unknown word might well be adequate. Additional phonic skills to be taught include final consonant sounds as related to individual as well as a combination of letters. Medial vowel sounds may also be taught as needed. The social studies teacher sets the stage for pupils to achieve vital knowledge, skills, and attitudinal objectives. To achieve these objectives, pupils need assistance when reading is being emphasised as a learning opportunity related to relevant ends in unit teaching. Phonics, many times can be taught as needed, not as an isolated skill. When feasible, we recommend this approach.

There are selected syllabication skills that might be taught to pupils to unlock unknown words. These syllables need to be important and are frequently used in reading content. For example, the syllable 'un' appears in many words with rather high frequency, such as in unimportant, unfit, unreliable, unable, and unlikely. Pupils need help, in certain situations, to identify and pronounce words correctly due to syllables which are prefixes, such as 'un.' Common syllables as suffixes may also cause problems for pupils in recognising unknown words. Pupils may need guidance in recognising words containing suffixes, such as 'ful' in cupful and roomful, among other words (Ediger, 1997, 18-27).

READING FOR A VARIETY OF PURPOSES

There are numerous kinds of reading materials that pupils need to read proficiently presently as well as in the future at the work place. Reading subject matter content, narrative content, and creative ideas require reading for a variety of purposes. The social studies teacher should assist pupils to read for diverse purposes or reasons. We will now discuss different, relevant purposes in reading.

Pupils should become proficient in reading for facts in the social studies. There are many facts that are relevant for pupils to know in the social studies. For example in a social studies unit on the Middle Ages, learners may read and recall meaningfully, the following facts:

1. many people lived on a manor.
2. the manor was a farm owned by a lord.
3. peasants performed the difficult work on the manor.
4. the lord usually lived in a cattle, surrounded by a moat.
5. the parish church was at the centre of life on a manor.

It is vital that pupils understand subject matter in each fact. Too often, facts are memorised for a test and then, perhaps, forgotten. This is most unfortunate.

A second purpose in reading social studies content is to read to follow directions. Many pupils fail to follow directions and thus do not complete an exercise or activity correctly. In society, we are asked to provide directors to a place by a stranger. These directions need to be given clearly and concisely. Pupils should have ample opportunities to learn to read and follow directions carefully. The directions may pertain to doing a work book exercise, completing a model, engaging in an art project, and/or taking a test. Pupils should read the directions carefully and then explain, at selected intervals, what they are to do. In many cases, the directions follow a definite order or sequence. Thus step one come first, then step two, followed by step three, and so on. Fluent reading is generally necessary to do an activity correctly from directions given (Ediger, 1991, 180-181).

A third purpose of reason for reading is for pupils to read sequentially a narrative account in social studies. After reading, proper order is very important in retelling these events. Otherwise, the narrative account may not make sense. For example, the order of presidents in the United States follow a specific sequence. The first president being George Washington and the last one being the present president. Naming the states in the union by dates when becoming a state requires a certain order in their listing. In problem solving, pupils first select a problem. Next, information is gathered in answer to the problem. An hypothesis is then developed which is tentative. More information is necessary to test the hypothesis in a realistic situation. The original hypothesis might then be revised and a new one developed. There appears to be a certain order to follow when engaging in problem solving in the social studies. Certainly, the pupil could not begin with an hypothesis since there would be no problem for which an hypothesis is needed. Thus, there is a certain order that needs to be followed in doing problem solving activities.

A fourth purpose in reading is to skim subject matter content to note if it is relevant. When looking for proper nouns, subject matter may be skimmed and not every word read on a page. Proper nouns begin with capital letters, always. Common nouns begin with lower case letters unless they begin a new sentence. As a further need for skimming when reading in the social studies, the pupil may skim to secure names, dates, and places in order to answer questions. Names do begin with capital letters as a distinguishing feature. Dates are numerals and do stick out in context. Places, such as cities, states, nations, and countries have capital letters for the beginning letter of each word. Thus, there are distinguishing characteristics when skimming subject matter which provides assistance in locating desired information. In using the index to a social studies text or reference book, the pupil does not read every entry, but quickly skims the entries until the needed one is found. When viewing the table of contents in a reference book, the pupil skims the chapter titles until the one necessary is located. Sometimes, of course, the reference book does not show materials in the table of contents that are needed, so the pupil must look in the index section to notice if needed entries are there.

A fifth purpose in reading social studies content is to scan materials that provide what one is looking for. For example, the pupil might scan the chapter titles, the topic headings, the subtopics, and the words in italics to notice if the desired content is there for an assignment. Not every word is read by any means, but the content being searched for is being scanned to see if the salient ideas are there. Once the salient ideas are noticed through scanning, the pupil may read further to notice if the content is relevant. Scanning as a skill in reading has many benefits to the learner. The pupil then scans until vital subject matter being looked for is in the offing.

A sixth purpose in pupil reading is to develop main ideas. In the development of main ideas, pupils indicate in one sentence what has been read, covering several pages on the intermediate grate level, as an example. Many pupils on that grade level, as well as adults, find this difficult to do. The main idea expressed truly needs to cover, in general, what was printed on the several pages. Thus the main idea is general and covers considerable content in print form. The main idea con be checked by having pupils give supporting details. These details need to support the main idea to be valid. Thus the main idea given does not hold water, so to speak.

A seventh purpose in reading social studies content is to have pupils read to achieve a summary. Here, the reading activity must lead pupils to draw conclusions covering that which has been read. The conclusion needs to cover what is vital and relevant in content read. Summarising is a complex act of reading. Pupils then need to relate ideas and finalise the subject matter with concluding statements. Summarisations cover previous content read emphasising relationship of significant ideas. A summary may be appraised in terms of having adequate supporting ideas from what has been studied in an ongoing unit of study in the social studies. Reading and writing certainly are related to each other. When pupils write, they must have content to write about. Reading social studies subject matter might well provide the content for summary statements. As the summary is written, pupils in a committee may debate what is relevant and what is irrelevant to record. Paper and pencil may be used. Generally, on the intermediate grade levels, there are learners who are proficient in using the word processor to type the summary. If not, the teacher may do the typing as the content is provided by learners in a collaborative setting. Revising the rough draft may also be stressed. Pupils need to realise that quality work should be in the offing in all that is done. Writing summaries of what has been acquired in social studies is no exception. Much reading is required before, during, and after writing the summary statements.

When reading and writing summaries, pupils need to be able to identify words correctly and attach meaning to what has been written. Meaning theory is salient to stress in reading in the social studies (Ediger, 1997, 104-107).

An eighth purpose involves reading diary entries. Many pupils do write diaries at home, but do not maintain writing these entries for an extended period of time. We suggest that pupils individually or collaboratively write diary entries pertaining to what has been learned on a daily basis in the social studies. The entries are dated. Taking turns in writing these diary entries avoids boredom and sameness in learning opportunities pursued. Reading and writing are interrelated. Revising and modifying what has been written will be in the offing. If done collaboratively, team work is very important. The talents of each pupil need to be used with no one left out or shunned. Each pupil should feel that he/she belongs to the group and is accepted as a human being having much worth. Recognising the talents of each participant is important so that esteem needs are being met. Individuals like to have belonging and esteem needs met. It certainly is an uncomfortable feeling to be minimised and not being able to participate actively in an ongoing learning activity. Important items need to be recorded, such as excursions taken and fascinating learning opportunities in the classroom (Ediger, 1997, 188-190).

A ninth purpose involves reading in an analytical manner. Here, the pupil with teacher guidance divides into component parts what has been read to view each facet with a skeptical attitude. The learner needs to separate the accurate from the inaccurate, the factual from fantasy, and the parts from the whole. Evaluation of the components needs to be thoroughly assessed. After the inaccurate has been separated, for example, from the accurate, the pupil is in a better position to use what has been learned. The pupil then has taken apart the whole and examined meaningfully what is accurate so that it may be better understood.

A tenth purpose for reading is to read in an imaginative manner. Pupils with teacher guidance need to come up with new ideas. New arrangements may be made of the previously acquired content. Novel ideas may come forth which are used to provide background information to write creative prose and poetry.

An eleventh reason for reading in the social studies is to read for problem solving purposes. If the problem pertains to appraising the worth of a given written product, criteria for the appraisal need to be developed. The learner should be heavily involved in writing each criterion. The problem was to write criteria for the appraisal and this involves higher levels of cognition. When evaluating the worth of each criterion for evaluation, pupils with teacher guidance brainstorming the values of each.

THINKING, MULTIPLE INTELLIGENCES, AND READING IN THE SOCIAL STUDIES

Sternberg (1997) determined levels of thought for pupils to exhibit in learning. For social studies, Sternberg indicated the following, as an example:

Memory. Remember a list of the factors that led to the Civil War.

Analysis. Compare, contrast, and evaluate the arguments of those who favoured slavery versus those who opposed it.

Creativity. Write a page of a journal from the viewpoint of a soldier fighting for one side or the other side of the Civil War.

Practicality. Discuss the applicability of lessons from the Civil War to countries today that have strong internal divisions, such as the former Yugoslavia.

The social studies teacher may use the above model to have pupils think on different levels of complexity, such as memory, analysis, creativity, and practicality.

The theory of multiple intelligences is important in educational practices when having pupils reveal in diverse ways what has been learned. Pupils might then reveal what has been learned, not through testing only, but also through seven intelligences identified by Gardner (1993). These intelligences are the following:

1. verbal/linguistic such as in reading and writing.
2. logical/mathematical.
3. visual/spatial.
4. musical.
5. bodily/kinesthetic.
6. interpersonal.
7. intrapersonal.

Thus, there are numerous ways to reveal what has been learned in social studies. For example number one intelligence above—verbal/linguistic—the pupils may show content learned through the writing of related prose and poetry. Number three above—visual/spatial—pupils might want to indicate subject matter learned through art products and projects (Ediger, 1996, 101-103). With multiple intelligences theory, the door has been opened to pupils in using talents and skills to show to others depth and breadth of learning in ongoing lessons and units of study.

Conclusion

There are numerous skills and abilities involved in teaching when producing quality readers in the social studies. Reading, as one learning activity, needs to be emphasised since it is a highly useful skill presently in the curriculum as well as in the future work place. Pupils then need to learn word recognition skills, such as phonics and syllabication. Contextual clues also are valuable to use to identify unknown words. Different plans in reading subject matter exist and these need to be adapted to each learner's potential in learning to read proficiently. Individualised reading, shared reading, experience charts, and use of basal, among other recommendable procedures, are excellent to use providing pupils benefit as optimally a possible from the procedure used. The learning style of the individual pupil is important to use as a basis for determining under which conditions pupils learn best in the social studies. For example, selected pupils learn best on an individual basis whereas others achieve more optimally in group or collaborative settings. The teacher's position is complex indeed with research data coming out continuously to assist in teaching pupils to learn as much as possible (Ediger, 1998, 137-144).

References

Ediger, Marlow (1997), *Social Studies Curriculum in the Elementary School*, 4th Edition. Kirksville, Missouri: Simpson Publishing Company, 93-97.

Ediger, Marlow (1998), *Teaching Reading Successfully in the Elementary School*. Kirksville, Missouri: Simpson Publishing Company, 94-95.

Ediger, Marlow (1988), *Language Arts Curriculum in the Elementary School*, Kriksville, Missouri: Simpson Publishing Company, 21-22.

Ediger, Marlow (1996), *Elementary Education*. Kirksville, Missouri: Simpson Publishing Company, 229-233.

Ediger, Marlow (1988), *The Elementary Curriculum, Second Edition*. Kirksville, Missouri: Simpson Publishing Company, 1-6.

Ediger, Marlow (1998), *The Holy Land*. Kirksville, Missouri: Simpson Publishing Company, 1-10.

Ediger, Marlow (1996), *Essays in School Administration*. Kirksville, Missouri: Simpson Publishing, 101-105.

Ediger, Marlow (1997), *Teaching Reading and the Language Arts in the Elementary School.* Kirksville, Missouri: Simpson Publishing Company, 18-27.

Ediger, Marlow (1991), *Relevancy in the Elementary Curriculum. Second Edition.* Kirksville, Missouri: Simpson Publishing Company, 180-181.

Ediger, Marlow (1997), 'Meaning in the Social Studies,' College *Student Journal*, 31(1), 104-106.

Ediger, Marlow (1997), 'Social Studies and the Middle School Student,' *Journal of instructional Psychology*, 24(3), 188-190.

Ediger, Marlow (1998), 'Issues and Technology Use in Reading Instruction,' *Reading Improvement,* 35(3), 137-144.

Ediger, Marlow and Digumarti Bhaskara Rao (2000), *Teaching Reading Successfully.* New Delhi, India: Discovery Publishing House.

Gardner, Howard (1993), *Multiple Intelligences: Theory into Practice.* New York: The Basic Books.

Sternberg, Robert J., (1997), 'What Does It Mean to be Smart?' *Educational Leadership*, 54 (6), 20-24.

Lakshmi, L.B. and Digumarti Bhaskara Rao (2000), *Reading and Comprehension*, New Delhi, India: Discovery Publishing House.

7

Writing in the Social Studies

Writing is a basic in the social studies that can be stressed throughout the different curriculum areas. Written work needs to emphasise writing for a variety of purposes. There are many kinds of purposeful writing activities, including creative, expository, and narrative—each with its diverse subdivisions. Pupils need to enjoy and appreciate different writing experiences that contribute to a better understanding of the social studies.

Social studies teachers need to stress the concept of writing in the social studies. A quality curriculum advocates that learners write across the curriculum. There are numerous purposes in writing. Individuals write for a variety of reasons. Pupils need to perceive that writing taught in school has utilitarian values. What is emphasised as objectives in school can be used in society. The teacher must determine where a pupil is presently in writing achievement and assist the learner in making continuous progress. Each pupil then needs to attain optimally.

There are numerous component parts in writing content for others to read. Ediger (1995) wrote:

There are numerous separate academic disciplines that may be taught in the school setting. The following language arts areas, among others, might then be taught separately from other academic areas...

1. grammar
2. spelling
3. oral communication
4. reading
5. literature
6. punctuation
7. formal writing
8. creative writing
9. handwriting
10. listening.

When viewing the above separate subject areas, it is quite obvious that the teacher could relate curriculum areas so that fewer isolated subjects are taught. For example, items four and five above could easily be correlated. Pupils then would study reading skills within the literature curriculum. To further decrease the isolated language arts areas, the teacher might well bring in oral communication skills (item three above) as the content in literature is being discussed in the classroom setting. Listening skills (item ten above) could definitely be brought in as the content in literature is being discussed. What has been read and discussed in literature may be dramatised creatively or pantomimed; these are additional language arts skills, not listed above that may be stressed in ongoing units of study. Much correlation, fusion, and integration of the language arts can easily be emphasised here. Presently, the integrated model of curriculum development is in vogue. If pupils perceive that knowledge is related, they will tend to retain previously acquired subject matter for a longer period of time as compared to learning subject matter in isolation, such as isolated facts.

DEVELOPING EXPERIENCE CHARTS

Primary grade pupils may experience a rich writing curriculum through the use of the experience chart. To provide readiness, the teacher may have selected objects on an interest centre. For example, the following objects from the Middle East provide a model:

1. a shepherd's flute used for entertainment while herding sheep.
2. a cloak and baggy trousers worn by bedouins.
3. a drum made from goat's skin stretched over a jug made from clay.
4. a bedouin coffee pot.

Pupils had not seen these objects before and appeared highly curious as to their use and origin. A map of the Middle East was shown to these first grade pupils. Questions were definitely invited from pupils during the discussion. The resulting experience chart reveals the kinds of thinking learners were engaged in. The teachers then recorded the following comments of pupils after discussing objects from the interest centre:

We blew into the shepherd's flute and were not able to make a sound. It was fun though to do so. The drum made soft sounds when we hit it with the palm of our hands. The cloak was too large to fit any of us properly. We looked at the wide baggy trousers and marveled how it looked. We really enjoyed sitting in a circle and pretending that coffee was being drunk using the bedouin coffee pot.

Pupils were guided by the teachers to notice that talk can be written with the use of letters (graphemes) to represent sounds (phonemes) within the framework of words and sentences. Talk (oral communication) came entirely from learners for the experience chart. Each teacher was a guide and stimulated pupils to speak and listen to the ideas of others. After the experience chart had been completed, pupils read the content as the teacher pointed to words, phrases, and the entire sentence, in sequence. If young pupils cannot do their own writing, they can enjoy seeing the teacher record their ideas. When pupils are ready to do their own writing they should write their own experience charts. This can be done one any age and achievement level.

WRITING OUTLINES

When readiness is in evidence, the pupil should achieve skills in writing an outline. A good outline is useful in giving an oral report to others. Why? The speaker then has better organisation in presenting content to listeners. Sequence is inherent in presenting the subject matter orally. Then too, if a pupil forgets content, he/she may view the outline at that point and present information sequentially.

Each outline should have title followed by ordered major divisions with Roman numerals. Subdivisions should have sequential capital letters of the alphabet to show that each subdivision is directly related to its main division. The details are shown by Hindu-Arabic numerals under their subdivision.

A major reason that pupils forget what has been learned is that subject matter is perceived as being isolated. Relationship of content is then lacking. Developing outlines as a learning opportunity, among others, should assist pupils to integrate ideas acquired through reading, in particular. Subordinate ideas are then related to main ideas as well as quality in logical order of content should be in evidence.

Within a committee setting, pupils may share ideas acquired from an outline. Constructive evaluation of the outline using appropriate criteria may be a part of the committee endeavours. Peers learning from each other can be an excellent way of growing and achieving. When engaging in evaluation, pupils use that which has been learned. With use made of content acquired, pupils retain subject matter for a longer period of time.

WRITING, VARIETY, AND BOOK REPORTS

There are numerous library books which relate directly to ongoing social studies units of study. If the selection is large enough, library books may be harmonised/correlated with the basal textbook. Thus a pupil might choose which library book to read based on his/her present level of attainment. Those who read well may select the more complex library books to read. Pupils who possess fewer skills in reading proficiency may choose library books on an easier reading level. The learner is the chooser. Content read by pupils may then be shared in the current lesson being pursued in class. Learners individually might have read on transportation, communication, family life, education, urban and rural areas, agriculture, and recreation in the unit being pursued. Ideas read can then be shared with others as the lesson progresses in unit teaching. We recommend that basal textbooks be used along with individualised reading. Different sources might then be contrasted and compared such as library book versus textbook subject matter. In making these comparisons, higher levels of cognition might arise in the process. Thus problems identified, questions raised, and critical thinking emphasised in the process might guide leaners to appraise sources of information more adequately.

What pupils have read from a library book in terms of content may be appraised, not only by contributions made in classroom discussions, but also with the use of the following activities:

1. making a mural covering major ideas in the library book. A few sentences may be written to describe the mural.
2. presenting an oral report with the use of an outline.
3. developing a related diorama. The scene in the diorama should be described in writing.
4. writing a summary of main ideas covered in the library book.
5. constructing one or more models. Each model made needs to have a summary of ideas contained therein.
6. drawing sequential pictures directly related to the contents in the library book. Clarification of content in these illustrations may be achieved with brief written statements pertaining to each.
7. painting in water colour a scene emphasising a broad theme from the book read. The broad theme with selected subordinate ideas should be written and attached to the art product.
8. engaging in writing a formal dramatisation with specific play parts pertaining to a library book read.
9. stressing committee work in written summaries produced when several pupils have read the same book. Multiple copies of a library book in paper back form has become increasingly popular in many classrooms.

10. conducting a survey pertaining to a particular facet of what was read from a library book, such as voting behaviour toward candidates running for election, and writing up the included findings.

When reading self selected library books, pupils tend to enjoy the contents and feel a sense of ownership of the social studies curriculum. Many purposeful writing experiences for learners may follow as a result of reading. These activities need to be challenging, meaningful, and purposeful.

WRITING DIARY ENTRIES

Pupils with teacher guidance should have ample opportunities to write up experiences from each concluded lesson in social studies. Each day's entry should be dated. Rotation of committees and individuals writing the diary entries need to be emphasised so that boredom and routineness does not become a part of the pupil. Developing and maintaining learner interest in writing is important. Learners should be encouraged to keep personal diaries so that practice in writing is stressed continually.

What goes into the diary entries for a lesson in social studies that has been completed must be

1. salient and relevant. Trivia needs to be minimised.
2. directly related to the lesson presentation.
3. important to the learner(s) in that the committee and the individual pupil reflect upon perceived significance.
4. stimulating so that problems and questions are identified.
5. depth oriented so that main and subordinate ideas are written. Shallow misunderstood content should be eliminated.

We will write a sample of diary entries as an example pertaining to a unit on the Middle East. These include the following:

October 13. We studied about the wall surrounding East Jerusalem. The wall was completed in 1542 when the Ottoman Empire ruled the Middle East. Previous walls were built by King Solomon (about 980 BC) and Nehemiah (444 BC). Inside the wall are many very small shops, much like in medieval days. Thus there is a small shop for selling shoes, another for selling spices and grain for food, and still another for selling souvenirs. Hawkers sell tea to drink and fresh garden crops, among other items. The contents in the video tape we viewed showed this city to be bustling and noisy. With traditional Arabic dress, men wear cloaks and head dresses. The latter is kept in place with an agal, a rope-like material, which fastens the cloth like head dress to the head.

October 14. We studied about the Dome of the Rock, a Moslem Mosque completed in 691 AD. This mosque is octagonal and has a golden plated dome. Prior to entering the mosque, devout followers perform ablutions, that is they wash the faces, feet, and hands before entering this holy place. Here, devout Moslems pray five times a day while facing Mecca, the birth place of Mohammed and the holiest city of Islam. From this place too, Mohammed ascended into heaven and came back to earth again, according to devout followers of Islam.

October 15. We discussed the Western Wall, adjacent to the Dome of the Rock, which is the only remnant of the ancient Jewish temple. This wall goes back to the days of Herod the Great. Herod was a ruler of the land of Palestine, a part of the Roman Empire. The Western Wall was a part of the entrance to the ancient Jewish Temple. The Temple was destroyed by the Romans in 70 AD. The natural rock is large indeed in the Wall. Devout Jews pray here each day. Orthodox Jews wear traditional clothing such as the men wear long black coats, black trousers, and a large broad brimmed black hat. Many have cork screw curls on each side of the head.

October 16. A video tape was introduced by the teacher on the Church of the Holy Sepulcher, located inside the walled city of Jerusalem. Inside the church is the traditional Golgatha where Christ was crucified, according to devout Christians. Golgatha is a hill inside the Church of the Holy Sepulcher. Nearby is the rotunda which has the tomb of Christ. Here, devout Christians come to the place of entombment of Christ. The Church was built in 1542 after the Crusaders had captured the old city of Jerusalem. The crusaders held on to Palestine until 1187 when the Moslems recaptured it.

Pupils need to have experiences individually as well as in committees to write diary entries. Quality standards should be stressed when the teacher appraises learner progress in writing. Pupils individually need to attain continuous progress in written work.

WRITING LOGS IN THE SOCIAL STUDIES

The teacher should guide pupil writing of log entries. These logs should assist pupils to summarise diary entries and other content gained in ongoing and completed social studies units. Learners need to achieve broader ideas in writing logs, such as attaining generalisations adequately. There are criteria which should be implemented in teaching—learning situations in writing logs. These are the following:

1. generalisations should cover more specific ideas acquired, including facts.
2. learners need to have ample opportunities to achieve content inductively or by discovery. Deductive or direct teaching is, of course, not omitted.
3. accuracy in writing generalisations is a must. Each generalisation may be checked as to its covering comprehensively of subordinate content including factual ideas.
4. the mechanics of writing such as punctuation, spelling, quotation marks, and indentation, among others, are secondary in importance as compared to ideas expressed.
5. sequence in recorded generalisations needs to be appraised in terms of logic and order.

Writing of logs can be a very valuable experiences for pupils. The log entries represent a purpose in writing and that being to summarise diary entries. Writing of logs challenges learners to write broad ideas which are supported by more specific content. It also provides practice for learners to review that which has been studied previously. A variety of reasons or purposes must be emphasised by the social studies teacher in having pupils write in the curriculum.

WRITING AND KEEPING JOURNALS

Journal writing has become popular in the social studies, Here each day, learners are given time to write what has been learned on an individual basis. What is written down represents the thinking and feelings of the involved pupil. Perhaps, five to ten minutes per day for writing journal items provide a learner with an additional worthwhile reason for relating content acquired with abstract symbols, such as written content. The teacher may or may not read the journal writing. In personal writing, the pupil might wish to share content written with others in a committee or with another learner. The choice should be up to the pupil. If the teacher believes that a pupil is wasting time rather than writing, he/she may desire to read the journal items. Best it is if the learner takes the initiative in wanting to share written ideas and impressions. We have the following suggestions to give to teachers of pupils in journal writing:

1. time on task in creative writing is salient.
2. pupils need to be motivated to share what has been written, not forcing learners to do so.
3. a log developed for writing to the pupil's part is important.
4. creativity and critical thinking skills need to be fostered within the learner.
5. problem solving endeavours are always necessary in writing.

Journal writing is stressed as a rather recent development in the social studies. The pupil here tends to own the curriculum in this case, since he/she is in control of what is written. We recommend much flexibility and openness in journal writing emphasis in the social studies.

WRITING A FORMAL DRAMATISATION

Pupils tend to like and role play in life. From basal textbooks or library books, the teacher may guide pupils to choose a selection on which to write play parts. The social studies has much printed content which lends itself well to the writing of a formal dramatisation. The selection chosen should have clearly expressed ideas which pupils can comprehend. Cooperatively, a committee may volunteer to write each part. Later on, others may write parts for a play in the social studies.

Learners need to work together in writing the play. Respect for the thinking of each committee member in writing the play is a must. Learning to work harmoniously within a committee is a very valuable skill to achieve. The thinking of each member in the committee is a very valuable skill to achieve. The thinking of each member in the committee is salient. The following are offered as suggestions to assist pupils with teacher leadership in writing a formal dramatisation:

1. ideas for the writing of the diverse play parts should come freely from each learner. Brainstorming can be a good procedure to secure these ideas.
2. each pupil needs to understand well what has been read from the textbook or other reference source in the social studies so that a related play can be written effectively.
3. appropriate attitude toward reading and writing as well as listening/speaking need to be in evidence when the play parts are written.
4. working harmoniously with each other is a must.
5. sharing, not ridiculing ideas, needs to be fostered.

The written play in its final form may and should be presented to peers in the classroom. How much of props and background scenery will be developed depends on goal attainment. Are these items salient to presenting the play? Do these items and their making have worthwhile educational values? These kinds of questions must be answered by the teacher. There is much that pupils need to learn in the school curriculum. A careful consideration on what has the most value for pupils in the social studies needs to be addressed and appraised (Ediger, 1998, Chapter Five).

CREATIVE WRITING IN THE SOCIAL STUDIES

Goals stressing creativity on the part of pupils need adequate emphasis in the social studies. Why? Life in school and in society demand that individuals be able to solve their own problems in a creative manner. Generally what has worked for others does not work for the self in a unique problem solving situation. Then too, improvements in inventions and technology by creative individuals have made life more enjoyable and fulfilling for most in society. Creativity is necessary for individuals to appreciate experiences and activities in the world of reality. Individuals and groups possessing creativity have brought to us the good, the beautiful, and the true, in many cases and situations. Creativity has also brought on devastating situations such as more capable instruments of war.

Writing of creative verse in the social studies has much to emphasise in ongoing lessons and units of study. First, pupils should have ample opportunities to write poetry. Writing poems can truly stress that which is creative and novel for the involved learner. Rhymed verse is fascinating to many pupils. Thus on the appropriate developmental level, pupils may write couplets in which ending words rhyme. The following was written by a pupil in a unit taught on the Middles East:

The Dome of the Rock

sits on a mountain top.

A triplet contains three lines with all ending words rhyming, such as in the following:

The Western Wall

is very old and tall

was used for a worship call.

A quatrain has four lines and all ending words may rhyme or lines one and two as well as lines three and four may rhyme The following is an example:

The Church of the Holy Sepulcher

is important to the worshiper

to which many come with awe

having feelings of sincerity in the raw.

In the above quatrain lines one and two rhyme as well as lines three and four have rhyme. Pupils tend to enjoy writing limericks when ready. A limerick is a combination of a couplet and a triplet. Thus lines one, two, and five rhyme. Also lines three and four rhyme. Limericks usually start with the words—'There once was——.' However, there can be inventive forms of verse written which have new standards as to what is inherent. A completely open-ended kind of verse to write is free verse. In free verse, there is no required rhyme nor number of syllables per line. The length of a free verse is also open-ended.

Poems may have a certain number of syllables per line such as haiku. Haiku has a five-seven-five number of syllables for each of three lines as is shown in the following written by a sixth grade pupil:

Eight gates in the wall
to enter the old city
of Jerusalem.

There are additional kinds of verse to write which have a certain number of syllables per line such as the tanka having a five-seven-five-seven-seven progression for each of five lines of verse. Actually, two more lines could be added tot he haiku to make a tanka.

Metaphors, similes, alliteration, and onomatopoeia may be added as ingredients to any written poem.

WRITING FOLKLORE

Social studies content lends itself well to writing diverse forms of folklore. The writing of legends, for example, may be stressed within any unit of study. Most have heard of Davy Crockett and his skills. There even was a very popular song which made it to the top, a few years ago, in popular music pertaining to Davy Crockett, a frontier scout in American History. In legends, Davy Crockett is portrayed as an excellent marksman who at age three could shoot a fly off the nose of a person. Legends stress real flesh and blood individual, past or present, who can do supernatural things. There are no limits to the imagination as to what a person can do in a legend.

In a unit on the Middle East, for example, a pupil could write a legend on one or more of the following:

1. Benjamin Netanyahy, Yitzhak Rabin, and Ehud Barak of Israel.

2. Yassir Arafat, President of the Palestine Liberation Organisation.
3. the late King Hussein and his son King Abdullah of Jordan; Hafez Assad, President of Syria; and Gamel Abdul Nasser, Anwar Sadat, and Hosni Mubarek, Presidents in sequence of Egypt.

Pupils need to secure adequate background information on a person prior to writing a legend. He/she then needs to think of interesting supernatural events that relate to this legendary person chosen. Sequence of content written is important for characterisation, setting, plot, and theme. Teachers need to guide pupils to read salient legends as well as discuss the ingredients that make for legends. Models of quality legends must be in the repertoire of the pupil. Here, the teacher could read entire or selections of a relevant legend to learners in the classroom setting. Additional kinds of folklore need to be understood prior to their actual writing. These should include myths, tall tales, fairy tales, and fables, Ediger (1995) wrote:

Use of the imagination is important for the... pupil. Why? Creative behaviour is necessary in school and in society. It is needed to identify and solve problems. New solutions are necessary. The tried and true may not work in a changing world. Thus, learners must develop unique, novel, and original means of human behaviour. Writing tall tales can be one learning opportunity that encourages creative thought...

Pupils were generally eager to share their tall tales with others. If a pupil did not want to share, this was the pupil's prerogative. Since enthusiasm is contagious, all ultimately shared.

USING THE WORD PROCESSOR

New Personal computers tend to be user friendly. Key board skills basically are quite similar as compared to the outdated typewriter. Each pupil must become computer literate. Computer literacy is sequential and should emphasise continuous progress. With the use of the word processor, a pupil becomes an owner of the curriculum. He/she does not react only to the contents on the monitor, but also decides what commands will be given to the computer. In the writing activities discussed previously, the pupil is the decision maker when content is placed into the computer.

It is the learner who decides titles, subject matter, order of the subject matter, style of writing, as well as other literary elements. The computer then serves the pupil, not the other way around. Thus in writing a legend, the pupil is the decision maker. The pupil then decides what shall go into the legend. The teacher is a guide, a helper, and a motivator, but not a teller or explainer of what is to be done. Corrections in writing can be quickly made and does not destroy interest in writing. With cut and paste, the pupil can rearrange the order of content rather quickly. Careful proofing by the learner of the written product is as important as ever. Spell check in the computer does not catch errors in homonyms, nor other errors with correctly spelled words that are incorrectly used in writing. With errors in punctuation, the pupils will need to catch and correct each mistake a result of proofing.

The following advantages of using computers in writing need to be emphasised:

1. spell check will catch all spelling errors and provide alternative words to the learners as to what is needed for each word in order that corrections may be made. The changes in most cases can be made in a matter of seconds.

2. all corrections made show on the monitor before the final document is printed. Thus a truly quality document may be printed even though initially, prior to proofing, the typing needed many corrections.

3. quantity and quality of types content can certainly be increased with the use of a word processor.

4. enjoyment in writing is furthered with personal computers being highly user friendly.

5. the pupil may focus more and more on ideas written rather than the mechanics of writing, especially correct spelling of words, with the use of the word processor (Schuncke, 1992).

Conclusion

Pupils need to experience variety in terms of the kinds of writing experience engaged in. Writing in the social studies should stress the concept of writing across the curriculum. Writing should stress positive altitudes and feelings of the involved learner. Subject matter should come from the pupil who has experienced a rich learning environment. Diverse learning opportunities assists the pupil to acquire relevant facts, concepts, generalisations, and main ideas so necessary in writing. Challenge for writing and encouragement form the teacher should guide the pupil to make continuous progress on an individual and group basis in writing.

Woolfolk (1990) quoted Lee Schulman's research on what expert teachers know:

1. they know the subjects they teach.
2. the general teaching principles that apply across subjects like the principles of classroom management, effective teaching, and evaluation...
3. the curriculum materials and programmes appropriate for their subject and grade level.
4. subject specific knowledge for teaching—those special ways of teaching that apply to certain students and particular concepts, such as the best ways to explain proportion and ratio problems to an accelerated algebra class.
5. learners and their characteristics.
6. the settings in which students learn—small groups, classes, schools, and the community.
7. the goals and purposes of education.

References

Ediger, Marlow (1995), 'Writing Tall Tales,' TAMS Journal, Vol. 22, No. 1, pages 33-34.

Ediger, Marlow (1995), 'Designing the Curriculum, The Progress of Education, Vol. 69, No. 12 pages 246-251.

Ediger, Marlow (1998), Teaching Reading Successfully in the Elementary School. Kirksville, Missouri: Simpson Publishing Company, Chapter Five.

Ediger, Marlow and Digumarti Bhaskara Rao (1996). Science Curriculum. New Delhi, India: Discovery Publishing House.

Ediger, Marlow and D. Bhaskara Rao (2000), Teaching Reading Successfully. New Delhi, India: Discovery Publishing House.

Ediger, Marlow and D. Bhaskara Rao (2001), Teaching Science Successfully. New Delhi, India : Discovery Publishing House.

Schuncke, George M. (1992), Elementary Social Studies. New York: The Macmillan Company, pages 177-199.

Woolfolk, Anita B. (1990), Educational Psychology. Fourth Edition. Englewood Cliffs, New Jersey: Prentice-Hall, Inc., page 12.

8

SOCIAL STUDIES CHILDREN'S LITERATURE

Literature for children can do much to enhance pupil learning in the social studies. A good selection of library books needs to be in the offing. Based on a variety of topics and reading levels pertaining to the thematic social studies unit being taught. Each pupil should then locate a personal book of interest and purpose as well as on his/her individual reading level of comprehension. The content obtained from reading library books may be used in discussions involving the ongoing lesson or unit of study. Library books may supplement the basal text, along with other materials of reading instruction, such as related reference books and computer technology. Each pupil needs to become a good reader so that optimal comprehension and higher cognitive levels of thinking are in evidence.

Children's literature has numerous contributions to make in ongoing social studies units. One student teacher whom we supervised in the public schools used children's literature entirely instead of basal textbooks. Here, learners would volunteer to say what they had read from a trade book in the social studies unit being pursued. There was no end to comments made by pupils. Basically the quality of responses from learners was good and reflected much enthusiasm. Generally learners held the title of the book up for all to see in the classroom when discussing ideas read. It appeared that many pupils had truly become hooked in the reading of trade books. We believe that trade books can provide subject mater for much of the social studies unit being pursued. Perhaps, it is good to bring in both the basal and trade books when teaching social studies. Basals, carefully chosen, should have much to offer pupils in ongoing units of study. We will start off with discussing how basal textbooks can successfully be used in unit teaching.

BASAL SOCIAL STUDIES TEXTBOOKS

The manual should have an objectives section from which the teacher may consider ends for learner attainment. Careful consideration must be given to each objective that is worthy for learner attainment. Those objectives emphasising higher levels of cognition should be stressed first in importance such as critical and creative thinking skills, as well as problem solving. There are word recognition skills which need emphasising. Prior to having learners read a selection form the basal, the teacher needs to preview the content to attempt to select new words which pupils need assistance in mastering. The manual section of the basal generally provides lists of words that may be new to learners for each chapter title. The teacher should look at these words and determine if any or all might be unknown to the involved pupils in class. Pupils should be able to pronounce words correctly and know their meanings, either in terms of definitions or within a sentence in context form. We would suggest that the teacher print in manuscript style for all pupils to see clearly, either on the chalkboard or on an overhead projector, each new word that learners will read in print. As each word is viewed by pupils while the teacher points to and pronounces it, learners say the same word correctly. Those pupils who can identify new words correctly from the chalkboard, hopefully, will also recognise the same word(s) when reading from the basal. Comprehension increases as pupils correctly identify words in print. Instead of printing the new words in isolation for pupils to learn to pronounce from the chalkboard or from the overhead, each word can be printed within a sentence. Perhaps, the new word should be underlined within that sentence. A more holistic approach is then involved in having pupils learn to recognise new words in print. The important point is that each pupil be able to pronounce correctly words read in context from the basal.

We have had teachers ask if phonics should be emphasised in reading in the social studies. We would say generally not. However, there are teachable moments when a pupil mispronounces many words that start with the 'm' sound, for example. We think the teacher then needs to emphasise that sound as the need arises in helping the learner to make appropriate grapheme-phoneme associations. Thus by having the pupil notice a series of words that start with the 'm' sound, the learner might make much headway in using the 'm' grapheme to relate directly to a specific sound (Ediger, 1997)

Along with introducing new words to pupils, the teacher should also assist learners to attain background information pertaining to what will be read. No doubt, when discussing the correct pronunciation and meaning of new words that pupils will meet in print from the basal, background information will also be discussed. We would suggest that concrete (objects and items) as well as the semiconcrete (pictures, study prints, and audio-visual materials) be used by the teacher to develop background information within learners prior to reading orally within a committee or silently in the social studies. For example if pupils are to read about a rain forest, semi-concrete materials pertaining to that topic might assist learners to understand this concept better. We also believe pupils should read for a purpose and that being to answer relevant questions. The questions may come from the teacher or from pupils themselves. Reading from the basal is then done to secure necessary information. Answers to the questions, established prior to silent or oral reading, need to be discussed. Meaning should be attached to content analysed in the discussion. Additional questions may be raised and appraised. What is important is that pupils attach understanding to content read and discussed. Also, higher levels of cognition should be emphasised. These follow up activities might well be sequenced through further experiences. They may include the following:

1. reading related trade books listed by the authors.
2. reading additional stories related to the same topic or title.

3. brain storming other settings, plots, and conclusions than those contained in the basal.
4. writing a formal dramatisation from the content read from the basal.
5. pantomiming selections from the text.
6. debating opposing values contained in the writing.
7. developing a college pertaining to one or more major ideas contained in the subject matter.
8. viewing and analysing imagery used in the story, assuming this is in the content.
9. dramatising creatively idioms contained in the reading selection.
10. writing a poem based on the basal reader content.

INGREDIENTS IN CHILDREN'S LITERATURE

Author's of trade or library books in the social studies put different interpretations into content written. One item is the setting of the story. All stories or novels take place in a given area or region. A certain season is also involved. The year of occurrence is also stated or inferred by the author. Pupils need to attach meaning to the setting of the story. Maps and globes should be used by learners to notice the setting. Generally, a certain sequence is followed in writing the setting. A setting written for young pupils might be quite short. Sometimes a setting can be quite lengthy for elementary age pupils. The important point here is that learners comprehend what a setting emphasises and why it is salient.

Second, pupils need to understand the concept of characterisation of a story. A good description of the characters assists the reader to know what kind of persons are in a story or library book. A character may change in time or a character may stay the same throughout the story. A character may be wealthy, have moderate income, or be on the poverty level. Characters may have positive or negative attitudes, or some place in between. There are many possibilities when characters are described by the author.

Third, pupils should become familiar with the concept of irony. With irony, things turn out differently than what the reader might expect. For example, an ideal parent or parents may raise a child who breaks the law frequently and is in prison frequently. Or, a policemen's son murders a fifteen year old. News accounts of recent happenings frequently have items that truly contain irony. The parent(s) then might be just opposite of their offspring. Literature contains numerous writings where irony is inherent. It appears to make for exciting reading when the writer has irony in his/her writings.

Fourth, pupils need to attach meaning to the concept of plot. Plots should be clear enough so that readers know what happened in the story or reading selection. A plot may be rather lengthy, medium in length, or short. The interest level of the reader should be high in order to complete the reading selection to ascertain the plot. Curiosity in knowing the plot is a must. A good writer is able to hold reader attention until the plot is revealed or inferred. Sequence of content leads to the plot.

Fifth, point of view is important in a literary selection. From whose point of view is the story told? In diverse literary selections, point of view may be provided by the main character telling the story. Other points of view may come from a child, an animal, or an outsider, among others. Pupils should definitely know from whose point of view the story is being told.

Sixth, writers have a theme that is presented in the literary selection. The theme is the underlying idea presented in the writing. The theme may relate to such ideas as the evils of war, greediness of human beings, good works performed by individuals and groups, or happiness being a continual goal of the human being.

If pupils understand ingredients placed in to literary selections, they should attach increased meaning to the human dimension in the social studies.

IMAGERY IN CHILDREN'S LITERATURE

Writers of literature empathise the use of imagery. There are two kings of imagery, similes and metaphors. Similes make creative comparisons between and among persons, things, and ideas. The following are examples of similes:

1. The boy ran like a bolt of lightening. The boy's running is compared to a bolt of lightening. A creative comparison is made. The word 'like' makes the connections in making the comparison. Another word that connects to make a creative comparison is 'as,' e.g. John runs as quick as a deer in the forest.

Metaphors omit the words 'like' and 'as.' Notice the following sentences, each containing a metaphor.

1. The dog, bolting with a flash through the door, licked his master's hand. Notice the creative expression 'bolting with a flash through the door' describing the dog's actions.
2. The cloud, rising in the sinking sun, looked beautiful. 'Rising in the sinking sun' presents a unique perception for a viewer to imagine.

Imagery is used by writers to portray and describe in novel ways that which cannot be done in a literal sense. Children's literature needs to be an inherent part of any social studies unit since the human condition is so prevalent in the humanities (literature) as well as in the social sciences (history, geography, political science, anthropology, sociology, and economic). An integrated social studies curriculum must be emphasised in the school curriculum.

IDIOMS, LITERATURE, AND THE SOCIAL STUDIES

Human beings tend to use numerous idioms when communicating orally or in writing. Perhaps, it is clearer, in may situations, to communicate using idioms than expressing literal content. Once learners, when ready, can locate and brain storm as many as idioms as possible. Perhaps, teams of pupils may compete against each other in attempting to find as many idioms as possible. An atmosphere of respect should permeate this activity. We will list some common idioms which pupils should attach meaning to in a sequential series of social studies units.

1. barking up the wrong tree.
2. placing it on the front burner.

3. having done one's homework.
4. catching fish and cutting bait.
5. beating a dead horse.
6. backing the wrong horse.
7. walking on water.
8. handling a person with kid gloves.
9. getting on the stick.
10. left holding the bag.

Idioms can be dramatised to show the figurative and literal meaning of each. Understanding of how idioms are used in diverse literary selections and in society is important (Tiedt, 1983).

CHILDREN'S LITERATURE VERSUS THE BASAL TEXTBOOK

There are selected writers in the social studies who believe basal textbooks to be too rigid and formal. Further criticisms are that teachers follow the textbook excessively. The basal presents one source of information which can be evaluated with the use of other references to appraise accuracy and thoroughness of content. Then too, there are criticisms about the text not providing for diverse reading levels of leaners. For some pupils, the content will be too complex to read. For others, the subject matter will lack challenge. To remedy these and other criticisms, library books may be used instead. The author believes that both basals and children's literature in library books should be inherent in quality social studies unit of study. At this point of our discussion, however, let us take a look at replacing basals with library books.

There must be an ample number of library books available for pupil reading that covers all facets of the present social studies unit being emphasised. If a unit on Australia is taught, for example, library books on farming, manufacturing, urban and rural life, trade, education, recreation, travel, geography, history, music, art, and religion of Australia should be in evidence. Thus the scope of reading materials on Australia must be broad so that learners truly can understand the people and nation of Australia.

Several productive units have been taught using children's literature instead of the basal textbook in grades three though six. I will discuss three library books, as an example, in thematic teaching by a student teacher and a cooperating teacher, working as a team, whom I supervised in a unit on 'Australia—the Land down Under.'

Three fifth grade pupils in a committee read *Australia. A Lucky Land.* by Al Stark (published by Dillon Press, Inc., Minneapolis, Minnesota). These pupils volunteered to develop a mural on subject matter acquired. A variety of art media was used on the three feet by four feet sheet of butcher paper, located on the classroom wall. Here, pupils with teacher guidance cooperatively planned and completed the mural containing scenes of Canberra, the capital city; a map of Australia; the national flag; agricultural crops and products consisting of sheep, wool, cattle, dairy products, wheat, and fruit; and manufactured products such as metals, transportation equipment, paper, foods, and home appliances.

Pupils took turns telling about their completed mural to classmates. Learners and their teachers from other classrooms were invited to see mural and listen to explanations and comments by pupils who developed the mural. Many positive comments were made of the neatness and attractiveness of the completed mural. Pupil knowledge of ideas expressed in the mural indicated that meaningful learning had taken place. We marveled at the good attitudes shown by pupils throughout the development of the mural.

For pupils in a committee read *We Live in Australia* by Rennie Ellis (published by The Bookright Press, New York). After its reading, these learners with teacher assistance planned a creative dramatics activity. Here, pupils played roles of workers in Australia. These workers included dredgers for digging coal in mines, members of parliament, sugar cane fields, cattle raising, a research scientist, postal workers, and travel agents for tourism.

Each participant checked the accuracy of the roles through reading from the basal textbook, encyclopaedia entries, computer software, and listening to a citizen of Australia tell about the world of work in Australia. Videotapes and slides taken in Australia were used in this presentation. The completed dramatic presentation was given to classmates as well as in five other classrooms. There was considerable interest shown by pupils from other classrooms and their teacher in the presentations given. Creative dramatics breathes life and reality into what is being studied in the social studies.

Three other pupils read *This is Australia* by M. Sasek (published by the Macmillan Company, New York). These pupils with the assistance of the student teacher and the cooperating teacher elaborated on each scene pictured in the library book by securing information from a variety of reference sources, including diverse audiovisual presentations, CD ROMS, resource personnel, as well as reading materials on Australia. Depth teaching and learning were used instead of survey approaches. Thus, pupil research went beyond the content as presented in the library book.

Additional information gathered by pupils, pertaining to selected illustrations with brief comments in *This is Australia*, were the following:

1. Sydney, the largest and the oldest city in Australia, containing Harbour Bridge, the Opera House, and King's Cross, as well as being the capital of New South Wales.
2. Taronga Zoo in Canberra with kangaroos, the wallaby, emus, penguins, the white stilt, black swans, the kookaburra, kingfishers, wombats, the echidna, lyre birds, and the koala bear.
3. Melbourne, the capital of Victoria and Australia's second largest city, containing St. Peter's Cathedral, the Royal Arcade Shopping Center, the Royal Botanical Garden, and the major financial district of Australia.

From the information gathered and summarised within the committee, pupils made a wall chart, four feet by five feet containing vital generalisations from each of the three above named cities—Sydney, Canberra, and Melbourne. Illustrations were drawn or photocopied pertaining to each generalisation directly related to these three cities of Australia. Each illustration was placed next to the related generalisation. Explanations of each city on the chart were given to classmates. Pupils individually had their oral presentations well in mind and listener attention to each presentation was exemplorary.

Pupils from other classrooms heard about the completed project and came to see the attractive wall chart on Sydney, Candberra, and Melbourne. As the visitors from other classrooms viewed the chart and asked relevant questions, learners revealed their interests in learning vicariously and on their very own. Their teachers also came in to see the wall chart. Teachers may certainly learn much from each other in the teaching of social studies.

From all three library books read by committee members and related projects developed with teacher assistance, involved learners appeared to show enthusiasm, motivation, and purpose. Energy levels for learning were indeed high in these situations. Pupils learned much about Australia and appeared to retain the content acquired since these learners related ideas achieved to new units studied sequentially.

What pupils read from their library books may then be brought into different discussions pertaining to the unit title of Australia. Thus if pupils are studying urban living in Australia, subject matter read by one or more pupils on that topic should be discussed. Pupils should choose their very own books to read unless they can not settle down to truly complete a library book. When learners choose their own books to read, they tend to choose those based on their own personal level of reading attainment. Learners then are not hindered in reading by library books that are to difficult or too easy to read. There are some exceptions to this statement. The teacher should then intervene to assist a learner in choosing a book to read. We have observed our own student teachers whom we supervised in the public schools.use library books instead of the basal textbook within a social studies unit of study. One problem, many times, is that schools do not have an adequate number of library books for a single unit title so that these books might substitute for the basal.

WHAT CHILDREN'S LITERATURE CONTRIBUTES TO LEARNERS

Children's literature comes in many forms. Thus pupils can read biographies, authobiographies, fictional accounts, factual accounts, encyclopaedia entries, magazine articles, animal stories, people from other lands, folk lore (myths, fables, tall tales, legends, fairy tales, and other imaginary content), diverse nations on the planet earth, values clarification, multicultural topics, and other areas of information to numerous to mention. Content read should ideally relate in one way or another to the social studies unit title being stressed in teaching and learning. There are numerous contributions that children's literature can make to pupils.

First, pupils cannot travel to different nations on the face of the planet earth. However, they can experience vicariously from others who have. Second, experiencing something directly can be too costly and negative. Yet through reading one can safely experience things vicariously. Third, children's literature can enrich and expand one's own boundaries and borders. Broadening of experiences is then in evidence. Fourth, sheer enjoyment of reading encourages further pursuits to read. Thus positive attitudes can be developed within learners toward reading. Fifth, subject matter is learned which assists pupils to attain more adequately in any curriculum area. With the present day emphasis upon the integrated curriculum, books that pupils read dealing with the social studies may also relate to subject matter acquired in other curriculum areas.

Conclusion

Children's literature and the social studies need to be integrated so that holism is involved in pupil learning. A variety of kinds of reading materials should be available to learners so that each social studies unit might be meaningful and interesting. Individual differences among pupils' abilities and achievements must be adequately provided for. Reading content is a vital way of learning, along with concrete and semiconcrete materials use, in teaching-learning situations. Reading is one activity, an important one, to guide pupils to attain salient objectives.

References

Bhaskara Rao, Digumarti and Digumarti Pushpa Latha, eds. (1998). *International Encyclopaedia of Women*, 5 Volumes, New Delhi, India: Discovery Publishing House.

Ediger, Marlow (1997), *Social Studies Curriculum in the Elementary School,* Fourth Edition, Kirksville, Missouri: Simpson Publishing Company, Chapter Six.

Ediger, Malrow (1997), *Teaching Reading and the Language Arts in the Elementary School,* Kirksville Missouri: Simpson Publishing Company, Chapter Five.

Ediger, Marlow and D. Bhaskara Rao (2000), *Teaching Reading Successfully*. New Delhi, India: Discovery Publishing House.

Tiedt, Iris M. (1983), *The Language Arts Handbook*. Englewood Cliffs, New Jersey: Prentice-Hall, Inc., Chapter Eight.

9

GROUPING FOR INSTRUCTION IN THE SOCIAL STUDIES

The social studies teacher needs to group pupils so that optimal achievement is possible for each learner. Pupils differ from each other many ways such as abilities, interests, motivation, purposes, and subject matter knowledge. It behooves the social studies teacher to study each pupil carefully in order to determine which type of grouping will best benefit the learner to attain needed knowledge, skills, and attitudes in the social studies. Groups should be flexible and subject to change when necessary. Rigidly is not a part of modern day procedures for grouping in the social studies. Purposes and reasons for placing a pupil into a group change and should be based on learner needs. When a group has served its purpose, it should be disbanded or modified, and a new group formed. Each pupil needs to be accepted and respected. Which kinds of groups might then be established to aid pupils to achieve as much as possible individually as well as collectively (Ediger, 2000)?

INTEREST GROUPS IN THE SOCIAL STUDIES

The teacher may have pupils volunteer to join an interest group. In an ongoing lesson or unit of study, a pupil may wish to develop a relief map based on important areas being studied. If pupils are studying a unit of 'Visiting the Middle East,' they may participate in making a relief map of the West Bank of the Jordan to include The Sea of Galilee, the Dead Sea, the Jordan River, old and new Jerusalem, Bethlehem, Nablus and ancient Samaria, Hebron, The Negeb, Jericho, as well as Bethany.

The relief map may be made of strips of old newspaper about six inches long by one inch wide. These strips need to be soaked in water overnight. A paste may be made of an equal mixture of flour and water. The strips of paper should then be dipped into the paste and placed on a plywood section, two feet by three feet in dimension. After the paper mache' strips have dried, they should be painted with different colours of tempera paint which harmonise with each colour on the accompanying legend. A study of maps and globes by pupils with teacher guidance will provide background information on the making of a relief map. When observing maps and globes as models for developing the relief map, pupils feel the geographical features as they are being placed on the plywood. Learners need to paint these elevation features, using different colours on the model map, harmonising with the legend.

Pupils, when engaged in learning about maps and globes, should be very familiar with the five fundamental themes in geography, identified by the National Council for Geographic Education—NCGE, (Boehm and Petersen, 1994):

1. Location. Absolute location of a place using latitude and longitude grid lines for references on maps and globes.

2. Place. Physical characteristics including land forms, climate, soils, vegetation, and animal life. Human characteristics include language, population, settlement patterns, as well as economic activities.

3. Human—Environment System. Human activities that affect the natural environment such as altering the environment with waste products as well as using it for purposes of earning a living and developing places to live and dwell.

4. Movement. Movement of peoples in history, including the use of diverse means of transportation. Forces of a nature also stress movement such as wind, weather, and natural disasters.
5. Regions, Uniformity of an area in terms of physical characteristics, such as a desert, as well as cultural regions including the use of a language such as Arabic, or general agreement on religious beliefs, such as Islam.

Each pupil needs to have opportunities to develop well individually in terms of lesson and unit presentations as well as work collectively on diverse projects. There needs to be balance between individual versus committee endeavours in the social studies curriculum.

ABILITY GROUPING

There needs to be ample opportunities for pupils to work within a committee in which pupils have similar abilities, also called homogeneous grouping. Gifted/talented pupils may then wish to work on a challenging problem within the framework of unit teaching based on themes. Internet sources, CD ROMS, textbooks, library books, among other references, should be used. There are numerous fascinating problem areas which may be identified in a unit on the Middle East. With appropriate background information within a thematic units in social studies, gifted/talented learners may identify problem areas such as the following to solve:

1. why do news reporters never talk about the security of the Palestinians when working out some kind of a peace settlement between Arabs and Jews on the West Bank of the Jordan?
2. will a settlement have minimal chances of succeeding when Palestinians are to receive such a small share of the West Bank in governing small enclaves such as Bethlehem, Ramallah, most of Hebron, and Nablus, among others?
3. NATO forces with United States leadership have just completed at this writing the bringing back of Albanians

into Kosovo Province, after the latter were forced out by the Serbs of Yugoslavia, also called Serbia. Will Palestinians living the refugee camps since 1948 in Egypt, Syria, Lebanon, and Jordan, also be able to return to their former villages in what is now Israel, formerly called Palestine before 1948.

4. why does the United States provide at least $3 billion dollars in aid to Israel each year but none to the Palestinians?
5. is the United States an honest broker for peace between the Palestinian Arabs and Israel, or are there too many biases here?

The above are a few examples of fascinating topics for gifted/talented pupils to explore in problem solving (Ediger, 1998, 57). Average achievers as well as slow learners may also work on topics with problem identification and solution activities. A major area of concern here is that all pupils need to be accepted in a positive manner, and each learner is cared/provided for as much as possible. All human beings have great intrinsic value and need full opportunities for optimal development.

REMEDIAL GROUPS IN THE SOCIAL STUDIES

Areas of needed deficiencies of pupil learning need to be identified by the social studies teacher and remedies found. Each learner needs to experience the best possible sequence in learning so that failure is greatly minimised, and ideally eliminated. However, even the best of social studies teachers find diagnostic and remediation procedures necessary in ongoing lessons and units of study. The following areas are commonly selected whereby pupils individually indicate deficiencies:

1. word recognition techniques in reading social studies content.
2. comprehension difficulties when reading for a variety of purposes.
3. metacognition skills to monitor one's own reading skills and comprehension of content.

4. lack of background information when readiness for reading needs to be in the offing.
5. inability to relate reading the written work in the social studies (Ediger, 1997).

Regardless of the homogeneous/heterogeneous grouping controversy, each pupil needs to be accepted and respected to develop a feeling of belonging in order to attain as optimally as possible.

MINILESSON GROUPING IN THE SOCIAL STUDIES

The social studies teacher needs to evaluate when a minilesson should be taught pertaining to a perceived need. For example, when Jewish settlers have confiscated Arab land to build a new housing area on the West Bank of the Jordan, such as on the Har Homa hill located directly south of the walled city of Jerusalem, and there is resistance by the local Arabs, violence might well erupt. The teacher may desire to take time to teach a specific lesson on this incident. The teacher then chooses to teach a relevant minilesson on a current happening in the news.

CURRENT EVENTS IN THE NEWS

Each day there are newspaper, TV, and radio news items on the Middle East area of the world. Pupils need to be well informed on their present optimal achievement level. Lev Vygotsky (1978) offered the Zone of Proximal Development Theory in assisting pupils to achieve individually and collectively as well as possible. Here, the teacher is to determine where a pupil is presently in achievement. This present level is compared with a reasonable ideal that the teacher has in mind for pupils to attain. The gap between the present achievement level and the ideal makes for a gap (the zone of proximal development) that needs adequate attention and provision by the teacher. A variety of learning activities need to be used to minimise/eliminate the gap. Thus, the social studies teacher may need to provide adequate readiness for pupils in order that they benefit from the new current events news item. The following methods may be used in fulfilling the zone of proximal development concept:

1. explaining to learners ideas that would take care of the difference between present pupil achievement and the ideal desired by the teacher.
2. showing and discussing and audio-visual aid that enhances pupil understanding of the new subject matter.
3. raising questions requiring pupil responses that provide readiness for the new learnings.
4. dramatising content necessary for understanding what is new in ideas to be learned.
5. reading aloud to pupils which provides subject matter for learning which is deficient in the zone of proximal development.

A good current events curriculum keeps the social studies updated and can be stimulating to pupils as well. Quality sequence is needed here in that the social studies teacher must take care of the gap between what learner's know and where they might be in optimal achievement.

To indicate what pupils have learned, a variety of procedures may be used. Using paper/pencil tests favours those who are inclined to do well due to possessing verbal intelligence. Gardner (1993) indicates additional underlined intelligences in which pupils may reveal and show that which has been learned, such as in the following whereby the writer provides the social studies description pertaining to the identified intelligence.

1. ***logical/mathematics.*** Logical thought certainly may be used by learners to indicate what has been learned. Thus, in a unit on the Middle East, pupils might do research and come up with a logical approach as to what would make for some degree of fairness in resolving the dilemma between the Palestinian Arabs versus Israel over the status of the walled city of Jerusalem that Israel captured in the 1967 Six Day War.
2. ***visual/spatial.*** Individually or collectively, pupils may develop a quality mural, diorama, collage, and/or

montage pertaining to religious beliefs of Jews and Arabs in the Middle East. The art project might then include illustrations of The Dome of the Rock and the Mosque el Aqsa with their minarets. The Synagogue of Jerusalem located in new Jerusalem as well as the Jewish Wailing Wall (also called the Western Wall and the only remnant of the ancient Jewish Temple), and the Tomb of David, located inside the walled city of Jerusalem. Much research and planning needs to be done too make these art projects.

3. ***musical.*** the social studies teacher, after writing a brief current events item, may secure assistance from the music teacher in terms of putting the lyrics into musical notation. The resulting musical composition may be sung by learners. Within a classroom, there are pupils who, in degrees, possess musical intelligence. Pupils need to be challenged to compose music if musical intelligence is there. The writer attended a National Council Social Studies Convention a few years ago in which a professor handed out photocopied compositions in which the songs had content on the Civil War. When looking at the lyrics, there certainly was much subject matter covered on The Civil War in the many duplicated compositions handed out to each participant.

4. ***body/kinesthetic.*** Physical education might well become an important part of any social studies lesson or unit of study. We had university students choose a learning experience to perform in front of our graduate class in Social Science in the Elementary School. A set of four university students planned as well as executed a folk dance pertaining to the fiords of Norway. The folk dance based on geographical concepts, such as fiords, was directly related to a resource unit developed by these students on the Scandinavian Countries of Europe. The unit was taught that Fall to pupils in their respective public schools.

5. ***interpersonal.*** Pupils here may do exceptionally well in committee or group endeavours. Collaboratively, learners may plan and engage in an activity which relates directly to the current unit being studied in the social studies. Learners here are high achievers in collaborative work. Standards for doing group endeavours need to be developed and implemented. They are necessary for group work to be of high quality and where each pupil achieves as optimally as possible.
6. ***intrapersonal intelligence.*** Here, pupils achieve at a high level when working alone on a task relating to achieving social studies objectives. In educational literature, too frequently, the merits of committee work, collaborations, cooperative learning, and other forms of group work are praised to the point of leaving out individual work or intrapersonal intelligence. To be sure, both cooperative learning and individual achievement need to be stressed since in society, both kinds of endeavours are in evidence. People do things within groups as well as use their individual spare time in one way or another. With individual endeavours, the homogeneous/heterogeneous controversy becomes unimportant. With intrapersonal intelligence, the learner chooses tasks within a lesson/unit of study to persevere in and hopefully succeed.
7. ***naturalism.*** this intelligence stresses the world of science and objective endeavours. It does not take much time in classrooms to notice highly motivated and knowledgeable pupils in science. Science correlates well with the social studies. There are well known scientists whose life and times may be studied in history. An individual/committee endeavour might involve pupils making a time line as to the dates and what was discovered by scientists sequentially. A labelled illustration may be drawn above each date on the time line to show the person who made the scientific contribution. A good current events programme in school, when providing for intelligences emphasising naturalism, will stress what is happening

in the natural environment, such as mud slides, earthquakes, floods, tornadoes, cyclones, hurricanes, and monsoon rains.

In current events instruction, large groups, committees, and individual tasks may be stressed in grouping in the social studies.

GROUPING AND USING AUDIO-VISUAL AIDS

There are numerous quality audio-visual aids which may be shown to pupils so that they may achieve vital objectives. Audio-visual aids used in teaching and learning may include, videotapes, slides, filmstrips, films, pictures, objects and items, CD ROMS, and study prints, among others. How might pupils be grouped to achieve as much as possible individually?

First, the class as a whole may be introduced to the AV subject matter to be viewed. The class may be homogeneously or heterogeneously grouped. The major point here being that each pupil learn as much as possible and that all learners are respected/accepted. Nothing feels worse than to be minimised and ridiculed. The social studies teacher has an important responsibility to guide learners to develop well socially and be accepting of others. Each pupil needs to posses feelings of belonging and have talents identified and rewarded.

With the class as a whole viewing and later discussing the content acquired, the teacher must notice if each and every pupil is paying attention and learning as much as possible. Small groups might also view an audio-visual presentation with appropriate readiness, depending on the purpose involved. Ability grouping or mixed achievement levels may be stressed in the small group, depending upon the involved purpose. There are times when an individual learner may observe an audio-visual aid; there needs to be time available for pupils to view a presentation again if the need/desire exists. It is surprising how much can be learned anew if the AV presentation is 'reviewed'.

With AV learning opportunities, the teacher needs to be certain that

1. pupils have the needed background information in order to understand the contents in the presentation.

2. pupil interest is developed and maintained.
3. pupil purpose or accepted reasons are there for their viewing.
4. pupil comprehension is maximised.
5. pupil's higher levels of cognition are activated such as using analysis, synthesis, and evaluation of what has been viewed.

FLEXIBLE DISCUSSION GROUPS

Ample opportunities need to be given to pupils for discussing subject matter acquired, be it from an AV presentation or from reading, among other learning activities. With discussions, all pupils should be involved actively to participate. No pupil should be denied the opportunity to discuss. If a pupil ties to dominate or intimidate others, the teacher needs to model correct behaviour and modify negative behaviour. Democratic procedures are a must in any discussion group. Thus, pupils with teacher guidance need to do the following:

1. respect the thinking of others.
2. stay on the topic being pursued.
3. ask questions pertaining to what is no understood.
4. comment on relevant information in the ongoing discussion.
5. think creatively and critically as well as identify vital problem areas.
6. let each participant participate.
7. avoid disturbing any member in the discussion group.
8. evaluated in a positive manner the quality of ideas presented.
9. do not interrupt others in communicating ideas.
10. work for the good of the total group, but do give recognition for individual work well done. The group as well as the individual is important in school as well as in society.

Discussion groups are held depending upon the involved purposes. If a current events item provides the basis for a discussion, the class as a whole may be involved. The whole class may not provide adequate opportunities for individual participation. Thus, a smaller group may be necessary, such as five members. The members of this group may volunteer membership based on personal interests as to the topic to be pursued in the discussion. If highly complex subject matter is to be discussed, the group could be made up of those with high abilities. Pupils of lesser achievement then may make up other discussion groups. If all can achieve as much as individual abilities permit, then heterogeneous groups may be formed. From the discussion group in which a learner is involved, an individual project may be decided upon for the pupil. Several individual projects may then arise from small group discussion.

Social studies teachers need to develop rational balance among large group, committee work, as well as individual endeavours. Pupil's possess different styles of learning in that group and individual tasks need adequate plans for learning in the social studies (Dunn and Dunn, 1979). No pupil should be held back from learning as much as possible. Political and social agendas should not hold pupils back from achieving as much as individual interests, abilities, and purposes permit. Regardless of abilities, each person needs acceptance and rewards for whatever can be accomplished in an optimal way.

MODELLING AND GROUPING

Learners need to observe quality role models. The social studies teacher is an important model for pupils to emulate. Thus, he/she needs to be very cognisant of one whom pupils will emulate. Learners, too, may present good patterns of behaviour worthy for pupils to consider as positive models. Children growing up are looking around in school and in society for those whom they would like to imitate, accept, and pattern their beliefs, values, and attitudes. A person who shows perseverance in what is done presents a good and positive role model. Individuals need to persevere to achieve goals in life. The perseverance needs to be there to realise objectives in life. There are obstacles and hindrances that keep individuals from accomplishing and achieving, but perseverance is a trait that comes in as being very valuable to attain vital ends. Giving up can be very costly in life's journeys. Opportunities may be there only once to latch on to, and then no longer be there. Each day of schooling is very important for pupils. Time wasted cannot be made up. If it can be made up, time is taken for that and not for new learnings.

Groups may be formed by the teacher to model selected behaviours so that pupils realise important objectives in the social studies. What might the social studies teacher model for pupil emulation?

1. How to select an important problem in an ongoing lesson/unit of study.
2. How to choose reference sources that relate directly to the chosen problem so that solutions may be found.
3. How to develop an hypothesis, based on the information gathered.
4. How to assess the hypothesis as to its worth.
5. How to analyse and synthesise subject matter within the framework of problem solving activity.

Another area that we feel many people fall down on is to be a good member of a discussion group. Sometimes, people reveal rude and inconsiderate behaviour. A few may get together and intimidate others while agreeing among themselves upon railroading an agenda during the discussion. We believe that teachers can do a good job of indicating to learners in the classroom what roles members should play during the discussion. The following roles can be modelled by the classroom teacher within a discussion setting:

1. How to keep members in straying from the topic to be pursued.
2. How to keep a discussion moving forward within the framework of all participating and no one dominating.
3. How to build positive attitudes towards each other in a discussion setting.

4. How to clarify in a discussion that which is not understood.
5. How to separate salient from non-salient ideas.

Much time can be wasted if discussion group members do not follow selected ideals. We believe that being able to discuss well and be accepting of others is a vital part of the social studies corniculum.

Flexible groups need to be formed for modeling selected behaviours. A group may be formed which is based upon needs of learners. For example, those who need help in using an index in a book may have this behaviour modelled by the teacher. Sequentially then, the social studies teacher models how to use the index to obtain necessary information. Perhaps, the class as a whole needs to have a model presented for using the index of a text. The class then might be either ability grouped or have mixed achievement levels. If a small group of talented learners needs a role model for developing a bibliography, then ability grouping might be used. However, there are always pupils who show much perseverance in school work and might also wish to be included here. It is indeed difficult to define who should be placed in a specific group of learners to accomplish a goal. The major criteria to use in grouping is to have each pupil learn as much as possible. This is a professional responsibility of the teacher of social studies. Pupils need to be challenged and encouraged to learn as much as each possibly can. Certainly, there are pupils of different abilities and talents and they need to realise their optimal achievement, nothing less. Expecting too little or too much of any pupil is not recommendable. Pupils do need to set high goals, but at same time it is possible with perseverance to be successful in goal attainment.

If a set of pupils can benefit from seeing the teacher model phonics learnings in reading social studies subject matter, then the teacher should model appropriate skills for these pupils to attain. A group can then be formed to observe and use these learnings to become better readers. Groups formed for observing role models may be disbanded when no longer functional or useful.

PEER GROUPING IN THE SOCIAL STUDIES

Peers can do much to help other learners to achieve. Thus, two or three may read social studies content by changing off sequentially. As one is reading aloud, the other peers may follow along in their own textbook. Those having problems with word recognition may obtain assistance within the peer group. Questions may be identified and discussed to increase comprehension. Peers need to understand that they need to stay with that task at hand and not digress. Politeness is very important in the peer setting. Selected pupils do not learn from peers if there is rude behaviour therein. What is import in peer learning is that pupils assist, not hinder achievement. The goal in peer teaching is to guide pupils to achieve vital objectives in the social studies, not for the sake of having peer interaction. The peer group may be homogeneous or heterogeneous depending upon what helps these learners most in achievement.

Peer teaching might also be used. Here, one peer teaches the others in selected problem areas such as using picture clues in reading. The goal here is to have a peer teach the others, based on need, how to identify an unknown word through the use of a related picture in the specific social studies reading selection. A peer may also pronounce unrecognised words to a learner, once the latter has spent ample time in attempting to identify a word. The teaching peer must first let pupils use diverse skills in word recognition before pronouncing orally the unidentified word. The purpose of peer teaching is to help pupils learn as much as possible, not to stress peer teaching per se (Ediger, 1995, 56-58).

INDIVIDUALISED TASKS IN THE SOCIAL STUDIES

The bebate on how to group pupils for instruction becomes unimportant when a learner pursues a learning opportunity on his/her own. Ample opportunities need to be given to assist each pupil to achieve individually on an optimal basis. Reading in the social studies might stress an individualised programme in which a pupil chooses which library book to read as these choices are made sequentially. There need to be numerous library books on diverse topics pertaining to a social studies unit. The library books may then emphasise history, geography, anthropology, economics, sociology, and political silence. Biographies, autobiographies, primary sources such as letter and diary entries from internet sources, as well as poems and plays that relate directly to the present social studies unit being taught might well provide learning opportunities for pupils. Each book is written for children and may be fictional or non-fictional. Books that deal with children of other lands are very popular. Here, among other things, pupils, from the story read, may identify the geographical location of the involved nation on a map/globe, foods eaten there, types of homes/houses possessed, kinds of work performed by adults, the language(s) spoken, religious beliefs of these people, and the kind of government existing within the country being read about. Child centered materials are then in the offing. Learners individually may pick a book to read which is on their very own reading and interest level. The library book chosen then needs to be written on the recreational or instructional level of reading, not the frustrational level. The social studies teacher selects all the library books for pupil reading and places them in a reading corner in the classroom. The child then.

1. selects a library book to read from among an ample number.
2. reads the book silently to the self, until it is completed.
3. asks for assistance in word recognition if necessary.
4. has a conference with the teacher at intervals to check word identification skills as well as comprehension of subject matter.
5. may choose peers to share the contents when reading aloud in passing the library books from one child to the next in the group.

Library book content may be brought into the discussion when the lesson from the basal social studies text is being discussed within the class as a whole.

PROJECT METHODS OF INSTRUCTION AND THE SOCIAL STUDIES

Activity centered approaches of teaching and learning are being emphasised with the project method of instruction. Pupils with teacher assistance then need to plan the project that relates directly to the ongoing social studies unit being taught. For example, if a unit is being taught on the Middle East, pupils in a committee might wish to make a model of the walled city of old Jerusalem. A large cardboard box may be used for the wall. The eight gates leading into the old city need to be cut neatly into the model cardboard box. The turrets on the top of the box also need modelling. Tempera paint amy be used to show natural rock divisions used then in wall building by the Ottoman Empire in 1542. The winding streets and very small shops may also be included in the model of the old city of Jerusalem. Pupils need many audiovisual aids to use as examples in making this city. As they study the walled city in detail, they will become increasingly interested in related factors, such as the long rule of Sultan Sulieman, the Magnificent in the Ottoman Empire, 1526-1566 (Ediger, 1993, 156-157).

Diverse kinds of grouping may be used for instruction such as the following (Ediger, 1995, 135-139):

1. homogeneous if there are like minded pupils being artistic in intelligence.
2. homogeneous/heterogeneous if the project is based on pupil interest.
3. mixed ability levels if so planned by the teacher assigning classmates to a group.
4. friendship grouping whereby learners being friends may volunteer to be on a committee. A major problem here may be that one or two pupils are always left out by not being chosen in any friendship committee (Ediger, 1995, ERIC # ED386319).
5. cross grade grouping if this is possible. We believe that some time in the social studies should be given for cross grade grouping so that individuals become increasingly flexible in working with people of diverse age levels, since this is done in society.

LEARNING CENTRES IN THE SOCIAL STUDIES

When supervising student teachers and cooperating teachers in the public schools, we have noticed where pupils generally worked only at learning centres in social studies units of study.

Then too we have observed where teachers use one or two centres per unit of study as enrichment for pupil learning. The teacher(s) developed the centres, perhaps, eight centres for a set of twenty-two pupils in a classroom. Centres individually have task cards indicating what pupils are to do and learn. One centre had the following tasks for pupils to choose from:

1. write a quatrain on urban life in the Middle East.
2. pick a library book to read and then draw an illustration pertaining to a main idea from your reading.
3. read and tape record in your own words a recent news report from the Middle East.
4. read about and dramatise with two other pupils a scene depicting bedouin life when using the hands to eat rather than knives, forks, and spoons.
5. develop a mural with three other classmates on village life in a small Middle Eastern community.

All needed materials, basically, are available at a centre to complete the tasks selected from the task card. There should be ample tasks at the different centres so that pupils may choose sequentially what to complete and what to omit. The social studies teacher encourages, guides, and assists each pupil to optimalise time on task. The pupil is the chooser and the decision maker as to learning opportunities to work on in sequence. Individual and cooperative learning activities are in the offing. Activity centered approaches may be selected by the learner as well as those that are quite abstract. The goal is to have a variety of learning opportunities for learners individually to select from so that personal needs of instruction are met in an open-ended curriculum. In some ways an ideal is expressed here in that a pupil may select as well as omit that which does/does not meet personal needs.

Conclusion

There are many approaches to use in grouping pupils for instruction. Each procedure must be evaluated in terms of does it assist pupils to achieve as much as possible individually. When looking at that one criterion—does it assist or help pupils individually to learn as much as possible—and secondly, do pupils respect all and accept each learner as individuals having intrinsic values, then the need to pay attention to the following is minimised:

1. segregated grouping due to racial factors.
2. bias toward pupils of a particular gender.
3. cultural and national origin biases toward pupils, including those of diverse religious persuasions (Ediger, 1994, ERIC ED368625).
4. dislike of pupils of a certain socio-economic level.
5. prejudice toward individuals who are very unique and novel.
6. a lack of respect for individuals with opposite sexual preferences as compared to the dominate group in society.

Quality and new methods of evaluation need to be developed and used to ascertain which plan of grouping for an individual does assist the learner to achieve as optimally as possible and yet develop respect for others in the classroom setting as well as in society (Ediger, 1994, 169-174).

Reference

Bhaskara Rao, Digumarti, ed. (1996), *Global perceptions on Peace Education*, 3 Volumes. New Delhi, India: Discovery Publishing House.

Boehm, Richard G., and James F. Petersen (1994), 'an Elaboration of the Five Fundamental Themes in Geography,' *Social Education*, 58 (4), 214-218.

Dunn, Rita S., and Kenneth Dunn (1979), 'Teaching Styles/Learning Styles,' *Educational Leadership*, 36(4), 238-244.

Ediger, Marlow (2000), *Teaching Science in the Elementary School, Second Edition*. Kirksville, Missouri: Simpson Publishing Company, Chapter Nine.

Ediger, Marlow (1998), *The Holy Land*. Kirksville, Missouri: Simpson Publishing Company, 56 pp.

Ediger, Marlow (1997), *Teaching Reading and the Language Arts in the Elementary School*. Kirksville, Missouri: Simpson Publishing Company, Chapter Three.

Ediger, Marlow (1995), 'A Study of Values,' *Clearing House*, 69 (1), 56-58.

Ediger, Marlow (1993), 'A Grade Six Project in the Social Studies: The Wall of Old Jerusalem,' *Canadian Social Studies*, 27 (4), 156-157.

Ediger, Marlow (1995), 'To Every Action There is an Opposite and Equal Reaction,' ERIC # ED386319.

Ediger, Marlow (1995), 'Cooperative Learning and Heterogeneous Grouping,' *Reading Improvement*, 32 (3), 135-139.

Ediger, Marlow (1994), 'Measurement and Evaluation,' *Studies in Educational Evaluation,* 20 (2), 169-174.

Ediger, Marlow (1994), 'Teaching Religion in the Public Schools, ERIC # ED368625.

Vygotsky, Lev (1978), *Mind and Society*, Cambridge, Massachusetts: Harvard University Press.

LEADERSHIP IN THE SOCIAL STUDIES

Each pupil must attain optimally in the social studies. Teachers need to guide learners to achieve quality objectives. Learning opportunities for pupils should be selected by teachers which provide for individual differences and guide each learner to achieve as much as possible. Quality appraisal procedures should be in the offing to determine how much pupils have learned.

Leadership is needed to assist teachers to do an excellent job of teaching social studies. The principal/supervisor must provide the necessary leadership.

PROVIDING LEADERSHIP IN THE SOCIAL STUDIES

The school leader be it the principal or supervisor needs to observe teaching-learning situations frequently in the classroom setting. The leader must praise teachers for doing a good job of teaching. Praise for quality teaching can spur teachers on to greater efforts. Teaching suggestions are provided by the leader to teachers so that pupils more fully attain the objectives of instruction in the social studies. The leader becomes a catalyst for improving the social studies curriculum.

To be a leader, one needs to possess expert power in that knowledge, experience, and attitudes are there to modify, revise, and improve what is presently being done. Rewards for good teaching are then in the offing in terms of deserved praise. The leader knows how to reward and which approaches to use to reinforce that which is positive. All teachers should then have ample opportunities to be rewarded due to emphasising excellence in teaching the social studies. The leader too is able to suggest learning activities to teachers in a non-threatening way. These activities and teaching suggestions reflect the professional repertoire and knowledge base of the leader. Learning opportunities guide pupils to achieve objectives in the social studies. Which procedures might the leader of the social studies curriculum use to guide teachers to optimalise learner attainment?

LEADERSHIP AND THE SOCIAL STUDIES

Staff development is a very salient item to stress in updating the social studies. Problems salient to teachers need to be identified and solutions sought. The leader may survey social studies teachers to determine that which should be stressed in staff development. From the survey, problems common to teachers provide a basis for emphasising staff development. The writer has supervised student teachers for nearly 30 years. In speaking to teachers in these public schools, the following problems are mentioned most frequently in teaching the social studies;

1. Teaching for outcomes rather than processes.
2. Using an integrated team to teach pupils in which social studies and each academic discipline therein becomes fused and correlated.
3. Emphasising the use of criterion referenced tests (CRT's).
4. Stressing pupil-teacher planning of objectives, learning opportunities, and appraisal techniques.
5. Implementing project methods of instruction.

Teachers may volunteer to serve on a committee to solve one of the identified problems listed above. Adequate reference materials need too be available to participants in staff development programmes. Consultant assistance should be in the offing to guide problem solving activities. Progress reports may be given from each committee to others within appropriate intervals of time. Conclusions reached should be tried out in the regular classroom. Teachers who try out the new ideas need to discuss within staff development programmes how well the new procedures worked out and suggestions need to be given to make necessary modifications.

If a new curriculum is being proposed for the school, the leader must.

1. present it meaningfully to teachers.
2. answer questions raised in a clear, concise manner.
3. respect the thinking of participants.
4. invite discussions and active participation.
5. try to improve communication among leaders and faculty.

New curricula should not be forced upon teachers. Acceptance of ideas by involved faculty is a must.

Workshop methods to improve the social studies have been quite effective if quality procedures are used. A social studies workshop must have a theme. The following themes have been used in workshops observed by the writer;

1. using learning stations in teaching-learning situations.
2. creative writing in the social studies.
3. emphasising art work in the social studies.
4. developing readiness for reading content.
5. organising the social studies to optimalise pupil achievement.

Once the theme has been decided upon, workshop participants in a general session need to identify problem areas to solve. Pertaining to the theme of using learning stations, the following problems were selected by participants;

1. how are the diverse stations introduced to pupils so they have an inward desire to participate actively in sequential learning activities?
2. what is the role of the teacher when learning stations are in evidence?

3. When should the teacher intervene in guiding pupil achievement to emphasise time on task?
4. which procedures should be used to assess pupil achievement at the diverse stations?
5. can tasks at the stations be developed cooperatively between pupils and the social studies teacher?

At a workshop, there needs to be standards to assist teachers in working effectively on a committee. These standards could include participants staying on the topic being pursued, respecting the thinking of others, and being conscientious in quality of ideas presented. Adequate reference materials and consultant assistance should be in the offing. Progress reports may be given by each committee to others participating in the workshop. The writer has noticed how interested committee members can be in progress being made by other committees. Mutual sharing of ideas between and among committees is recommended highly in the workshop setting.

In addition to the general session and committee endeavours, participants should also have ample opportunities to work on a problem on an individual basis. Thus participants individually have chosen areas for study such as the following;

1. how to work effectively with pupils who are participating in committee endeavours.
2. how too stress the addition of anthropology and sociology into social studies units.
3. how to implement portfolio methods of appraising learner performance.
4. how to assist main streamed mentally retarded pupils in the social studies.
5. how to maintain a quality learning environment when project methods of instruction are being used.

Social studies teachers may perceive individual endeavours as being extremely worthwhile since the participant can now work on something that is perceived important individually.

Workshops need to be appraised by participants in terms of meeting teacher needs. A rating scale or checklist may be used together with an open ended procedure whereby participants can write in necessary comments. Results from the rating scale and the checklist should be used to improve future workshops.

FACULTY MEETINGS AND STAFF DEVELOPMENT

Faculty meetings can be quite beneficial to participants in improving the social studies. Agendas for faculty meetings should contain vital items to discuss, not trivia. All faculty and staff should have salient roles in determining that which should go into an agenda. Each needs to ask himself/herself, 'What do I believe should be an agenda item?' The agenda should be in the hands of participates two days before the faculty meeting. Thus participants have had ample opportunities to think about solutions to identified problem areas. One school that had a series of faculty meetings to improve the social studies had discussed the following with related solutions implemented in the classroom;

1. teachers with principal leadership identifying key concept and generalisations for pupils to attain.
2. guiding pupils to read with greater meaning and understanding from the basal social studies textbook.
3. using a variety of reference sources in the classroom.
4. helping pupils to use software and other technology more effectively in teaching-learning situations.
5. assisting learners to perceive purpose in learning.

In classrooms, teachers should have ample opportunities to try out relevant ideas discussed in faculty meetings. A vital point here is to have teachers provide feed back to the rest of the faculty on how well the teaching suggestions worked out in the classroom. Application and use needs to be made of quality ideas in teaching and learning.

LEADERSHIP AND THE PROJECT METHOD

Project methods represent an activity centered curriculum. The student is an active participant, rather than a passive recipient of facts and information. Active participation in the social studies emphasises strong learner involvement in choosing goals, activities and experiences, as well as appraisal procedures. The social studies teacher becomes a guide, stimulator, and resource person, not a dispenser of subject matter (Ediger, 1998, 54-59).

Project methods of instruction place stress upon the student being a responsible being in establishing goals, planning to attain goals, implementing the plans, as well as evaluating the quality of the project (Ediger, 1997).

THE PROJECT, STUDENT, AND THE TEACHER

A stimulating learning environment is needed to encourage students to select a project on an individual basis or as a committee endeavour (Ediger, 1997, 188-190). Quality bulletin board displays, objects on an interest centre, and carefully chosen audio-visual aids as learning activities, can become motivators for learners to pursue and develop a project. Students receive ideas for project development when pursuing ongoing lessons and units of study. After viewing and discussing materials in the classroom setting, questions are raised by learners. Each question becomes purposeful due to students having an inward desire to learn. To pursue the purpose, students need to plan sequentially what to do to attain the purpose or solve the identified problem. Well developed plans are needed. What is planned needs to be carried out to completion. Effort and ingenuity are necessary in working toward task completion. Carrying out the plans then would come in sequence, after the planning component. A creative being perseveres and does not give up along the way when pursuing a task to completion. A final step is to evaluate the completed project. There are selected criteria to use when evaluating the project. Among others, the following criteria appear salient:

1. Was neatness and accuracy involved in the completed project?
2. Did each committee members actively pursue responsibilities on the committee?
3. Were committee members able to work harmoniously with each other?
4. How would committee members operate if the project would be done differently?

5. Did each member of the committee achieve as optimally as possible? (Ediger, 1999, 233-240).

Specific projects will now be discussed in stressing a unit of study on 'The Middle East' (Ediger, 1998, *The Holy Land*).

1. Students with teacher guidance could made a model of The Mosque of Abraham in the city of Hebron. A cardboard box measuring 12 inches wide by 18 inches long with a height of ten inches may be used. The Mosque originally was built as a fortress in the days of the Roman Empire, approximately 2000 years ago. A minaret can be designed and cutout from the scrap cardboard. (From the minaret, devout Moslems are called to prayer five times a day). The minaret is then attached to the box representing the Mosque. Reputable encyclopaedias contain pictures of the Mosque of Abraham. Inside the Mosque are tombs of the patriarchs Abraham and his wife Sarah, Isaac and his wife Rebecca, as well as Jacob and his wife Leah. A Mosque is a place of worship for devout Moslems. Moslems face toward Mecca in Saudi Arabia, the birthplace of the Prophet Mohammed, when praying.
2. Learners might plan with the teacher how to portray the Church of the Nativity, located in Bethlehem. Thus, a mural might be planned and completed, using a variety of art media. This Church has its importance as the place where Christ was born, according to devout believers in the Christian religion. Bethlehem is located 13 miles north of Hebron. The mural can be exhibited along with the Mosque of Abraham, among other class projects, developed by students. Students from other classrooms, as well as parents, should be invited to observe that which students have completed. Selected audio-visual aids provide visuals and history of the Church of the Nativity.
3. Students with teacher guidance may plan a model of the wall around east Jerusalem. A cardboard box may be used to portray the wall. With proper safety rules, the box may be cut so that the top shows the contour

of the walled city. Students can use a watercolor brush with brown tempera paint to show the natural rock in the wall. The wall around east Jerusalem is two and one-half miles in length. It was built in 1542 when the Ottoman Empire ruled the land of Palestine. Openings in the wall may be cutout to show well known gates such as the Damascus gate, Herod's gate, and the Jaffa gate. Much research can be completed by students to learn about the long history of east Jerusalem, as well as many other well known sites in the land of Palestine. Studying the history of these gates, especially the Golden Gate, can fascinate many students.

4. Students may make a relief map of Palestine using an equal mixture of flour and salt, adding enough water to make a thick paste. The mixture should be placed on a piece of plywood, 18 inches by 24 inches. On the relief map, students may shape the Dead Sea, located approximately 1300 feet below sea level. The Dead Sea has no outlet, thus making for 25% salt and mineral content in its waters. The sea of Galilee, located 67 miles north, provides water for the Dead Sea. It has fresh water. The Jordan River connects the Sea of Galilee in the north with the Dead Sea in the south. The Jordan River winds like a ribbon and is approximately 200 miles in length with its curves and turns. The Sea of Galilee is about 600 feet below sea level. Thus the muddy water from the Jordan River flows rapidly from the Sea of Galilee into the Dead Sea in its rapid descent. These geographical facts make for a fascination of their very own when students make a relief map of the land of Palestine. These, among other geographical features of Palestine, can be placed by students on the relief map.

Place geography activities are also vital for learners to participate in (Ediger, 1998, 133-146). On the above named relief map, students may put in the location of Jerusalem. East Jerusalem has a fascination of its very own. It is a walled city with walls two and one-half miles in distance to surround it. Approximately, five miles south is the city of Bethlehem. The Church of the Nativity is located on a hill in Bethlehem. Inside is the grotto area where, according to devout Christians, Christ was born. Other familiar cities to place on the relief map include Hebron, West Jerusalem, Samaria, Jericho, Bethany, Haifa, and Tel Aviv. The history attached to each city and village is very important to the land where three religions were born.

5. Students with teacher guidance may make dioramas. A three dimensional model is then made of selected sites. The Western Wall, also called the wailing wall, is located inside the walls of east Jerusalem. The western wall as the only remnant of the ancient Jewish temple, according to devout believers in Judaism. This wall dates back to the days of Herod the Great, approximately 2000 years ago. The western wall is used for worship services by devout believers in Judaism. By studying models of and reading about the wall, students can make a related diorama.

A second diorama to make would emphasise the Dome of the Rock , a Moslem Mosque (built 691 A.D.) located directly east of the western wall. Approximately, 100 yards south is The Mosque El Aksa (built 706 A.D.). Between these two mosques, according to devout Moslems, The Prophet Mohammed ascended into heaven and returned back to earth again. The Dome of the Rock and The Mosque El Aksa are located inside the walls of east Jerusalem. Right on the east side of the wall of Jerusalem is the Golden Gate. This is the only gate that is closed on the entire wall surrounding east Jerusalem. The Golden Gate will remain closed until the Messiah returns to earth again, according to devout Moslems, Christians, and Jews. By and through studying models of all scenes from diverse reference sources, students can receive information on constructing replicas for the dioramas.

Conclusion

Problem solving is involved in using the project method of instruction. Ediger (1996) stated that the project method including problem solving procedures deemphasise the following:

1. pupils learning subject matter for its own sake.

2. passive learners in the classroom receiving content in lecture or explanation form.
3. large group instruction provided by the teacher or a team of teachers.
4. mastery learning or management systems of instruction with its precisely stated objectives selected prior to instruction.
5. rote learning and drill activities for students.

Each student needs to achieve as optimally as possible in knowledge, skills, and attitudes when participating in the project method. As projects are constructed and developed, much reading and writing are involved. Arithmetic is used to measure projects planned and implemented. Principles of science are brought in when learning about the Sea of Galilee, the Jordan River, and The Dead Sea. Art work is emphasised with the framework of making models, murals, and dioramas. Truly an integrated interdisciplinary curriculum is then in evidence. Ediger (1995) wrote the following:

An actively involved student in learning then determines the project to be pursued. The project possesses the interests of the involved learner. Effort is put forth to pursue and complete the project. Committee endeavours are relevant. Social theory emphasises that students learn to work together in completing one or more projects.

After the purpose has been chosen, the student or committee plans the purpose. Careful planning is necessary so that a quality project becomes an end result. The teacher guides, stimulates, and motivates students to develop as well as plan the purpose. After careful planning has occurred for the project, implementation of the plans comes in sequence. Meticulous, creative work is necessary to develop the project. Finally, the completed project needs to be evaluated in the evaluation process.

During the time the project was conceived as a purpose, as well as its completion, students engaged in relating reading, writing, listening, and oral communication activities. These learning activities were instrumental to the solving of a problem which was to develop and complete the project. An integrated curriculum was in evidence.

REFERENCE

Ediger, Marlow (1997), Social Studies Curriculum in the Elementary School. Kirksville, Missouri: Simpson Publishing Company, Chapter One.

Ediger, Marlow (1998), *The Holy Land.* Kirksville, Missouri: Simpson Publishing Company, 67 pp.

Ediger, Marlow (1998), 'Social Studies: Processes Versus Products,' *The Philippine Educational Quarterly*, 27 (1), 54-59.

Ediger, Marlow (1999), 'Appraising Learner Progress in the Social Studies,' *College Student Journal*, 33 (2), 233-240.

Ediger, Marlow (1998), 'Social Studies and the Middle School Student,' *Journal of Instructional Psychology*, 24 (3), 188-191.

Ediger, Marlow (1996), *Elementary Education (A Collection of Essays).* Kriksville, Missouri: Simpson Publishing Company, page 2.

Ediger, Marlow (1995), *Philosophy in Curriculum Development* Kirksville, Missouri: Simpson Publishing Company, pages 80-81.

Ediger, Marlow (1998), 'Maps and Globes in Social Studies,' *Middle States Council for the Social Studies 1998 Yearbook.* University Park, Pa.: Pennsylvania State University, 133-146.

Ediger, Marlow and D. Bhaskara Rao (2001), *Teaching Science Successfully.* New Delhi, India: Discovery Publishing House.

Marja, Talvi and Digumarti Bhaskara Rao, Eds. (1996). *Educational Leadership and Social Changes.* New Delhi, India: Discovery Publishing House.

Social Studies and Democracy in the Classroom

Writers, speakers, and practitioners emphasise democracy and democratic living in the social studies quite frequently. Beliefs differ greatly on what is meant by democracy and democratic living. Perhaps, social studies educators need to get together for a planned series of meetings to clarify meanings therein. Logical positivism, as a philosophy of education, advocates that sharp disagreements in educational thinking are due to careless use of language in most cases. Thus the word 'democracy' is vague and has little meaning unless clarity in language is involved. Clear and distinct ideas are then necessary to bring meaning to concepts of democracy in the social studies. The writer will first review different schools of thought in teaching social studies and ask selected questions about each.

SOCIAL STUDIES AND STATE MANDATED OBJECTIVES

There are social studies educators who recommend that objectives for instruction be chosen on the state level. Thus social studies educators would be selected by the state department of education or other equivalent group to select objectives for learner attainment in the public schools. Much study and thought must go into this venture. Relevant objectives need to be chosen. Ultimately the objectives in their final form are available to teachers for implementation in the classroom. Classroom teaches select the learning opportunities for students to attain the objectives. Criterion referenced tests developed on the state level are used to measure learner progress. The criterion tests measure against the stated objectives, Validity in testing should then be in evidence (Ediger, 1999, 233-240).

There are numerous questions that arise pertaining to state mandated objectives. Among others, the following questions are relevant when thinking about democracy in the curriculum.

1. When objectives are developed on the state level, a hierarchical method of teaching is emphasised. How do this harmonise with teacher and student involvement in choosing objectives in the social studies?
2. Why are more localised efforts shunned by the state in selecting quality objectives of instruction?
3. How well might teachers be able to choose learning opportunities that harmonise with state mandated objectives? It may be difficult for teaches to locate teaching materials that are valid for the stated objectives.
4. Can teachers provide adequately for individual differences when they have not been involved in choosing objectives?
5. Should teachers be involved in selecting appraisal procedures to evaluate learner progress?

BEHAVIOURISM AS A PSYCHOLOGY OF LEARNING

Behaviourism with its precise, measurably stated objectives chosen prior to instruction has had much influence in education. Preciseness in the writing of objectives has much appeal to selected social studies educators. After instruction, the student either has or has not achieved one or more objectives. When viewing the behaviourally stated objectives, it is clear as to what the teacher will be teaching. Vagueness and ambiguity are eliminated in determining what will be taught. Testing learners as to what has been learned matches and harmonises with the precisely stated objectives. Instructional management systems (IMS) developed on the local district level advocate using behaviourism and its precise objectives. Questions that need answering pertaining to behaviourism and its precise objectives of instruction are the following:

1. The chances are better that teachers will be more actively involved in choosing objectives for instruction in IMS as compared to state mandated objectives procedures. IMS is generally developed on the local district level and could involve *some* teachers in its planning. Should all teaches be involved in selecting objectives since the selection made affects those who use IMS approaches in teaching learning situations
2. Can students achieve optimally if some one else chooses objectives, learning opportunities, as well as evaluation techniques for the former?
3. Can teachers sequence learning opportunities for pupils so that more optimal attainment is in evidence? A logical sequence is in evidence if teaches sequence activities for learners.
4. Do students fell left out of the curriculum if someone else continually makes decisions for them?
5. Does learning become rote in nature if criterion referenced tests are used to measure against the precise objectives?

FILL INCLUSION IN THE SOCIAL STUDIES

Mainstreaming or inclusion is recommended and advocated by many educators in the social studies as well as in other curriculum areas. According to PL 94-142, handicapped students are to be taught in the least restricted environment. Many have interpreted PL 94-142 to mean placing all handicapped students into the regular classroom. In the past, prior to 1976, handicapped student were taught in classrooms separate from regular learners. The teacher-student ratio in special education classrooms was relatively low, perhaps five or six to one ratio depending upon the type of handicap involved. In the regular classroom, the student-teacher ratio is much larger, perhaps twenty five to one a suggested average. In special education classrooms, students should be able to receive better individualised instruction as compared to the regular classroom. However, many parents want their children to be in the regular classroom with normal students. Here, the beliefs are that a better quality of instruction is in the offing. Then too, more sophisticated knowledge is presented in the regular classroom as compared to a special education classroom. Subject matter, for example, will be more complex as presented to learners in the regular classrooms as compared to that of learners in a class for the mentally handicapped (See National Council for the Social Studies, 1994). Questions that may be raised pertaining to full inclusion of students into the regular classroom are the following:

1. Are regular teachers prepared and educated to teach diverse kinds of handicapped students such as a deaf or blind learner?
2. Is the quality of teaching better in regular classrooms as compared to classrooms for the handicapped?
3. Do regular classroom teachers receive adequate aid service to assist in teaching main streamed learners?
4. Why are an inordinate number of minority students in special education classrooms? There certainly are implications here for a lack of educational opportunity due to poverty. In the societal arena, the divisions are great indeed between the haves and the havenots. The havenots may live in 'war zones.' Here, guns and drug sales may abound. Safety and security of young people are not the order of the day. Rather, violence and aggressiveness are in evidence.
5. Should a behaviourally disordered student who is main streamed ruin the teacher's and other student's opportunities to teach and learn? The implications here for quality teaching are the selected students may not fit into the regular classroom.

RESTRUCTURING THE SCHOOLS

Many educators speak and write about restructuring the public schools. It is difficult to determine what restructuring the schools means. How would the social studies differ from what now exists if restructuring were in evidence? To be sure any institution needs improving. Education including the social studies curriculum needs improvement. It appears, however, that social studies educators disagree much as to what should be in the social studies. Previously, the writer discussed the pros and cons of state mandated objectives, behaviourism as a psychology of learning, and full inclusion. Other issues in the social studies include the following:

1. Process objectives (problem solving, critical thinking, and creative thinking) versus a subject centered curriculum (facts, concepts, and generalisations). Which should receive primary stress?
2. Psychological versus a logical curriculum. The former stresses student-teacher planning in objectives, learning activities, and appraisal procedures whereas the latter emphasises the teacher ordering objectives, activities, and evaluation techniques.
3. National goals versus locally selected objectives for student achievement. Perhaps, a broad question to ponder upon is 'Who should choose goals in the curriculum—the local level, the state level, or the national level (Education 2000, National Governors' Conference of 1989) decision making?'
4. Cooperative learning versus individual endeavours in achieving objectives. The former stresses committee work and harmonising individual talents with those of others in the group setting. The latter stresses individual work to attain cognitive, affective, and psychomotor goals. Cooperative efforts may hinder achievement of those more talents and gifted learners in that the slower achievers can not use their individual abilities optimally without much assistance. The talented and gifts continually may then need to help others within

the cooperative learning setting. Whichever procedure is used in teaching, students individually need to attain optimally. Perhaps, cooperative learning emphasises more of social development rather than cognitive objectives, Both kinds of objectives are salient and need adequate emphasis in the social studies. Balance among cognitive, affective (including social development) and psychomotor ends needs to be in evidence.

5. Activity centered versus subject centered social studies. The testing and measurement movement has emphasised students achieving worthwhile subject matter. What is taught must be measured in terms of test results, be it norm referenced or criterion referenced tests. Activity centered approaches in teaching stress a hands on method of instruction. Learning by doing such as constructing, dramatising, engaging in art work, making models, and developing murals pertaining to what has been learned is stressed. The basics such as reading, writing, and arithmetic enter in as needed in ongoing lessons and units of study. A subject centered social studies curriculum places major emphasis upon using the textbook in teaching-learning situations. Other kinds of activities may be used to clarify and enrich. Psychomotor objectives predominate in a hands on approach in the social studies. Cognitive goals enter in when reading, writing, and arithmetic become a part of the curriculum. Affective objectives are in evidence if learners like and enjoy ongoing activities and experiences. In a subject centered approach, cognitive ends predominate. Mental development becomes salient. Mind is real and needs optimal nurturing. Learning of content then becomes of utmost importance.

6. Testing to determine learner achievement versus port folio procedures of appraisal. Testing to notice student attainment has been very important in the social studies. Advocates of testing to notice student

attainment receive much attention in educational literature. Claims are made that the lay public and selected educators want to know in quantifiable terms the amount of learner achievement in the public schools. Results can be provided in terms of percentile rank of each student. Results may also be given in standard deviations, quartile deviations, grade equivalents, and/or the per cent of items a student got right on a test.

Port folio approaches to notice learner achievement contain a variety of products for observers to appraise. Thus art products, snapshots, construction items, tape recordings, and written products become a part of the port folio of an individual student. A representative sample of learner products should be inherent in the port folio. Students could definitely be involved in ascertaining the contents of a port folio (Ediger, 1994, 219-220)

Conclusion

There appears to be wide disagreement on what is meant by restructuring the school which includes the social studies. Points of view here may be placed on a continuum. Perhaps, there needs to be numerous philosophies involved in restructuring the schools. Students differ from each other in many ways including interests, abilities, purposes, and motivation. Thus it takes different philosophies to guide each student to attain more optimally.

Democracy as a way of life and in school must have a more consistent philosophy than that which is stressed in the many approaches stressed in educational literature and in actual teaching practices. Do state and national goals for learner attainment emphasise democratic theory? If goals in education for students are developed on the state or national levels, then learners have no input into the curriculum. Should students have opportunities to choose objectives, learning activities, and evaluation techniques when emphasising democratic philosophy of thought? Teacher input into state and national goals is also non-existent. There needs to be recommendations and implementation for student-teacher planning in the social studies. Democracy as a philosophy and as a way of life needs implementation in the social studies.

REFERENCES

Bhaskara Rao, Digumarti, ed. (1997). *Success Story of a Primary Education Project.* New Delhi, India: APH Publishing House.

Ediger, Marlow (1995), *Philosophy in Curriculum Development* Kriksville, Missouri: Simpson Publishing Company, Chapter Two.

Ediger, Marlow (1999), 'Appraising Learner Progress in the Social Studies,' *The College Student Journal*, 33 (2), 233-240.

Ediger, Marlow (1997), *Social Studies Curriculum in the Elementary School—fourth Edition*, Kriksville, Missouri: Simpson Publishing Company, Chapter Three.

National Council for the Social Studies (1994), *Curriculum Standards for Social Studies.* Washington DC: NCSS.

Ediger, Marlow (1994), 'Social Studies and the Affective Dimension, ' *Journal of Instructional Psychology*, 21 (3), 219, 220.

Jayasree, K. and Digumarti Bhaskara Rao (1999). *Correlates of Achievement.* New Delhi, India: Discovery Publishing House.

Rathaiah, L., Digumarti Bhaskara Rao and P.K. Rao (1997). *Achievement Correlates.* New Delhi, India: Discovery Publishing House.

Rao, Digumarti Bhaskara (2001), *International Encyclopaedia of Human Rights*, 7 Vols. New Delhi, India: Discovery Publishing House.

12

Technology in the Social Studies Curriculum

There is strong emphasis placed upon use of modern technology in the elementary school curriculum. Technology is very strongly used in all facets of society, and elementary schools should not lag behind what is stressed in the societal arena. The elementary pupil of today will be expected to achieve in a heavily endowed work place involving technology. Many factories and farms have been strongly automated. Fewer workers are continually needed in these work places. Machines automatically do work that was formerly done with the use of human muscles and physical work.

Generally, people think of farming as stressing that very heavy manual labour is done continuously. Egg production, as one example, has eliminated most of the manual labour that was formerly done. Today, the eggs fall down from the cages, onto a conveyor belt. A person at the end of the long row presses a button and all the eggs come down to where this worker is located. A machine is even available to pack the eggs into a crate. The feed goes down a conveyer belt every fifty minutes so that the laying hens have plenty to eat in order to produce eggs. The feed is augured automatically from a bin outside the laying house. Water also goes down the troughs continually for laying hens to drink.

A truck comes to pick up the crates of eggs two times a week. The owner largely manages the laying house operation to see that all machines are working properly. Not all farm work, by any means is automated to this extent. In contrast, any person who has cut, baled, and hauled hay realises the heavy use of muscles that are presently involved here.

Being nonsmokers, we have observed at a cigarette factory where everything is automated including quality control. In other words, when the cigarettes have been packaged, the machine will cull out what was not done properly. Workers are there, few in number to notice when involved machines are not working properly. They are then responsible for repair work when needed or to obtain assistance if someone else needs to do the work.

Menial work that requires human feats pays very little money, but even here the manual labour done by a human being is rather minimal, such as in fast food restaurants. At these fast food restaurants, there is a lot of movement and motion by workers in getting fast food orders fulfilled. No doubt, these workers get tired after being at the task, but the labour is not intensive.

When growing up on a farm, as mentioned above, farmers would shovel wheat by hand, since grain augers had not yet been perfected adequately. Shoveling grain by hand with a scoop is labour intensive. The grain auger took most of the human efforts out of shoveling wheat since the wheat was now augured rapidly, fifty bushels in three minutes, using an attached electric motor to the auger. What does this discussion have to do with the use of modern technology in the elementary school classroom?

PERSONAL BELIEFS ABOUT TECHNOLOGY USE

There are selected criteria from the psychology of learning that need emphasis in having pupils work with technology. We believe that technology should capture pupil interests in learning. Activities here should be fascinating to engage pupil interaction. These interests should provide for effort in pupils desiring to achieve, grow, and develop. There is little time for misbehaviour if pupils are interested in the task at hand. We have noticed, for example, first graders who had little interest in drill and practice in arithmetic using paper and pencil. And yet when a hand held calculator or computer programme was emphasised, these learners truly showed interest and fascination in learning. Interest is a powerful factor in learning since attention to the task at hand makes for increased achievement (Ediger, and Bhaskara Rao, 1996)

Second, We believe that technology may assist learners to perceive purpose in learning. If purpose is lacking, there will be little incentive for pupils to learn. Goal centered pupils achieve more than those who fail to perceive objectives in learning. We have observed many pupils who did not like to check long division problems using paper and pencil. Again, when the checking was done rapidly and accurately with the calculator or computer, there seemingly was even joy in doing the checking to see if the long division problem had been worked correctly. It appeared that pupils saw purpose, not drudgery, in checking these long division problems (Ediger, 1994, 24-25).

Third, we believe technology can assist pupils to attach meaning to ongoing lessons and units of study. What pupils learn then should make sense, not be nonsense tasks. There are numerous programmes in computer use which guide pupils to achieve an objective. These numerous ways stress if one procedure is not understood, there are other approaches which will guide pupils to attach meaning. It is so important that pupils understand what is being learned. Many of us have learned that to divide fractions, we need to invert the divisor and then multiply. This mechanical procedure made no sense to us in grade school and in high school. There should be meaning in why 'the divisor is inverted and then multiply.' With clear illustrations together with the abstract numerals on the monitor, pupils may well understand and attach meaning as to why to 'invert the divisor and multiply.' What is learned should make sense and not merely be committed to memory.

Computer programmes should assist pupils to perceive knowledge as being related, not in isolated bits (Ediger, 1996 25-27). We noticed a delightful programme on a monitor with high pupil enthusiasm working on the Egyptian system of numeration when studying a social studies unit on the Middle East. Here, pupils were fascinated to learn that individual strokes represented the numerals from one through nine. Further interests were shown in the following features of the Egyptian system of numeration:

1. each heel bone of an ox, shaped like an arch represented a value of ten. Nine heel bones represented a value of ninety.
2. each coiled rope represented a value of 100. There could be as many as nine coiled ropes to represent a value of 900.
3. each lotus flower represented 1,000. The pattern is that nine lotus flowers represent a value of 9,000.
4. each bent finger represented a value of 10,000. Nine bent fingers represent 90,000.
5. each tadpole represent 100,000; thus nine tadpoles represent 900,000.

We present this information, as an example, to show that computer programmes along with other technologies can definitely assist pupils to perceive that knowledge is related. In this case, social studies and mathematics can definitely be related so that the learner perceives the interrelationship of subject matter. Morris and Pal (1976) wrote the following pertaining to Jerome Bruner's thinking on the relationship of knowledge.

...since human beings seem to be able to store more information than they can spontaneously recall, the main problem in human memory is that of effective retrieval. Bruner is convinced that the key to effective retrieval is organisation of information. He contends there is sufficient evidence to support the assertion that, in general, any information organised around the interests and the cognitive structure of the learner can be most efficiently recalled. Hence, the only means by which we can reduce the quick rate of loss of human memory is to organise facts according the basic principles and concepts from which they were inferred. Further, 'the very attitude and activities that also seem to have the effect of conserving characterise figuring out or discovering things for ourself also seem to have the effect of conserving memory.' In addition to these effects, the learning experiences resulting from self-discovery give us an increased awareness of the connections and continuities between what we learn and what we do. As a result, we are likely to see our activities in a broader context and thus gain more control of our acts in relation of an end in view. In learning by discovery, knowledge already possessed by the learner is used to gain new insights and, and in the process old knowledge becomes reconstructed.

Being very strong on learning by discovery, Jerome Bruner, stresses organising information around the interests and cognitive structure of pupils. Discovery conserves or saves what has been learned previously. Pupils need to use knowledge to obtain new insights thus connecting what we learn and what we do. There are many key ides Bruner presents here for learners to relate knowledge and increase memory/recall. The use of technology such as video-tapes and software programmes can and do assist pupils to relate knowledge inductively and thus retain content for a longer duration of time.

Fifth, the use of technology can certainly assist to provide for individual differences among pupils in terms of achievement in diverse academic areas. When pupils work on computer programmes, they can definitely work at their optimal rate of achievement individually. Thus, in a tutorial programme for example, pupils need to possess readiness factors such as having adequate background information. The learner then may move forward on the programme at an as optimal rate as possible. Comparing this learning situation with viewing a video-tape, the contents in the latter may move forward too rapidly or too slowly.

Sixth, technology and its use might well guide pupils to develop wholesome attitudes toward learning. Pupils seem to be fascinated with interacting with technology. We have observed pupils in classrooms with little interest in achieving in mathematics, as an example, until it is time for the learner to work with the computer. Here, the pupil interacted with drawings and abstract related numerals on the monitor. Problem solving was stressed here for a fifth grade pupil emphasising finding the volume of a cone. The drawings were excellent and the hints given in finding the volume were sequential to permit the learner to determine the needed answer. Later, another pupil also came to the computer to solve additional problems cooperatively. The interest was high and the two learners worked together harmoniously. The joy that comes in working with others truly has its values for pupils.

PHILOSOPHY OF EDUCATION AND TECHNOLOGY

We are strong believers in teachers, not only stressing the psychology of learning, but also the philosophy of education in technology use. There are selected philosophies that teachers need to understand and use in teaching-learning situations.

A first philosophy and its use we would like to discuss is experimentalism. Experimentalists believe strongly in a changing environment. Changes occur in all facets of the social/natural environment. Rather rapid changes have occurred such as in technology. When we first started teaching, there were no word processors on our campus. Typewriters was abundant. Electric typewriters quickly replaced the manual typewriters. Word processors rapidly replaced the electric typewriters. Changes can and do occur rapidly. There is hardly anything, objects as well as ides, where change does not occur.

With change, new problems arise. These problems need identification and delimitation so that they can be solved. An hypothesis is developed in answer to the problem. The hypothesis is tentative, never an absolute. Each hypothesis is to be tested in a lifelike situation. Problems, hypotheses, and tests of hypotheses are done in context within a practical situation. Experimentalism is utilitarian, not abstract nor theoretical. Pertaining to John Dewey and his beliefs on change, Ediger (1995) wrote the following:

John Dewey (1859-1952) lived during a period of rapid change. When he was born and even until the early 1900s, the automobile basically did not exist. When he died in 1952, manufactured automobiles, as a whole, were very dependable with hydraulic brakes, heaters, and even a few with air conditioners. Electricity had its beginning in home and factory use in the early 1890s and was highly refined with its uses in 1952, with electric ranges, dishwashers, clothes washers, and driers. Changes have occurred from zero automobiles in 1859 to more highways and interstates being built to take care of the large number of automobiles in use in the present time. In 1859 horse drawn farm equipment was utilised to plow, harrow, disk, and seed the farm land. By 1952 farm tractors had electric lights, hydraulic brakes, and could pull a plow with four to five shears in plowing the land. Tremendous changes then occurred from 1859 (year of birth) to 1952 (year of death of Dr. Dewey).

With these and many other changes, problems arise. Problems need identification and careful delineation in the school curriculum, as well as in society. Each problem is vital. Information acquired in school needs to be utilised to solve problems. Knowledge is not attained for its own sake, but is instrumental to the solving of identified problems. In society also, information is secured from a variety of reference sources, useful to solve each chosen problem.

From the data gathered, directly related to the problem, a hypothesis is developed. A hypothesis results for each identified problem. The hypothesis is tentative and subject to change through testing. Testing is done in a life-like situation. The results of the test may confirm or refute the hypothesis. Minor revisions of the hypothesis may also be needed. Generally, change will occur rather continuously.

Experimentalists believe that one can only know experience. One cannot know the real world in whole or in part as realists advocate nor does one know ideas only, of what exists out there in society, as idealists stress. With the world of experience as experimentalists believe, one identifies and solves necessary problems. Eichelberger (1989) wrote the following pertaining to pragmatism, also called experimentalism:

> The relationship between knowledge and reality (truth) that is used by researchers today is that of the pragmatist, which states that all knowledge is produced by human beings and that we can never distinguish between knowledge and truth. In empirical research, this means that if something works in practice then it is true, or we can assume that it is true. A truth (knowledge) that is not supported by further empirical study will be modified or discarded.

How does any philosophy of education relate directly to the use of technology? We have noticed numerous computerised programmes that are excellent for pupils to use in problem solving. Thus pupils in context have identified a problem for which they wish to have or find a solution. A software programme carefully selected might well provide data to test a hypothesis. Generally, additional technological sources will be used to evaluate an identified hypothesis in answer to a problem. However, there are numerous programmes which may provide information in the problem solving arena. Then too, there are simulated programmes which tend to be lifelike and real. These entire software programmes go through flexible steps of problem solving. A delightful computerised simulation is Choice or Chance (1984) which contains the following sequential content on the Age of Exploration:

Little is know of Hudson's life before his travels as an explorer began in 1687. During his sailing career, he sailed for both the Dutch and the English.

Hudson's Voyages in 1687-1688 were founded by an English trading company, the Muscovy Company. His goal was never reached. In 1689 Hudson was hired by the Dutch East India Company, also a trading company, to lead another expedition. He again headed northeast hoping to avoid the ice floes. After the crew and supplies were in place, the ships set sail from Amsterdam, Holland on April 6, 1689. Their goal: find a northern route to Asia. Follow their journey (a relevant map is shown on the screen):

* Sail north and east to Novaya, Zemla, and an Island in Russia.
* Crew threatens mutiny, but Hudson convinces them to sail southwest.
* Arrive at the coast of Maine and cut a mast for the ship on July 18, 1689. Some trading was done at that time. Sail south, along the coast to what is called the Chesapeake Bay. Arrived on August 3. 1689.
* Sail north along the coast to what is now called the Delaware Bay
* Continue to sail north along the coast until a large inlet is spotted.

Imagine that you are Hudson. Use the map, called Dutch Exploration, to help you make decisions consider the geographic factors presented and how they affect your decisions on the map page. You are now ready to sail upstream and explore. Good Luck! As you continue further into the inlet, a large Island is seen. The Island is covered with oaks.

Strong saltwater tides occur. a suitable harbour with a depth of 4-5 fathoms is seen. The inlet is continually windy. Do you wish to

a. settle in this area?

b. explore further upstream?

c. return to Amsterdam?

Feedback is then given on the screen pertaining to choice(s) made. Additional content is presented so that new sequential decisions need to be made by students. The *Choice or Chance* simulation

1. relates history and geography.
2. brings reality into the programme
3. emphasises active involvement on the part of learners.
4. presents background information to pupils before decisions are considered and made.
5. involves a logical sequence in that the programmers present sequential problems for pupils to consider.
6. stresses low risk on the pupils' part interacting since the materials are not first hand, but are reality based.

Changes in technology abound. Rose and Fernland wrote:

During the 1980's, computer assisted instruction (CAI) was an important part of classroom use. Teachers, department chairs, and district technology coordinators purchased commercial and public domain programmes in the subject areas, stored on one or more floppy disks, including drill and practice programmes, tutorials, simulations, and games. During the next decade there were four major changes that improved CAI: (1) the decline of the use of floppy disks, replaced by the enhanced storage capability of CD-ROM and videodisc, (2) enhanced interactivity in software in which students play a more active role, (3) sophisticated graphics, video clips, colour and sound, creating a multimedia presentation no long dominated by screens of text; and (4) the growing marriage of CAI and telecommunications, allowing a seamless transition from single computer use to collaborative work with distant partners and access to internet-based sources.

The use of CAI in the social studies classroom continues to be strong, although such use is being eclipsed by the tool uses of computers; word processing; communications, research, and multimedia production. CAI is available on the internet, a helpful tool for teachers who want to review the product and consult other teachers who have used the programme with their students. CAI has greatly improved in creatively and quality; many programmes offer motivating experiences for students in analysis, problem solving, and decision making.

IDEALISM AS A PHILOSOPHY OF EDUCATION

Previously, it was mentioned that experimentalist believe we can know experiences only from the physical and social world. Idealists state that we receive ideas only, not experiences; nor can we know what the real world is like in whole or in part as realists indicate. Idealism is an idea centered philosophy of education. Mind is real and needs to receive nourishment through quality ideas in different academic disciplines. There are numerous tutorial programmes with computer use that stress learners achieving important concepts and generalisations. Knowledge objectives predominate, according to idealism as a philosophy of teaching and learning. Ediger (1997) wrote the following:

Idealism is a more traditional approach in making decisions as compared to experimentalism and existentialism. According to Idealists, individualists cannot know the world as it truly is in terms of a objective reality. Each person, however, obtains ideas pertaining to objects and items in the environment. The mind brings order to what is observed and seen. Thus, of all facets of human development that is significant to develop, the mind or intellectual achievement must come first. Rich learning experiences will need to be in evidence to guide pupils to achieve maximum development mentally. Thus experiences may well be selected in terms of leading pupils to attain universal ideas and knowledge of the Absolute (God). These universal ideas need seeking and finding. Any person may not achieve perfect understanding of these universal ideas and of God. However, each person may continually move closer in achieving ideals of universal ideas and of the absolute.

From the thinking of idealists, the following implications apply for teaching and learning:

1. broad generalisations need emphasising that have much use to the learner in terms of mental and moral development.

2. quality ideals for pupils to emulate need adequate emphasis in the school curriculum.
3. intellectual objectives should receive primary stress in the curriculum.
4. quality course work in literature and history, in particular, should guide pupils to achieve worthy generalisations.
5. abstract ideas are more important to emphasise as compared to the concrete and the semiconcrete.

Key ideas in understanding idealism in teaching and learning are written by Bigge (1982) in the following statements:

The heart of Idealism is the belief that basic reality consists of ideas, thoughts, minds or substantive selves, not physical matter. Since priority is given to minds, minds have bodies, but bodies do not have minds. Idealism usually carries with its view the ideas of the subsistence (the superexistence) of God, who also is basically mind or self. The universe is an expression of intelligence and will; its order is due to an external, spiritual reality. For idealists, people are just good-active substantive minds; they are absolutely real selves endowed with free will or genuine moral choice. This philosophy has ancient roots; it dates back to Socrates (469-399 BC) and Plato (427-347).

Idealism is really idea-ism. The source of this title is based on Platonic thought. For Plato, ideas alone were genuinely real; they consisted of immaterial essences. That which people perceive is a shadow of reality; each thing that they perceive gets its existence from its Thingness; an idea. A book is a book because of its being more or less an imperfect replica of Bookness. A woman is a woman because she is a replica of Womaness. Plato's assumed world of "eternal verities" considered of the True, the Good, and the Beautiful.

We can trace the development of Idealism by listing some of the leading philosophers who contributed to this position and stated a leading idea that each has contributed to the philosophy. Socrates believed that children are born with knowledge already in their minds, but they need help to recall this innate knowledge. Plato contributed the idea of ideas, which are the universal forms of all existing things and are the essence of reality. St. Augustine

(350-430) held a dualistic (mind-body) theory of humanity within which the mind or soul is the set of the force of goodness.

What then are the implications of idealism for teaching and learning in the classroom involving computer use? I have been selected excellent software packages which stress an idea centered curriculum. It seems as if for each academic area, there are tutorials which might well assist any pupil to achieve subject mater knowledge.

These software packages should assist pupils to

1. achieve abstract content which is challenging and yet attainable.
2. learn content in depth with emphasis placed upon mental development of pupils.
3. acquire subject matter which makes sense and has meaning.
4. relate relevant content from an academic centered curriculum.
5. attain vital facts, concepts, and generalisations in each academic discipline.

An idea centered curriculum might also guide pupils to use what has been learned in problem solving. This belief assists in relating idealism with experimentalism.

EXISTENTIALISM AND THE CURRICULUM

Existentialists are very much concerned about the every day life and its anxieties of individuals. Individuals are concerned with choices that need to be made regardless if the desire is there to make these decisions. There is dread, fear, anxiety, and uncertainty in making choices. Many existentialists believe life to be absurd and ridiculous. There is dread in choosing when so many alternatives are available in the making of these choices. People do not live in a subject centered world, nor in a world of science. Rather they live in an openended world where there are no standards in and of themselves. These standards, rules and regulations, need to be developed. Human beings make their own world; there are no absolutes nor are there given rules to live by.

People, past and present, have developed standards to go by in life, but these are human made in an open environment where people, individually and collectively, develop the kind of society they wish to have. Pertaining to existentialism, Ozman and Craver (1990) wrote:

> Because the individual human is so important as the creator of ideas, existentialists maintain that education should focus upon individual human reality. It should deal with the individual as a unique being in the world, not only as creator of ideas, but as a living, feeling being. Most philosophies,... existentialists charge, tend to focus upon only a cognitive being. The individual is this, but he is also a feeling, aware person, and existentialists think that this side deserves attention.

Which impilcations in the curriculum might follow some of the tenets of existentialism?

1. pupils individually need to choose freely, from among alternatives, those learning activities which are purposeful and meaningful.
2. content in the curriculum should reflect human feelings of loneliness, alienation, anxiety, and tension.
3. personal feelings of the pupil should be reflected in ongoing lessons and units of study. These feelings might well be expressed in art and construction projects, as well as of personal writings of learners.

The pupil needs of realise that choices do need to be made. If others make decisions for the personal self, choices are still being made, but the individual has abdicated responsibility in the decision making arena. Choices made do involve dilemma decisions, but authentic decisions must be made. Coercion is definitely not a part of the decision making philosophy of existentialists. Quality decisions made do not always make for good human relations. Alienation may also be an end result. The individual always needs to consider the consequences of choices made. Moral decisions made in a free environment is the goal of existentialists. Individuals should remember they are responsible for choices made; no one else can assume this responsibility. Choice are subjective, not objective by any means.

With technology in the curriculum, existentialism advocates

1. individuals selecting from among others computer programmes to complete. The individual should also choose which tasks to engage in when additional forms of technology are used.
2. the human condition with all of its uncertainties and anxieties should be stressed in the technology curriculum.
3. the pupil needs to have ample opportunities to study situations in which dilemmas are present. Decision making is not clear cut nor an absolute. Content in technology can emphasise these ideas.
4. the learner needs to express his/her feelings in diverse projects and activities. Thus a variety of writing experiences, fine arts and practical arts activities, speaking and reading learning opportunities, as well as listening may be stressed as evaluation techniques as well as enrichment activities in the technology curriculum.
5. heavy pupil involvement and choice in the technology curriculum should always be in evidence with existentialism as a driving philosophy in education.

REALISM AND THE TECHNOLOGY CURRICULUM

Realists are strong advocates of individuals knowing in whole or in part what the real world is like. Their model comes from the world of science and mathematics. Precision and extreme accuracy are major tenets of realism as a philosophy of education. Thus the realist is strongly interested in having pupils achieve precise, measurably stated objectives in each curriculum area. With these kinds of objectives, carefully chosen by teachers and other educators, pupils do or do not attain each objective as a result of instruction. Learning activities selected by the teacher harmonises with what pupils are to learn as contained in the stated objective(s). Evaluation techniques need to be aligned with the stated objectives. Validity is then in evidence in testing and measurement. Reliability needs to stress test-retest, split half, and/or alternative forms of appraisal. Results from pupil tests should indicate numerical data such as percentile ranks, per cent of items correct, standard deviations, quartile deviations, and standardised scores. Subjectivity in testing is definitely not wanted. Rather objectivity in testing is advocated to determine what any one pupil has learned as a result of teaching.

Pertaining to realism, Wild (1995) wrote the following:

The child, of course, should be interested in what he is learning. But it does not follow that whatever the child is interested in is, therefore, valuable. This is absurd. The skill of the elementary teacher lies in eliciting the interest of the child in the right things, especially in grasping the truth for its own sake. At the early stages no psychological or rhetorical technique should be neglected which is capable of strengthening this urge. When a mathematical principle has been understood, the child's attention should be drawn at once to the problem this enables him to solve. No opportunity should be lost to point out the principles of pure science which underlie modern technology. Language and grammar should be taught at essential phases of that mysterious process of apprehension by which the actual structure of things is mentally reflected an expressed, and by which such knowledge is achieved.

Realists do place very strong emphasis upon the following in teaching and learning situations.

1. carefully selected ends for pupils to achieve need to be written in precise, measurable terms.
2. learning opportunities chosen by the teacher align with the ends or objectives mentioned in number 1 above.
3. pupil achievement in having attained the precise objectives are measurable presented in numerical terms.
4. the models of mathematics and science with its accuracy and specificity should be incorporated into the curriculum.
5. research studies can provide much data on what learners should study such as, for example, which words pupils should master in spelling. Many excellent

studies have been made which indicate the words pupils use most frequently in functional writing. Words that are misspelled in these writings provide a scientific basis for determining practical words to be chosen by the teacher for pupil mastery.

Technology needs to be matched with the chosen objectives of instruction in lesson plans and units of study. After the use of technology in teaching and learning situations, the teacher may measure what pupils have learned. The results are given in numerical terms, not vague subjective data. The objective results may be reported to parents to indicate learner achievement in the school curriculum.

LEADERSHIP IN TECHNOLOGY USE

Teachers need to be and are leaders in curriculum development. They select objectives, learning activities, and appraisal procedures. Teachers organise the classroom for instruction. Organisational work includes grouping pupils for instruction, disciplining pupils, as well as devising a schedule for teaching. Technology is definitely involved in making curricular decisions. For example, there should be an ample number of software programmes in the learning activities section to guide pupils to achieve objectives. Definite leadership skills are necessary here. In addition to the classroom teacher, the principal plays a vital role in curriculum development.

Ritchie (1996) wrote the following pertaining to reasons why the use of technology is minimal in schools:

* A lack of administrative support
* Inadequate staff development and technological support
* Low quantity, quality, and access of technologies in the classroom
* Non-existent or cursory plans for adopting and implementing technology into a school
* The failure to allocate a technology coordinator to help train teachers and coordinate the technologies
* A lack of funds and personnel to maintain equipment
* Continual assessment of content acquisition through traditional methods

* Establishment of a broad participatory clientele to establish a technology culture (Hoffman, 1996).

From the above statements, it is quite clear that school administrators need to understand and value technological use in the classroom. School administrators should perceive the necessity of implementing technology use in the classroom so that pupils may achieve more optimally. No doubt, there are school administrators who lack quality experiences with technology and therefore do not see the need for pupils supervisor should avail themselves in learning more about technology and how to integrate its use into the school curriculum. Talking to and learning from classroom teachers should assist the school administrator in realising the importance of technology in a modern elementary curriculum. Staff development programmes in using technology in the curriculum should be in the offing. Teachers and administrators need to realise the importance of an updated curriculum. The school of today and the work place of tomorrow should not be in isolation from each other, but rather become integrated entities. Definite goals in inservice education using technology are musts! These goals and experiences for participants need to be chosen carefully. Relevance and importance are two concepts that need careful consideration when inservice education programmes are developed and implemented. The goals of the workshop need to be clearly stated and should be cooperatively developed by workshop participants. There should be a large group session to hear a speaker or two who introduce vital inservice education goals. In the large group session, participants need to identify problem areas pertaining to the use of technology. Cooperative endeavours and committee work should follow to solve identified problems from the large group session. Consultants need to be available to assist in clarifying ideas and raising important questions to consider. A hands on approach should be in the offing. Individual endeavours need to also be pursued in the inservice education programme. Participants individually have concerns that need addressing with consultant assistance. There should be opportunities to try out what has been studied in the inservice education programme to the level of application in the regular public school classroom. Feedback from the classroom to participants in the inservice education programme is a must!

There need to be definite plans to integrate technology into the school curriculum. This should not be left to chance, but rather quality goals and plans have been developed to use technology to its fullest in teaching and learning situations. Teachers need to have easy access to technology in lesson plan and teaching unit construction. A trained and educated coordinator of technology use can assist teachers to educate children for more optimal achievement. The coordinator of technology needs to develop good human relations with teachers with the latter having access readily to technology.

Adequate money needs to be budgeted and used to develop a curriculum with technology as a guiding principle. The lay public needs to be informed continuously about the merits of using technology in the classroom to assist each pupil to achieve as optimally as possible. The school culture reflects the importance of technology use with pupils, teachers, and administrators indicating its importance to child growth and development in the school setting.

Maskin (1996) wrote the following:

Promoters of computers in the classroom claim that exposing pupils to Web sites, e-mail, and newsgroups promises more than the means of securing a job in the next century. Technology boosters also predict that the use and mastery of the internet and the World Wide Web will produce affective changes that can be measured to produce increased student self-esteem and confidence. Whether working at home or in school, as an individual or in a cooperative learning or team setting, students will become "infotectives", i.e. independent thinkers, researchers, inventors, inquirers, capable of solving problems that often required the active direction of a teacher or supervisor... .

In expanding the learning environment to include data bases, computer networks, and other library resources throughout the world, the internet makes it possible for students to shape their own education. Once the easy accessing protocols are learned, the student can dive into these resources in the comfort of his or her home and/or library without the constant supervision and intervention of the teacher. Lao Tzui's' dictum, 'He who teaches least teaches best,' describes a student centered teaching, learning, and assessment environment in which the student can access information from multiple perspectives and learn to use this information to solve complex problems.

Freedom, however, also opens up the possibility of choice. The emerging information technologies can just as easily be used to access sports trivia as they can explore issues being debated in Congress or at the World Bank. Many students, if left to their devices, might choose to spend hours surfing the "Net for their own enjoyment rather than using it to complete a school assignment. The job of the teacher, therefore, is to involve students, individually or in teams, in internet projects that are fun to do and skill enhancing. Students exposed early on to such educational endeavours are more likely to fell comfortable and confident in Drucker's knowledge based society... .

We are convinced that internet connectivity empowers students, gives them a research advantage, and generally gets them excited about learning.

We are truly in an information age in which there are so many outstanding sources of content for pupil acquisition. Pupils need to have ample opportunities to secure a variety of subject matter on a topic. It does cost money to have the latest of technology in our schools. But can we afford to be without it? Pupils today, in a few years, will be in the work place where the information age will even more be clearly defined as compared to today. Pupils of every race, creed, and religion must have the chances in an equitable manner to be able to use the latest in data securing sources. The upper income level pupils will have these opportunities of obtaining information through World Wide Web Internet in the home setting. Other pupils also should have equality of opportunity to use state of the art sources to obtain information.

Pertaining to the future of technology, Mehlinger (1996) wrote the following:

Without going into detail regarding specific pieces of hardware, we can say with confidence that schools should expect more *integration, interaction, and intelligence* from future technology. In their early days in school, computers and video were regarded as separate entities, and it was assumed they would stay that way. In fact, we can expect a continuing integration of these technologies.

Voice, data, and images will be brought together into one package. One current example of this process is desktop video. In a single, relatively inexpensive unit, one has telephone (voice), computer (data storage and manipulation), and video (sending and receiving moving images) capabilities. Those who use the machine can talk to people at a distance, exchange documents, work collaboratively, and even see collaborators on the screen.

Technology will also become more interactive. In the field of distance learning, rather than strictly rely on one-way video and two way communication, teachers and students will see another simultaneously, thereby making distance learning more like face-to-face classroom interaction. Computer based instruction will also be designed to respond to learners' Interests and abilities, giving them greater control over what they need to learn and the pace at which they will learn it. And computer searches, which can be bewildering to the casual observer, will become easier and more responsive to what a user needs. Greater interactivity will make instructional programmes even more powerful then they are today.

Finally, technology will have greater intelligence. This intelligence will be displayed in several ways. First, the technology will have more features and greater capacity. Second, it will have the capability to learn from the user, so that it can customise its services to fit the user's learning style and interest. Future technology will provide not only data bases but knowledge bases. And technology will be able to stay abreast of that information most valued to the user and alert him or her to its availability.

Integration, interaction, and intelligence. These are three features we can expect of technology in the future. And they will change the way technology is employed in schools.

Conclusion

From the psychology of learning, there are numerous criteria recommended for teaching pupils. These are that interest needs to be developed within pupils for learning, purpose should be there on the learner's part to achieve, meaning should be inherent in ongoing lessons and units of study, relationship of knowledge is salient in the instructional arena, individual differences among pupils need to be provided for, and good attitudes need adequate emphasis.

Four philosophies of education were discussed and need to be appraised so that the best one(s) are used to meet individual pupil learning styles. These philosophies are experimentalism with its stress upon pupil problem solving; idealism with its emphasis upon an idea centered curriculum advocating learner's achieving abstract subject matter; existentialism with values placed upon the individual pupil selecting, from among alternatives, learning opportunities to pursue; and realism with its stress upon pupils achieving measurable stated objectives.

The future seemingly looks bright for use of technology in the classroom. The use of World Wide Web and Internet, e-mail, faxing, and the electronic bulletin board, among others, will guide pupils to attain vital objectives of instruction. Desktop videos, as a truly modern device in technology, integrate voice, sound, and the pictorial.

References

Bhaskara, Rao, Digumarti, ed. (1997), *Education for the 21st Century.* New Delhi, India: Discovery Publishing House.

Bhaskara Rao, Digumarti, ed. (2001), *International Encyclopaedia of Science and Technology Education*, 11 Volumes. New Delhi: Discovery Publishing House.

Bigge, Morris L. (1982), *Educational Philosophies for Teachers.* Columbus, Ohio: Charles E. Merrill Publishing Company, pp. 25 and 26.

Choice or Chance (1984), Chicago, Illinois: Rand Mc Nally and Company.

Ediger, Marlow and D. Bhaskara Rao (1996), *Science Curriculum.* New Delhi, India: Discovery Publishing House, Chapter Three.

Ediger, Marlow (1995), *Philosophy in Curriculum Development.* Kirksville, Missouri: Simpson Publishing Company, pp. 86-87.

Ediger, Marlow (1997), *Social Studies Curriculum in the Elementary School.* Fourth Edition. Kirksville, Missouri, p.241

Ediger, Marlow (1994), 'Teaching Science,' *Investigating*, 10 (3), 24-25, published by the Australian Science Teachers Association.

Ediger, Marlow (1996), 'Personalised Science Instruction, *Prism,* 5 (1), 25-27, printed by the Newfoundland and Labrador Teachers Association.

Eichelberger, Tony R. (1989), *Disciplined Inquiry: Understanding and Doing Educational Research.* Write White Plains, New York: Longman, Inc., p. 11.

Hoffman, Bob (1996). 'School Technology Integration: An Automated Needs Assessment and Planning Tool.' in *Technology and Teacher Education Annual.* edited by Robin, Price, Wilis, and Willis. Charlottesville, Virginia: Association for the Advancement of Computing in Education.

Maskin, Melvin (1996), 'Infotectives on the Infobahn: Designing Internet-Aided Projects for the Social Studies Classroom, *National Association of Secondary School Principal's Bulletin*, Vol. 80, No. 582, pp. 59-69.

Mehlinger, Howard D. (1996), 'School Reform in the Information Age,' *Phi Delta Kappan.* Vol. 77, No. 6, pp. 405-406.

Morris, Van Cleve and Young Pai (1976). *Philosophy and the American School.*: Houghton Mifflin Company, p. 378.

Ozman, Howard, and Samuel Craver (1990), *Philosophical Foundations and Education*, Fourth Edition. Columbus, Ohio: Merrill Publishing Company, P. 249.

Rao, Digumarti Bhaskara and K. Vijaya (1995), *A Text Book Evaluation.* Ambala Cantt. India: The Associated Publishers.

Ritchie, Donn (1996), 'The Administrative Role in Integration of Technology,' *Bulletin of the National Association of Secondary School Principals*, Vol. 80, No. 582, p. 43.

Rose, Stephen A., And Phyllis Maxey Fernlund (1997), 'Using Technology for Powerful Social Studies Learning, *Social Education*, Vol. 61, No. 3, pp. 161-162.

Wild, John (1955), *Modern Philosophies of Education.* Chicago, Illinois: The National Society for the Study of Education, p. 31.

13

MAPS, GLOBES AND THE SOCIAL STUDIES

The purpose of writing this chapter is to provide a model to assist teachers in helping pupils achieve optimally in map and globe use. There are many reasons for pupils to develop a good knowledge of maps and globes. The world appears to be 'shrinking' in size due to better means of transportation and communication. For example, I traveled from New York City to Beirut, Lebanon in fourteen days by freighter in 1952; now, a person can take a nine days tour, which includes transportation, to the Middle East and back. Air transportation makes it possible to travel in ten hours what it took fourteen days to do in 1952. With direct dialing and fax messages, instant messages can be received in the Middle East as they are sent from any place in the United States. I believe it is more imperative than ever before for pupils to have a good knowledge of maps and globes.

Military threats between two superpowers—the United States and the former Soviet Union ended in 1991. There seemingly are always critical areas of the world where threats to war are a possibility. Bosnia, formerly a part of Yugoslavia, has received much attention in the news. The three opposing sides—the Serbs, the Croats, and the Muslims—have been able, in degrees, to work out major problems as to who gets what in Bosnia. Israel and the Palestinians have started to move forward in small steps to resolve major problems pertaining to the West Bank of the Jordan which the former captured in the six day 1967 war. To briefly mention one more trouble spot presently on the face of the earth, the civil war between the Tutsis and the Hutu of Rwanda had made for much destruction and devastation. After fleeing Rwanda, the Hutu are going back in small numbers to Rwanda.

In developing meanings on the pupil's part pertaining to maps and globes, the following questions arise when teachers plan for teaching:

1. Which specific nations, cities, continents, oceans, rivers, lakes, and areas should pupils be able to locate.
2. Should the use of maps and globes be stressed in separate units of study or should map and globe learning be emphasised within ongoing units of study?
3. Which criteria should be used by teachers in selecting salient concepts and generalisations that pupils should develop?
4. Which learning opportunities may be provided to guide pupils in developing important map and globe understandings, skills, and attitudes?
5. How can balance be established and maintained between inductive versus deductive teaching involving pupil use of maps and globes?
6. How might pupils to motivated to identify and solve relevant problem areas involving maps and globes?

Pertaining to another problem area as to when maps or globes should be used, Michaelis (1980) wrote the following:

The globe is the most accurate representation of the earth's surface; it should be referred to whenever questions arise about relative location, size, distance, direction, and shape of land masses and water bodies. Because the globe, like the earth, is a sphere, it has properties that cannot be found one any one flat map. It shows (1) distances between places in correct proportion, (2) correct shape of land mass and water bodies, (3) areas in correct proportions, and (4) true directions. When a sphere is transferred to a flat surface, some distortion is inevitable; in many flat maps, distortion is greatest at the outer edges.

The globe should be used in conjunction with maps whenever distortion creates problems and misconceptions arise. Such misconceptions as the belief that Greenland is larger than South America (it is about one-eighth as large) or that the shortest distance from San Francisco to Moscow is across the Pacific (a polar route is shorter) can be avoided by referring to the globe. The relative position of continents, the shapes of land masses, and the size of various regions, should be checked against the globe.

PLACE LOCATION ON MAPS AND GLOBES

Elementary age pupils receive letters from penpals, friends, and relatives. The source of the letters can be identified by locating these places on maps and globes and relating these locations to the local city, community, or area. E mail messages are also sent and received by pupils.

Pupils who collect stamps could bring all or part of their collection to school on selected days. They may locate the place of origin of these stamps on maps and globes. We have noticed pupils become interested in place geography when they relate their hobby to an ongoing social studies unit.

Children may bring labels to school from fruit and vegetable containers as well as from cereal boxes. The place of manufacturing or packaging may be located on maps and globes. Many items purchased in stores come from foreign nations. The place of origin of these products provides excellent opportunities for pupils to learn place geography. It is indeed excellent if these place location activities mentioned so far can be related directly to ongoing units of study in the social studies. This, however, may not be possible in selected situations. For example, if pupils are studying a unit on Argentina, Brazil, and Chile, the situations referred to above may not pertain to these nations. Teachers might bring in labels from food products and items from different nations and states that could fill this vacuum so that each region or area being studied can be referred to in terms of imports or products exported to places being studied in social studies.

Pupils can certainly learn much in place location in a quality current events programme. News happenings lend themselves well to place location. Thus events occur in a state, nation, or region. Each current events item is enriched through place geography experiences. The Middle East area of the world is mentioned frequently in news papers and magazines television, internet, Infotrack, and radio reports. Nations such as Egypt Israel, Jordan, Syria, Lebanon, Saudi Arabia, and Palestine provide much news. These nations and their respective capital cities may be located on maps and globes.

Many pupils travel within a state in the United States. Highway maps be used to show the route travelled. Pupils with teacher guidance may trace the route taken when walking to school or riding on a bus to school be it from within a city or from a rural area.

There are numerous creative thinking activities possible in making use of maps and globes. We have observed pupils with teacher guidance plan an imaginary tour within a state, several states, and abroad. One pupil in a fifth grade class planned a tour from Kirksville, Missouri to the Mark Twain Museum and the Rock Cliff mansion in Hannibal, Missouri. After visiting Hannibal, the tour group would travel onto the Amana Colonies in Lowa. A map was drawn using a highway road map as the model. The route was traced from Kirksville to Hannibal and then on to the Amana colonies in Lowa. A travel brochure was made which included neat, attractive drawings of Mark Twain Museum and Rock Cliff Mansion in hannibal and also the seven colonies of Amana, Lowa. This display along with others developed and completed by pupils was observed by other classrooms of learners who also wished to have learning experiences such as these.

A student teacher and cooperating teacher whom I supervised in the public school had their pupils take an excursion to a farm showing sheet and gully erosion and means used to remedy these situations such as planting trees and grass, terracing, and strip cropping. A county road map was used to trace this route. Later pupils made a map showing the location of the farm visited.

How difficult or how easy should objectives be for pupil achievement in developing map and globe skills? I have listed the following guidelines to follow in establishing objectives (Ediger 1995):

1. the objectives should be new goals to achieve, not that which has already been acquired by pupils.
2. objectives need to be achievable and yet challenging to learners.
3. the objectives must engage learners by stressing what is of interest to the pupil.
4. the objectives might well encourage learner purpose and motivation.
5. the objectives shall guide pupils to attach meaning and understanding to what is being learned.
6. the objectives may well advocated depth learning by pupils, not survey approaches.

USING MAPS AND GLOBES IN UNITS OF STUDY

Social studies teachers need to make full use of pupil opportunities to learn map and globe knowledge and skills pertaining to ongoing units of study. If, for example, pupils are studying a unit on the Middle East, what should they learn in a meaningful way? We would like to pinpoint here the West Bank of the Jordan with examples of rich learning opportunities for learners.

1. The walled city of Jerusalem being 2,500 feet above sea level.
2. Jericho, the oldest continuously inhabited city on the face of the earth, being 800 feet below sea level. Jericho is located eighteen miles east of Jerusalem!
3. The Dead Sea, the lowest place on earth in terms of elevation, being 1,300 feet below sea level and five miles southeast of Jericho.
4. The Jordan River, sixty seven miles long as a crow files or two hundred actual miles in length, connects the Sea of Galilee in the north with the Dead Sea in the south.
5. Mount Herman, located between Lebanon and Israel, is 12,000 feet in elevation, and has snow almost all year long on its surface.

6. Tel Aviv, being forty miles in a westerly direction from Jerusalem, is located on the shores of the Mediterranean Sea at sea level.
7. The Negeb, beginning about 30 miles south of Jerusalem, is a desert with less than five inches of rainfall per year, the same/similar amount for Jericho and the Dead Sea. Jerusalem has twenty-five inches of rainfall annually. Short distances among places in the Holy Land make for extreme diversity in elevation, temperature, and rainfall amounts.
8. The Judean Hills run from north to south throughout much of the land of Palestine, starting with Nazareth in the north to Hebron in the south. The Negeb begins soon after leaving Hebron which is still located on the Judean Hills.
9. The Plains of Esdraelen, located in a south-easterly direction from Nazareth are flat and known as the bread-basket of the Holy Land. These plains have excellent farm land in which modern farm machinery can be used. In the Judean Hills, the soil is good for grasing with valleys very fertile for growing garden crops. On these hills, there are many natural rocks making it difficult to use modern farm machines for farming. For example, a plow or disk might have broken parts when used for tilling due to the rocky soil.
10. The Jordan River is actually the result of earthquakes and erosion whereby this rift extends down to east Africa.

We have assisted pupils in the public schools in making a relief map of the Middle East when this unit is being studied. The student teacher and cooperating teacher and myself worked as a team here. We have a definite recipe for pupils to follow when making the relief map using an equal mixture of flour and salt with added water to make a thick paste. The modelling mixture is placed on a piece of plywood, approximately two feet by three feet in dimension. Pupils need to take careful note of a map showing the ten geographical features mentioned above. As each feature has been studied, pupils place the mixture of flour and salt with added water on the plywood sheet. Learners when take careful notice of where each geographical place is located and attach meaning as to what took place there, past and present, such as King David establishing the capital city of ancient Israel in Jerusalem in 1000 BC, whereas Omar, Caliph of the Muslim world, captured Jerusalem from the Byzatine Empire in 634 AD. Pupils need to establish meaning for places studied geographically in terms of events that transpired at these places in history.

It is very important that pupils follow posted rules when engaged in making the relief map, otherwise they may leave a mess that is hard to clean up. We have found the following rules developed cooperatively with learners facilitates teaching and learning in making the relief map:

1. three to four pupils should be maximum number working on a single map. Otherwise pupils may get into each other's way.
2. each pupil should participate actively in developing the relief map, but not dominate the situation.
3. learners need to respect and accept each other as human beings possessing much worth.
4. cooperative endeavours are wanted, not individualism as a philosophy of teaching.
5. pupils need to keep themselves as well as the furniture and equipment clean when working with the modelling materials.
6. difficulties experienced in making the relief map provides opportunities for problem solving, not arguments. Resolving conflicts is important in any endeavour.
7. learners need to work on the relief map until completion. This involves challenges and opportunities in budgeting for time and sequence in each class session.
8. pupils with teacher guidance need to arrive at criteria to appraise the quality of the relief map as well as

appraising the self on the pupil's part in having developed the relief map.

9. The finished product needs to be shared with the rest of the class as well as with peers from other classrooms.

10. a classroom newsletter should be sent home to parents to communicate what pupils are doing and achieving in the social studies.

In using commercially developed maps and globes in ongoing units of study, pupils need to attach meaning sequentially to the following concepts; meridians, parallels, latitude, longitude, bays, plains, plateaus, Tropic of Capricorn, Tropic of Cancer, the North Pole, the South Pole (Antarctic region), and Time Zones, among others.

Each of these concepts needs to be understood by learners in a meaningful way and used in contextual situations. Thus, the first named concept, above is 'meridians'. The teacher needs to show pupils on a map and a globe where the imaginary lines are called the 'meridians.' These lines run north and south and all meridians intersect at the north pole and at the south pole. Why are meridians important as reference lines? To locate any place on a map and globe, a point is placed on these north/south reference lines, directly on a meridian. But is this adequate? The answer is 'no.' There are many, many meridians or north/south reference lines. Another reference line is needed. This reference line runs in an east/west line and are called parallels. The lines are parallel to the Equator which is zero degrees. With the two imaginary lines on the map or globe, both representing the planet earth, the pupil can state the rather precise location of a city, state, or nation. A city on the map/globe, for example, is zero degrees from the Equator, meaning it is located directly on the equator. Longitude measures distances east or west of the Prime Meridian, located outside of London, England at Greenwich Observatory. To measure distances east or west of the Prime Meridian, one measures along a parallel. The Tropic of Capricorn is located twenty-three and one/half degrees south of the Equator. To measure from the equator to the Tropic of Capricorn, one measures along an imaginary line, which in this case, again is a meridian. The Tropic of Capricorn indicates an imaginary line on the planet earth which is the farthest place south in which the sun will be directly overhead at noon at any time during the year. In the northern hemisphere, this is the first day of Winter. Going north in the opposite direction to a place twenty-three and one-half degrees north latitude, one comes to a point known as the Tropic of Cancer. The Tropic of Cancer is the point in which the sun will be as nearly overhead at noon as possible. This time of the year ushers in the first day of summer in the northern hemisphere which is June 21. In between the Tropic of Capricorn and the Tropic of Cancer is the parallel known as the Equator. When the sun is as nearly overhead at noon, the first day of spring (March 21) or the first day of Fall (September 21) is in evidence. When speaking of the Tropic of Capricorn being twenty-three and one/half degrees in latitude, this means it is parallel to the equator on an imaginary line twenty-three and one/half degrees south. Simultaneously, the Tropic of Cancer, located twenty-three and one/half degrees north latitude is on an imaginary line parallel to the Equator.

It is quite obvious that the concepts 'meridians,' 'parallels,' 'latitude,' and 'longitude' have many generalisations inside each. Thus the concept 'meridian' contains, among others, the following generalisations:

1. it is an imaginary line running north and south on a map or globe.
2. there are many meridians; all intersect at the north pole and at the south pole. Mercator map projections do not show this intersection and thus distort the size of numerous nations.
3. to measure distances north and south of the equator, one measures along a meridian.
4. the farthest number in degrees that one can measure north of the equator is ninety. This is the north pole region. The Tropic of Cancer is located twenty-three and one/half degrees north of the Equator.
5. the farthest one can measure south of the equator is ninety degrees. This is the south pole region. The tropic of Capricorn is located twenty-three and one/half degrees south of the Equator.

6. to measure distances east or west of the Prime Meridian, one measures along a parallel.
7. there is a distance of fifteen degrees between regions for each hour of time difference. Thus is discussing Time Zones, in moving from east to west or west to east on a parallel, a difference of one hour in time is in evidence for every fifteen degrees in longitude. Longitudinal lines fifteen degrees apart measure one hour of time on the planet earth.
8. the low latitudes are between the Tropic of Capricorn and the Tropic of Cancer.
9. the high latitudes are located in the Arctic and Antarctic circles. From the North Pole and going twenty-three and one/half degrees south is the Arctic circle. From the South Pole and going twenty-three and one/half degrees north latitude is the Antarctic circle.
10. In between the low latitudes (Torrid Zone) and the high latitudes (Frigid Zone) are the middle latitudes (Temperate Zone).

Major concepts in geography pertaining to the use of maps and globes can be learned meaningfully and sequentially by pupils. It is best if the teacher starts with concrete experiences for pupils whereby they actually see a geographical scene first hand such as gully and sheet erosion and means to remedy these situations with the planting of grass, trees, strip cropping, and terracing. However, in many cases, this may not be possible. How many pupils have visited the Middle East by the time this unit is being taught? The chances are that none or very few have. Thus the teacher needs to lean upon semiconcrete materials such as audiovisual materials. The teacher should make learning as real and lifelike as possible. Using audiovisual materials in teaching and learning can make ongoing activities quite real and lifelike. The abstract terms then become meaningful to pupils with quality sequence and materials based on realia. Schuncke (1988) wrote the following:

Regardless of the phase the children are in the with their understanding of symbols, references should be made to the legend of the map. Initially, the children will construct their own. When they start using printed maps and their attention should be directed to the legend and to finding symbols identified in the legend. Then, as they become more sophisticated in their understanding of the symbols they can be helped to infer relationship among them (e.g., the relation of population and industrial centres).

The following summarises the sequence in which symbols are taught.

1. Children build models of their own environment, using three dimensional objects to represent things (primary grades).
2. Model environments are mapped by the children and symbols are drawn in a legend (primary grades).
3. Children are helped to identify symbols they encounter in everyday life. These symbols should be used on maps constructed by teachers or students (late primary, intermediate grades).
4. Pictorial symbols are introduced on commercially prepared maps. Children are taught to consult the legend (intermediate grades).
5. Semipictorial symbols are introduced (intermediate grades).
6. Gradually, adult symbols are introduced (late intermediate grades).

In using maps and globes, the teacher needs to ascertain where each pupil is presently in achievement. The pupil is always the focal point of instruction. Determining where each pupil is achieving presently needs to be emphasised before sequential instruction begins. Positive attitudes towards maps and globes might well be developed if pupils are ready for learning. For example, before pupils are to learn about the scale of miles, they should be evaluated in terms of what is known presently about this concept. The teacher may ask pupils what is meant by 'a scale of miles.' He/she should also ask how we may determine distances between two points using a 'scale of miles.' On a map/globe, the teacher may demonstrate how to measure the distance between two points or cities. The scale of miles on a map/globe may be given in the following ways on a legend:

1. a ratio, such as one inch equals 500 miles.
2. a piece of plastic whereby the length of that piece of plastic is 400 miles.
3. one inch on the map/globe represents 50,000 inches on the actual ground.

Approaches numbers one and two above are the easiest for pupils to understand and use. The teacher needs to assist pupils to use a plastic ruler to measure one inch on the map/globe accurately and then indicate how far that distance is. Learners should be guided to indicate other places that have that particular distance which in this case would be four hundred miles. Thus the learner is challenged to achieve from the known which is a distance of four hundred miles between two places. This item of knowledge/information is related to the new learning—the distance shown between two places on a map/globe. It might be just as easy for pupils to use a piece of plastic and then determine for each unit of that length what the distance between two points would be. If one of the plastic units is 400 miles in length, then two pieces would have a distance of 800 miles. The third procedure mentioned above to find distances between two places would be the most difficult. Even if the distance between two places on a map/globe is 50,000 inches on the ground, the fifty thousand inches need to be changed to a more meaningful indicator such as in miles or kilometers.

We have observed numerous situations in which pupils individually are given the names of two cities on a map/globe and are asked to estimate the distance between the two points. The estimate is an hypothesis and recorded by the involved learner. The hypothesis is then checked with actually measuring the distance between the two points. Learners seemingly are fascinated with estimating and then checking their responses.

Pupils love to work cooperatively in determining the distance between two points when given the names of two cities on a map/globe. Adequate readiness must be provided for pupils prior beginning this activity.

Cardinal directions for pupils to understand and use need adequate emphasis in terms of objectives and learning opportunities in the social studies. We recommend that a map always be on the north wall of a classroom. Thus east and west on the map harmonise with east and west in the out-of-doors. There should then be ample times when a wall map is on the floor of the classroom so that all directions on the map harmonise with the cardinal directions in the natural environment. Pupils need to orientate themselves properly so that the cardinal directions are consistent with that of the natural environment. There are diverse approaches here that the pupil may find helpful in determining directions:

1. in the northern hemisphere notice where the sun is located in relationship to where one is standing. In the afternoon, the sun will tend to be in the western sky, compared to being in the eastern sky in the morning.
2. orientate oneself to familiar landmark that is north from the school grounds. Then to one's left side is west whereas toward one's right hand side is east. Opposite of north and to one's back is south.
3. inside the classroom with the map being on the north wall as one faces the map, to one's left hand side is west and toward the right hand side is east. Toward one's back is the direction of south.
4. the cardinal directions should be printed neatly on cards and attached to the classroom walls showing north, south, east, and west respectively.
5. pupils need to learn familiar cities that are located in each of the cardinal directions from the local school.
6. games may be played in which pupils tell where a particular city is located in direction from the local city. The names of these cities are familiar to the learner. Or a direction may be given and pupils sequentially tell of landmarks located in the given direction.
7. the name of a pupil is called and he/she is asked to tell the direction of a learner seated at a certain location, away from home base of the responder.

TYPES OF MAPS

Pupils need to learn to work with a variety of maps due to the need for developing skills pertaining to each map. It is difficult to say which kinds of maps pupils will need to learn to read in society, presently as well as in the future. We would like to suggest the following:

1. ***A highway or road map.*** We believe most would agree that this kind of map is practical in learning to use. Drivers of automobiles are find it very helpful when travelling to be able to read a highway/road map. One can save miles and tension by choosing the best route to drive when the region is not familiar to the driver. We have known of people who took the long route when a shorter distance could have been driven. This situation resulted from not having essential knowledge and skills in reading a highway/road map.
2. ***A city map.*** Most people travel in a city where the streets are not familiar and a definite place needs to be found. A city map is very helpful to follow in finding one's destination in an unknown area. We have known people who have driven the wrong direction in a city and yet felt they were doing well in finding the proper location. Following a city map carefully might well avoid these kinds of situations.
3. ***A park map.*** Many visit parks in the United States and abroad during the summer months. It can be very helpful to be able to read a park map.
4. ***An agricultural products map.*** These maps can be very useful for pupils in understanding which crops and livestock are produced in a given region. Also, the learner can readily notice by viewing an agricultural products map in terms of how much is produced of major farm crops and livestock.
5. ***Natural resource maps.*** Here, Pupils may be guided by the teacher to observe petroleum produced, minerals mined, and other products obtained from the natural environment.

6. ***Contour maps of a given agricultural region.*** Pupils with teacher assistance may be guided to notice how farm land differs even within a small agricultural region. Thus farm land may be hilly, flat, eroded, possess wooded areas, be marginal for farming, have contours, farmed with strip cropping procedures, emphasise grassed waterways, have farms ponds, among other features. By studying these maps, pupils may see the need to conserve and use farm land wisely.
7. ***National maps.*** In travelling across the United States or India,, parents with their offspring have studied and used maps pertaining to an entire nation. These maps show interstate and federal highways that connect throughout the country. It is practical and utilitarian for pupils to learn to read maps of an entire nation since interactions occur frequently among people with in a country or state.
8. ***World maps.*** There is much interaction among nations on the face of the planet earth, which is depicted in world maps.
9. ***Rainfall maps.*** The maps will show pupils the approximate rainfall in a given region covering three months, six months, and an average yearly rainfall. The symbols used on the rainfall map may be interpreted by looking at the legend. For example, on the map in a given region, three measuring gauges may show the amount of rainfall in an area for one calender year. The legend indicated that each rainfall gauge stresses five inches of precipitation. Three gauges times five inches for each makes a total of fifteen inches average for the entire year.

There are globes available that also contain information mentioned above. The teacher and the school need to look at stated objectives of instruction and then determine if each of these kinds of maps and globes are needed. We definitely would not leave out computerised maps and globes for pupils to study. These maps and globes go along within a contextual situation when using programmed material. We have noticed pupils who are truly interested in maps and globes when using selected programme of study.

As a further note, pupils can certainly be involved in making their very own maps and globes in the classroom. Many times, a learner will remember what has be taught when making a model map. Thus in studying a unit on the local city, We watched learners in cooperative learning make an excellent map of the local park. This map was made in detail and appeared to very accurate. Inside of the park map, pupils indicated the roads, the swimming beach, the cabins, the boat house, the convenience store, and picnic areas. These features were drawn to scale and placed accurately in relationship to each other.

An excellent model of the planet earth may be made with covering a small beach ball with strips of papier mache'. The papier mache' needs to dry thoroughly before data is put thereon. What should go onto this newly formed globe, a representation of the earth? This depends upon what is being studied in the ongoing unit in social studies. If the Middle East is being studied, pupils may wish to put in the different nations of Egpt, Israel, Lèbanon, Syria. Jordan, and Palestine as they are being studied. Accuracy of presentation on the home made globe is very important. A purpose of making a globe is to have pupils pay strict attention to each specific place as its related data is put thereon. Thus as a river is being studied from one or more commercially prepared maps/globes, pupils make their own globes using a beach ball or balloon and attaching strips of papier mache' on this sphere. The river being studied is then out onto the globe. Elevation features may also be placed on the globe to show more accurately the contour of the river. Tempera paint may be used to put colour into the proper elevation of political boundary. In elaborating upon the fundamental themes in geography, Boehm and Peterson (1994) indicate the following stated in outline form:

1. Location

Absolute location such as using grids (latitude and longitude, different types of maps and globes (thematic maps show population, economic systems, climate zones, political divisions, and settlement patterns), map projections (to change from a spherical earth to a two-dimensions map sheet), as well as earth-sun relations (to determine climate, seasons, and time zones).

Relative location such as locations have geographical explanations as well as the importance of a location can change with history.

2. Place

Physical characteristics (land forms, climate, soils, natural vegetation, and animal life).

Human characteristics including religion, languages, population factors, settlement patterns, and economic activities.

3. Human-Environmental System

These include interrelationships between humans and environments, the role of technology (humans apply technology to modify environment, problems of technology (air and water pollution, waste disposal, and toxic materials), environmental hazards (natural-earthquakes, hurricanes, floods, volcanoes; human induced—nuclear disasters, oil spills, an heat pollution of water bodies), environmental limits (water, land, and natural resources), and adaptations (influence of the environment in making a living, house types, ways of life, and the appearance of the human landscape.

Ethics and values involve issues relating to management and protection of environmental resources as well as different cultural altitudes about the environment and its resources.

4. Movement

Transportation modes, movement in everyday, life, history of movement, economic stimulus for movements, as well as energy mass induced movements (weather, wind, ocean currents, folding and faulting, and landslides).

Global interdependence includes movement of goods, services, ideas, and foreign trade.

5. Regions

Uniform regions defined by cultural or physical characteristics.

The above enumerated items might well provide a quality

basis in determining objective pertaining to the teaching about maps and globes. Objectives need to be relevant, salient, and important for learners to achieve. They provide direction to the teacher in teaching pupils. Learning activities may then be chosen by the teacher to assist pupils to attain these objectives. Ultimately evaluation procedures selected may determine how well pupils have achieved the stated objectives. Ample opportunities need to be given pupils to identify and solve problems involving the use of maps and globes.

VITAL GENERALISATIONS FOR PUPILS TO ACHIEVE USING MAPS AND GLOBES

Which major generalisation should pupils achieve pertaining to the use of maps and globes? These should be chosen carefully with input from teachers, administrators, supervisors, and university professors. A listing of some major generalisations will be presented which pupils could realise inductively (Ediger 1986).

1. Pupils should realise that distances can be computed by using the scale of miles given on the map or globe. Maps and globes vary as to the number of miles that would be represented by one inch as given in a scale of miles.
2. Specific places on the earth can be located using the concepts of 'latitude' and 'longitude.'
3. North latitude refers to distance in degrees north of the Equator while south latitude refers to distance in degrees south of the Equator.
4. East longitude has reference to distance in degrees east of the Prime Meridian while west longitude relates to distance in degrees west of the Prime Meridian.
5. Distances north and south of the Equator are measured along a meridian while distances east or west of the Prime Meridian are measured along a parallel.
6. The earth rotates from a west to east direction once every 24 hours (causes for day and night can be shown by using a flashlight, a darkened room, and a globe which represents a model of the planet earth). The

imaginary line on which the earth rotates is called its axis.

7. The earth revolves around the sun approximately once in 365 and one/fourth days. On March 21 and September 21, approximately, .the sun is directly overhead at noon on the equator. Whereas on June 21, approximately, the sun is directly overhead at noon on the Tropic of Cancer located 23 and ½ North of the equator. On December 21, the sun is directly overhead at noon on the Tropic of Capricorn located 23 and ½ south of the equator. Other factors involved in determining temperature reading include elevation of land being considered, ocean currents, and nearness to bodies of water.

8. The axis of the earth points toward the North Star. On a bright and sunny day at noon each pupil can look directly at his/her shadow; he/she is facing north at this time. Pupils while facing north can be shown the position of the North Star as it would be at night.

9. Maps do not represent as accurately the surface of the earth as compared to globes. With the use of maps, however, a certain continent, country, or area can be studied more conveniently than a globe since it will represent a larger area.

10. Some of the symbols used in legends on maps and globes are standard symbols. For example, symbols on maps which represent hospitals, railroad tracks, and paved arc standard symbol. These are also symbols which vary in meaning from legend to legend in different maps and globes used.

11. Any circle has 360 degrees. There are twenty-four time zones in the world thus making each time zone have an approximate value of 15 degrees of longitude.

12. A hemisphere is represented by half of the earth: four hemispheres may be referred to—southern, northern, western, and eastern.

13. The direction of north on a map pertains to going

directly to the North Pole; whereas the direction of south means to go directly to the South Pole. There are different projections of maps so the direction of north may not always be 'up' on the map.

14. Low, middle, and high latitude refer to specific areas or parts of maps and globes, such as the low latitudes lying immediately north and south of the Equator while the high latitudes are located around the North and South Poles. The middle latitudes refer to those parts lying between the low latitudes and the high latitudes.

Each of the above enumerated items may be stated in terms of either general or measurably stated objectives. Teachers, principals, supervisors, and parents should choose what is vital for pupils to learn. Maps and globes may be taught as a separate unit or it may be integrated with other thematic units of study. In all social studies units, pupils need to study how to use maps and globes due to any happening or event occurring in a geographical region.

Douglass (1967) wrote the following pertaining to the use of maps and globes:

During the years the child is in school, teachers should encourage development of five abilities basic to all map reading activities:

1...develop concepts about direction.

2...develop concepts of distance and scale.

3...employ locational abilities.

4...interpret map symbols of various kinds.

5...draw inferences and develop generalisations from the study of a variety of different kinds of maps.

Conclusion

Social studies teachers need to choose what is salient for pupils to learn in the area of maps and globes. These objectives need to be stressed in teaching and learning. We recommend content on maps and globes be a part of thematic units of study so that content is perceived as being related by pupils.

However, there is merit also in stressing separate units of study on maps and globes. We have observed both approaches being used by classroom teachers in the public schools. Both approaches can make for interest, meaning, and purpose in pupil learning. Stimulating learning opportunities need to be in the offing to guide pupils to achieve relevant objectives. Learners should be actively involved in learning with goal centered learning opportunities. Engagement in learning in a wholehearted manner is advocated. Learners should not be passive individuals, but rather be thoroughly involved with the objective, learning activities, and appraisal procedures.

Technology needs to be brought into the map and globe curriculum as it assists pupils to achieve objectives more readily and in depth. Means and Olson (1994) wrote:

> For educational reform to take place, technology need to be integrated into a 'broad effort for school reform, and considered not as the instigator of reform or cure all, but as a set of tools to support specific kinds of instruction and intellectual inquiry.'
>
> Technology then becomes a tool for learning, not an end in and of itself. Thus there has to be a reason for using technology to achieve objectives in the social studies. The reason being to guide more optimal achievement among learners in ongoing lessons and units of study.

There are definite philosophies of teaching that may be stressed in map and globe learning. Ediger (1995) wrote about the following:

Experimentalism, as one philosophy, states that one can only know experiences. Individuals live in and experience society. The geography curriculum should then not be separated from the societal arena. School and society are one and not separate entities. Changes occur rather continuously in society... . With change, problems arise. Students with teacher guidance need to identify lifelike problems in society emphasising geography. Data from a variety of reference sources need to be secured. The data sources can be basal textbooks, audio-visual aids, direct observation, maps, globes, and software content. An hypothesis may then be developed. The hypothesis is tentative and subject to testing...

Idealism as a second philosophy stresses an idea centered curriculum. To an idealist, one can only know ideas pertaining to the natural and social environment. The teacher, as an idealist in philosophy orientation, needs to guide students to acquire much subject matter...

The teacher needs to possess much subject matter knowledge in the teaching of geography and be academically talented and inclined... .

Mental development of students is of prime importance. Cultivation of the intellect is the major goal in teaching geography. Mind is real and needs to be developed with the use of reputable textbooks, workbooks, worksheets, maps and globes, excursions, as well as audio-visual aids which emphasise academic learning. Ideas in terms of universal concepts and generalisations need acquisition by learners...

Realism, a third philosophy of education, emphasises that one can know the real world in whole or in part, as it truly is. The student may then receive a duplicate of that which exists in the environment. The geographical phenomena are known as they are and exist in and of themselves. With knowing the real world as it truly is/exists, measurably stated objectives become important. These specific ends represent the world in its totality... . The real world of geography then needs to be divided into measurable components so that students may obtain optimally on an individual basis. Each learner needs to achieve as much as possible in attaining the measurably stated objectives. The ends are precise so that it can be ascertained if a student has or has not achieved a specific objective... .

Existentialism, as a fourth philosophy of education, advocates the subjectivity of truth. Truth resides within the student. Learners individually need to have freedom to select objectives, learning opportunities, and appraisal procedures. Choices made are based on personal needs, interests, and convictions. The teacher here becomes a guide and stimulator of learning.

These philosophies need to be considered thoroughly in developing the geography curriculum involving maps and globes. Pupils individually need objectives, learning activities, and evaluation procedures that guide in achieving optimally in geography and its maps/globes emphasis.

References

Bhaskara Rao, Digumarti (1987). *Audio-Visual Teaching Aids*. Guntur, India: Nagarjuna Publishers.

Boehm, Richard G., and James F. Petersen (1994), 'An Elaboration of the Fundamental Themes in Geography, *Social Education*, Vol. 58, No. 4, pages 214-218.

Douglass, Malcolm P. (1967). *Social Studies: From Theory to Practice in Elementary Education*. New York: Lippincott Company, page 336.

Ediger, Marlow (1995), 'Objectives in the Elementary Curriculum,' *Philippine Education Quarterly*, Vol. 24, No. 1, page 19.

Ediger, Marlow (1986). *Social Studies Curriculum in the Elementary School*. Kirksville, Missouri: Simpson Publishing Company, pages 131-132.

Ediger, Marlow (1995), 'Geography in the Social Studies,' *Perspectives*, Vol. 27, No. 1, pages 9-10.

Means, B. and B. Olson (1994). 'Tomorrow's Schools: Technology and Reform in Partnership,' *Technology and Educational Reform: The Reality Behind the Promise*, edited by B. Means, San Francisco: Jossey Bass.

Michaelis, John U. (1980). *Social Studies for Children—A Guide to Basic Instruction*. Seventh edition. Englewood Cliffs, New Jersey: Prentice-Hall, Inc., page 381.

Schuncke, George M. (1988). *Elementary Social Studies*. New York: Macmillan Publishing Company, page 135.

14

CURRENT EVENTS IN THE SOCIAL STUDIES

It is very important to have a quality current events programme in the elementary school. There are numerous reasons given in having a good current events curriculum. There are many happenings on the planet earth which continually come over the news media. Thus there are new nations that spring up such as the nation of Bosnia, independent from the former Yugoslavia. There are new rulers or presidents in different nations. Wars are fought in diverse areas of the world. Natural disasters occur such as earth quakes, floods, hurricanes, tornadoes, and mudslides. It behooves teachers to guide pupils to locate where each relevant item of news happened on a map and a globe. News events always happen in time (history) and space (geography). A good current events programme updates ongoing social studies units and lessons. Change is a key word in current events. Pertaining to change, Doll (1982) wrote:

Science and technology are continuing to advance as new discoveries and breakthroughs are made in physics, chemistry, medicine, and other fields.

Bigness prevails in nearly everything: in government, labour, business, and agriculture.

Improved transportation and communication have brought

about travel at supersonic speeds and the transmission of messages to satellites.

The family has tended to disintegrate, so that striking changes have been wrought in family patterns of living.

Population seems to be growing out of bounds...

Social movements, that include integration of the races, mobility of our population, and movement of people from lower to higher socio-economic status are continuing, though the pace of these movements appears to have slowed.

A value crisis has gripped youth and adults, who have become less clear about what they realty believe.

The above named quote, copyrighted in 1982, is equally important today and will be so in the future. The only exception that I notice, perhaps, might be people moving from the lower to higher socio-economic levels in society.

Critical and creative thinking as well as problem solving can well be emphasised in a quality current events curriculum. Which are some possible questions that might be selected by pupils with teacher guidance in current events?

1. Which new leaders have arrived in different nations on the world scene? How did these leaders receive their offices?
2. Why have certain nations become friends that previously were enemies?
3. Which nations trade much with each other? Why is this the case?
4. Why have certain governments been overthrown as is indicated in news reports? Why does this happen?
5. Why are there wars between/among nations and within a nation?
6. Which nations receive aid from others? Why?
7. Which news events are happening on the state and local levels? Why are these events important?
8. Why do natural events occur such as reported

earthquakes, mudslides, floods, tornadoes, and hurricanes?

For each of the above enumerated items, pupils need to gather information from a variety of reference source including daily newspapers, weekly news magazines, radio and television news, and internet, among others. Critical thinking in current events involves choosing information sources that have valid answers to identified problems as compared to those that do not contain the necessary information. The content also needs to be appraised in terms of being vital versus the irrelevant, accurate versus inaccurate, factual versus opinion, as well as reliable versus unreliable information (Ediger, 1998, ERIC# ED 423519).

Creative thought emphasises originality in developing hypotheses for problem areas chosen in current events. Newness is also involved when creativity becomes apparent in organising and arranging information to support or refute an hypothesis. The hypothesis is an answer directly related to the identified problem area. Creative endeavours are involved when new problems and questions are identified.

What are needed purposes in a good current events curriculum? Wesley and Cartwright (1968) list the following possible achievable purposes:

1. To expand popular information.
2. To develop skill in locating reading materials on particular topics.
3. To promise the critical appraisal of information obtained from the radio, newspapers, magazines, etc.
4. To develop skill in resolving inconsistencies, contradictions, and errors.
5. To increase the ability to distinguish fact and opinion, between a major and minor event, between a principle and temporary trend.
6. To develop the ability to distinguish the significant from the trivial.
7. To develop the abilities to make valid generalisations.
8. To broaden and deepen sympathies.

9. To promote understanding and toleration.
10. To increase faith in the democratic process.
11. To vitalise citizenship.
12. To appreciate the interdependence of peoples and nations.
13. To promote the cause of world peace.

The above listed purposes may be used, as needed, to determine objectives in a quality current events curriculum. Teachers need to be creative in assessing and deleting objectives for learners to attain. I believe critical and creative thinking as well as problem solving to be at the heart of good objectives for pupils to attain in current events. A variety of learning activities need to be provided to achieve objectives. These activities should stress the concrete (reality with a hands on approach in learning): semi-concrete materials (illustrations, scenes on television, videotapes, drawings, electronic imaging, internet, electronic bulletin board, and diagrams, among others; abstract materials (all reading and listening materials containing current events items, such as newspapers, news magazines, cassette tape recordings, computer programmes, and internet printed items, among others.

ACHIEVING INTEREST IN TEACHING CURRENT EVENTS

How does a teacher develop and maintain interest on the part of pupils in current events? We have noticed in classrooms numerous approaches used successfully as interest factors pertaining to teaching current events. The teacher and pupils may bring pictures to put on a bulletin board. These very recent current event happenings are then placed around a world map. A piece of yarn should connect the news clipping with the place where the event took place. Thus a news report clipping on an earthquake should be attached with yarn to the geographical place of its location. The teacher might then teach directly from the bulletin board display as the need arises and pupils may study the news happenings on their own when convenient.

It is best if pupils have an inward desire to bring current events items to school. Intrinsic motivation is then in evidence. However, there are times too when it should be required for pupils to bring news clippings to school. Learners together with their parents may read these news items in the home setting and parents can become more involved in the school curriculum than is usually the case. Pupils then have background information to discuss in class when viewing these posted news items on the bulletin board as time is provided for current events instruction.

We have been a long time advocate of teachers having a radio in the classroom. We have observed radio use in having pupils listen to the news. The times for news broadcasts are specific so the teacher can definitely plan a specific time when pupils may listen to a broadcast. Background statements may be made by the teacher over what will probably be covered in a newscast prior to its occurrence. A few follow-up questions may be discussed after the newscast. There will and should be time given to relate these news items from the radio broadcast into the regular period given to an indepth discussion of relevant items in the current events curriculum. For depth learning, we recommend the following for pupils:

1. reading...those selections that pertain directly to the unit being taught. Readiness for reading should be stressed.
2. making a mural of related content.
3. developing posters of content being studied.
4. construction a model.
5. cooperating in doing an experience chart covering subject matter studied.
6. reading library books pertaining to the unit objectives.
7. viewing and discussing an audio-visual aid's illustrations and content.
8. dramatising subject matter read.
9. giving an oral report in class on a related topic. This report is evaluated in terms of quality standards.
10. discussing in a committee what was learned from a dramatics presentation.

Selected teachers have made the radio broadcast with its readiness and follow-up activities as the time designated for current events each day. This is especially appropriate for intermediate and middle school grade levels. What about primary grade pupils and their being actively involved in current events? There are primary grade pupils who have much interest in current events and this needs to be developed further. We need to observe the present achievement level of each pupil before determining what can be in terms of objectives for pupils to achieve in current events. Thus there are primary grade pupils who understand and are interested in current events items pertaining to the international, national, state, and local levels of happenings. We would suggest thoroughly that all of these levels be covered in depth of and in a good current events curriculum.

Primary grade pupils who are more interested in what happens locally and personally may report on these happenings in current events. Thus these pupils may report on a birthday celebration, a vacation taken in summer or travelling to take a nearby excursion over the weekend, a new addition to the family, and a new toy received, among other occurrences. News in the local area should be of interest to pupils on all grade levels. These happenings might emphasise a school board member election that is coming up, a bond levy or issue being proposed, a catastrophe in the community, natural disasters, and a new business being set up.

When discussing current events items with the class as a whole or in a committee setting. We have found the following standards helpful for pupils to follow:

1. each pupil needs to stay on the topic being discussed and not digress to other information.
2. learners must respect the thinking of each discussion participant.
3. it is important to listen to the ideas of others in the group.
4. all should participate actively in the discussion, but no one dominate the interactions.
5. content presented should be evaluated in an atmosphere of trust.
6. participants need to speak clearly and accurately in terms of concepts, generalisations, and main ideas

presented. There is considerable subjectivity in current events when making predictions and presenting one's own beliefs. This must be respected by all participants.

7. valid and reliable conclusions should be drawn from each discussion.
8. chairpersons may be elected or appointed by the teacher with rotation procedures; leadership might also emerge within a group without a chairperson.

Group/committee endeavours may follow listening to a radio news broadcast. We have also observed teachers who videotape newscasts in the home setting and these are played in the classroom with VCR at a suitable time for pupil viewing. With readiness for the TV newscast pupils seemingly are stimulated to listen to its contents. Follow-up activities can involve discussing relevant subject matter ideas. These could be summarised using a word processor and the document made available to each pupil. The compilation of documents from several discussions provide interest for pupils in that review of these ideas is possible. Ultimately, these documents may be bound for continuous pupil reference.

Current events newspapers written for pupils can have much appeal to learners. These papers are written by educators are as well as co-authored by individuals who are well versed as news reporters.

Newspapers written for pupils have an intended audience and that is the learner himself/herself. Many problems in word recognition have been taken care of when a child centered paper has been written, but to provide for individual needs, selected learners will still need assistance in identifying unknown words. Pupils will also need guidance in understanding the meaning of important words. This assistance should be given in context. Thus meanings of words are contextual and may vary from one context to another. Teacher assisting pupils in word identification should also stress the context within which the word is located, not in an isolated manner.

Ediger (1986) states there are selected questions that teachers need to ask themselves pertaining to developing pupil interest in current events:

1. Do I have a learning environment which stimulates pupil curiosity?
2. Are learning activities varied so that pupils will not lack motivation for learning?
3. Have I worked in the direction of guiding learners in wanting to learn rather then depending upon assigned learning activities only?
4. What evidence is there that pupils are actively involved in ongoing learning activities?
5. How often do pupils volunteer for completing additional work?
6. Is the quality of work from each pupil the beast that can reasonably be expected of him or her?
7. Do pupils have ample opportunities to participate in learning activities which are relevant to them?
8. Do I praise each pupil for doing better than formerly regardless of capacity and present achievement levels?
9. Do I provide a learning environment where each pupil feels he or she can achieve optimal development?
10. Do I help each pupil to respect the thinking and rights of others?
11. Does it appear that pupils have a positive attitude toward current events?
12. What should be changed so that each pupil will be motivated in wanting to learn in the area of current events.

THE SCHOOL ADMINISTRATOR AND THE CURRICULUM

Principals should provide leadership in curriculum development. When problem solving procedures are used in teaching and learning in the current events, a new philosophy of instruction may be ensuing. Principals should provide support and help in these areas. Ediger (1996) wrote:

Faculty members, as do all individuals in society, experience problems in developing and implementing the curriculum.

Administrative support needs to be in evidence for instructors who truly are innovative in improving course offerings. Innovations being tested in teaching/learning situations must:

1. guide learners to perceive purpose or reasons for learning.
2. assist students to attach meaning and; understanding to subject matter being acquired.
3. facilitate in the development of positive attitudes within each learner.
4. attempt to capture student interests.
5. guide students to achieve skills in critical thinking and problem solving.

Emotional support from administrators can do much to facilitate recommended curricular innovations. The principal of the school needs to be highly knowledgeable about the school curriculum, current events included. Leadership is needed to move from where the school is presently to where it should be. Quality human relations and trust are necessary. Positive feelings are necessary toward each other in the school setting so that adjectives of excellence, valid and good learning opportunities to achieve these ends, and reliable evaluation techniques that harmonise with the stated objectives may be implemented.

The proactive principal plans together with his/her teachers pertaining to that which should be in the curriculum. These plans are developed prior to experiencing conflict in the community over matters pertaining to teaching and learning. A normative approach is used herein that the principal and his/her teacher believe in selected trends in education that should be implemented. The reactive principal realises that certain happenings occurred which need remediation in the school setting. When reading, solutions are applied to the areas of deficiency.

Sometimes, the lines are thin indeed between a proactive as compared to a reactive principal. I attempted to show the roles of the proactive as well as a reactive principal in the following areas of the curriculum: problem solving, school-university collaboration, cooperative learning, school research, a common vision, parental input, staff development, a professional library, leadership to improve the curriculum, and needs in the curriculum. Hopefully, these vital areas will receive adequate attention in the school setting and each pupil will be assisted to achieve as optimally a possible (Ediger, 1966).

Certainly, the area of current events is vital for pupils in a democracy. We need well informed people so that quality decisions can be made personally as well as socially. A good current events curriculum should assist individuals to make better decisions to improve the self and society.

ORGANISING THE CURRENT EVENTS CURRICULUM

There are several ways of organising the current events programme. The teacher might have a separate subject approach whereby pupils bring news clippings to school for discussion. These clippings generally will not be related to the ongoing social studies unit of instruction. The news items should be relevant and assist pupils to achieve vital objectives of instruction.

A second approach is to have pupils bring in news items that relate directly to the unit in social studies being taught. Relating content when possible makes retention of information increasingly possible as compared to the separate subjects approach. It may not be possible to have current events items related directly to the unit that is being taught. Thus, there are relevant happeings occurring that are unrelated to the unit being studied presently by pupils. Whenever feasible, current events items discussed in class should relate to the unit of instruction that is ongoing.

A third procedure is to have a separate unit stressing a current events item. The happening is of utmost importance to spend a week, for example, in having it as a separate unit in social studies. The current events unit should be planned as carefully and as meticulously as possible. The objectives for the unit should emphasise vital content in terms of relevant facts, concepts, and generalisations. Skills identified for teaching should be important to learners. Attitudinal goals need to reflect such items as lifelong learning behaviours to be developed within learners. I believe that knowledge of current events is necessary for its own values as well as for developing good citizens who can make vital personal decisions and be involved in decision making in the community.

CONTROVERSIAL TOPICS IN THE CURRENT EVENTS

Controversial topics in current events pertain to issues which are vital for pupil study. Parents and the lay public might become upset if certain issues are discussed in current events, an yet, here is where pupils might well engage in higher levels of cognition when evaluating what has controversy. In controversy, there is a lack of agreement among participants in terms of what should be done. We certainly advocate that pupils have ample opportunities to view and discuss, in depth, controversial issues. Which are selected controversial issues that the lay public might have difficulties in accepting as having value in current events?

1. The prolife and prochoice movements are very strong in the United States. The former advocates believe in an anti-abortion stance. Some if these advocates equate abortion rights with murder. The prochoice advocates would let a woman decide if she wants an abortion or not. These advocates feel and believe that the involved woman should have the right of making choices whether the unborn should be brought to full life or aborted.
2. Gun control laws and legislation. Here, the issue seems to be how much freedom should individuals have in purchasing fire arms. Those opposed to most or all gun control legislation believe that hunters and sportsmen should have their rights in purchasing and controlling use of guns. We have seen slogans on signs saying, 'If guns are outlawed, only outlaws will have them.' Another slogan observed stated,' Guns do not kill, only people kill.' Another statement is quoted from the United States Constitution which says, 'Citizens and militias should have the right to bear arms.' It is difficult to know what the Founding Fathers of the United States constitution had in mind when this was written. At that time a war for independence was being anticipated and fought with Great Britain to obtain

independence from the latter. Militias and citizens had firearms to fight the British.

The gun control advocates point to the high level of murders, robberies, and other crimes in society committed due to the use of fire arms. The United States leads all industrialised nations in crimes committed involving fire arm use.

3. amount of federal money to be spent on welfare and social legislation. Advocates of the free enterprise system are very strong in advocating that people should work rather than being on welfare. Strong advocates of the free enterprise system believe people should be moved off welfare and onto jobs. To balance the federal budget, the free enterprise advocates advocate cutting spending from the federal budget. When cutting spending, federal programmes involving welfare costs and other social programmes go by the wayside. Sometimes the following slogan is stressed by free enterprise people, 'Let's get government off of our backs and out of our pockets.'

Toward the other end of the continuum, advocates state that there are barely enough jobs available for present day workers; certainly there will not be enough jobs to move people off of welfare when discontinuing unemployment payments. Many jobs do not pay enough money to support individuals presently as well as for those who move off of welfare.

4. increased federal aid to education. There has been a slogan by government officials on 'Lets not throw money at problems.' This statement had been made to justify not spending federal money on social programmes.

Conclusion

Pupils need a quality current events programme so that each learner may be well informed. In a democracy, citizens need to be highly knowledgeable pertaining to happenings that occurs locally, statewide, nationally, as well as internationally. Definite objectives need to be achieved by learners in current events. These objectives should stress understandings, skills, and attitudes. Learning opportunities should come from diverse sources so that pupils may achieve the identified ends. The teacher may select learning opportunities as well as pupils should also be involved in choosing activities and experiences. A logical curriculum is inherent when the social studies teacher sequences chosen activities for pupils. He/she orders the experiences logically moving gradually from the easiest to the gradually more complex experiences for pupils. If learners are engaged in determining the curriculum with teacher guidance, a psychological current events programme is then in evidence. Perhaps, both approaches need to be emphasised, the logical and the psychological current events curriculum. Certainly, the teacher has been trained to teach social studies and therefore has the wisdom, education, and capability in decision making areas. Also, pupils have their needs, interests, and purposes and should then have opportunities to study what is perceived as being personally beneficial. We believe all people should be highly knowledgeable of current events. Why? Current events knowledge enriches the self and can make for improved decision making in the societal arenas. All persons are members of society and its deliberations. Choices need to be made and decisions implemented when people are involved in determining the kinds of institutions wanted and the type of society needed. Knowledge of current events is also good for its very own sake. We have known many people who feel and believe that knowledge for its own sake is important as well as interesting.

Learning opportunities need to be aligned with the stated objectives of current events instruction. A variety of activities need to be in the offing such as using daily newspapers and weekly news magazines, internet, software packages, CD ROMs, children's newspapers, and resource persons, among others. Methods of learning in current events include using inductive and deductive approaches, problem solving, debates, readers' theater presentations, interviews, reading from diverse reference sources, interaction with software packages and internet, E-mail messages, audio-visual aids, as well as contract systems of learning. Pupils possess diverse learning styles and need accommodation for these differences.

References

Bhaskara Rao, Digumarti, ed. (2000), *International Encyclopaedia of AIDs*, 11 Volumes. New Delhi: Discovery Publishing House.

Doll, Ronald C. (1982). *Curriculum Improvement: Decision Making and Process*, fifth edition. Boston: Allyn and Bacon, page 41.

Ediger, Marlow (1997). *The Modern Elementary School*. Kriksville, Missouri: Simpson Publishing Company, page 171.

Ediger, Marlow (1996), *Essays in School Administration*. Krirksville, Missouri: Simpson Publishing Company, page 11.

Ediger, Marlow (1996), 'Comparing the Attributes of Proactive and Reactive Principals, *Education*, Vol. 117, No. 2, page 279.

Ediger, Marlow (1986), *Social Studies Curriculum in the Elementary School*, third edition. Kirksville, Missouri: Simpson Publishing Company, page 160.

Ediger, Marlow (1998), 'Reading in the Social Studies Curriculum,' *Resources in Education*, ERIC #ED 423519.

Rathaiah, Lavu and Digumarti Bhaskara Rao, eds. (1997), *International Innovations in Education*. New Delhi, India: Discovery Publishing House.

Wesley, E.B., and W.H. Cartwright (1968). *Teaching Social Studies in Elementary Schools*. Lexington, Massachusetts: D.C. Heath and Company, page 284.

15

Social Studies, Integrating School and Society

Too frequently, school and society are separated from each other. This results in the social studies becoming quite abstract for pupils. Learners might then acquire much abstract knowledge in terms of facts, concepts, and generalisations, but meaning here is minimised. For learners to be able to use what has been acquired, they need to have numerous opportunities to apply what has been achieved. Application should be made in the real world of society so that two separate realms, school versus society, do not exist.

THEMATIC SOCIAL STUDIES

Frequently, social studies themes on farming are taught on the primary grade levels. In this case, the content was much more complex and complimented what had been taught and learned at an early time in the schooling of the involved learners.

The student and regular teacher had grown up on a farm: I (Ediger) as the university supervisor had also grown up on a farm. Our goal was to provide pupils with an understanding of where food and fibre originally come from. In the city of twenty five thousand in population where the school is located, no pupil in the sixth grade classroom in this writing comes from the farm.

Ten pupils of the 26 pupils had grandparents that were or are farmers.

The teaching team decided to focus upon grain farming in the thematic unit in social studies. A bulletin board consisting of the following pictures was developed with the caption 'How would you like to farm?'

1. a new tractor and combine containing air conditioned cabs, power steering and brakes, and hydraulic lifts.
2. a farmer plowing the farm land with a plow on a three point hitch attached to the tractor.
3. a farmer cutting the wheat with the self propelled combine.
4. a truck with a hydraulic lift containing a load of wheat.
5. an auger augerring the wheat from the truck to a large grain bin.

Pupils were encourages to discuss among themselves the pictures on the bulletin board prior to the beginning of the thematic unit of study. Learners were then ready to ask questions in class during time for social studies. The teaching team found that pupils were truly interested in the unit of study and had numerous questions to raise. The following questions, among others, were raised:

1. what was farming like without air conditioning on tractors and self-propelled combines? A committee of five pupils volunteered to secure information in answer to the problem area.
2. what kind of tractors and plows were available before hydraulic lifts entered the scene in American farming? Three pupils desired to obtain information pertaining to this question.
3. how was wheat cut prior to the days of the combine? Three learners wished to find answers to this question.
4. how was wheat gotten to a grain bin before trucks with hydraulic lifts, and augers were used? Four pupils volunteered to serve on a committee to get necessary information.

5. what uses are made of wheat? Four learners asked they could make a collage showing these uses.
6. how large are grain producing farms, such as wheat farms? Four pupils indicated interest in this problem area.
7. what is the value of land per acre used for growing wheat and other grains? Three pupils expressed interest in securing needed information. This involved all pupils in the class setting.

Reference sources were discussed in obtaining information for problem areas identified above. Pupils could check with the teaching team for additional data sources. Rules were developed and pupils evaluated to determine if these standards were properly followed. Committee members could show what had been learned in a variety of ways. The approach used was considered the best means of sharing information acquired, be it in concrete, semiconcrete, or abstract methods. Both the student and the regular teacher monitored pupil progress and on task behaviour. Progress reports were given to the entire class after each work session covering a block of time consisting of 100 minutes.

Committee one above reported on tractors which had umbrellas to shade the operator. These umbrellas were used in the 1940's through the 1960's. A strong wind might tear the umbrella and make it worthless. The hot air from the tractor's exhaust further added to the heat of the farmer driving the tractor. Generally no umbrellas were used on tractors during the 1920's and 1930's. Before that time, draft horses were used to pull farm implements. Temperature readings need to be warm and hot for grain to dry before it is harvested. Ninety to one hundred degree Fahrenheit readings are ideal. Pupils drew pictures of each stage of development pertaining to the use of draft horses to the modern tractor with an air conditioned cab. Each picture was accompanied by a cassette recording pertaining to content in the drawing. Sources of information came from senior citizens who had been farmers, farm journals covering the decades in the report, general encyclopaedias, and the basal text, among other sources.

Committee # 2 reported on the kinds of tractors and plows available prior to the use of hydraulic lifts on tractors. These pupil had gotten pictures of tractors which had a drawer to hook on implements rather than on a three point hitch and hydraulic lift. Illustrations of horse drawn equipment was also shown to classmates. Horse drawn plows had one shear for plowing whereas a large tractor today can pull nine shears and pull them more rapidly as compared to horse drawn plows. A tractor does not get tired but draft horses do.

Committee #3 had borrowed a video tape from an implement dealer to show how wheat was cut before the days of the combine. Thus a grain binder cut the wheat and made bundles with twine to encircle each bundle. Farmers then took each bundle of wheat to make a shock. Usually ten bundles made a shock. The bundles were later pitched onto a wagon and pitched into a thrashing machine to separate the wheat from the straw and chaff. The wheat left the thrashing machine and was—into a wagon or pickup truck. A senior citizen came to the classroom and brought illustrations and snapshots of binders thrashing bundles of grain. He told of the heavy labour involved as compared to a modern combine with an air conditioned cab cutting and separating the straw and chaff from the wheat, all in one operation. The senior citizen told of how hot it was to pitch bundles one after the other into a thrashing machine. Members of the committee pantomimed the pitching of wheat bundles into a thrashing machine. They also dramatised shocking of bundles to make a shock. The senior citizen showed first how bundles were shocked to make a shock of ten bundles. The dramatisations here were video-tape and then viewed and evaluated by classmates. A chart was made by committee # 3 on the steps involved in cutting wheat with a grain binder, shocking the bundles, pitching them onto a wagon pulled by a team of draft horses or a tractor, and then pitched into the thrashing machine.

Committee #4 found information on shoveling wheat by hand with a shovel prior to the days of grain augers. They collected pictures from three implement dealers who sold grain augers. One implement dealer invited the class to come to his place of business to view farm implements. One auger augerred grain for a distance of forty feet after it left the truck box which held the grain. The auger augers wheat at the rate of one hundred bushels per minute from the grain box in the truck to the grain bin. There is very little human effort involved in moving the grain at this rapid rate of speed. The truck with the wheat needs to be backed up properly so that the wheat can run into a small box and then be augerred into the metal grain bin. Pupils on committee #4 had secured pictures of different sizes of grain bins from the 1000 bushel capacity size of the 1940's to the 100,000 bushel capacity size of the 1990's. Every item of farm machinery becomes larger and more efficient, making it so that farm size increases much with the advent of modern farm machinery. Pupils in class were amased to notice the increased productivity of farms with less than two per cent of individuals involved in farming today as a way of earning a livelihood, as compared to 95 per cent in 1800. A tabulation chart was made by committee #4 to show farm size in decades from 1800 to the present time.

Committee #5 made a collage to show uses of wheat in making bread, rolls, cereal, flour, and livestock feed, among other uses. Pupils were interested in learning that much wheat is exported each year to Russia, China, Japan, India, and Egypt, among other nations. A world map was traced to show in colour major nations that import wheat for human consumption and animal feed.

Committee #6 traced a map showing major wheat producing regions and indicated average size of farms. The average sized of a wheat farm was 700 acres. This size was compared to a farm of the early 1800's which averaged ten acres. A statesman had mentioned in the early 1800's his concern for all the time spent in growing grain with so little to show for all the efforts. I, as the university supervisors of the student and regular teacher teaching the lesson, gave a short slide presentation of our being in the Middle East area of the world for two years, as classroom teachers, and in this lesson showing how wheat is sown by hand in rock filled soil near Bethlehem in the Holy Land. The wheat when ready is cut with a knife and made into small sheaves, encircled with a strand of grain, not binder twine. The wheat bundles are then placed on a thrashing floor, which is a cleared place in which donkeys may tread out the grain. A wooden handmade pitch fork is used to throw the straw and chaff into the air. The air or wind blows the straw and chaff away. A pan is then used to separate, even further, the wheat from the chaff by throwing the contents in the pan upward to allow the wind to do the separating. The slides showing wheat harvesting by hand in and near Bethlehem was compared with using modern methods of cutting and harvesting wheat. Pupils then in committee #6 drew sequential pictures to display in the hallway outside the classroom door showing how wheat was harvested by hand.

Committee #7 had visited a realty office to determine the price of wheat and grain land used for farming. They were amazed at the range of prices paid for the land. Very level land sold for 1,000 dollars an acre, unless it was located near where industrialisation was in evidence. Then farm land was out of reach of pocket books of farmers. Hilly land suitable for grain production sold for five hundred dollars an acre. This kind of farm land usually has terraces to prevent soil erosion. Pupils here showed pictures of sheet and gully erosion if land was not properly taken care of. Hilly land needed to have grass, trees, terraces, and strip cropping to prevent soil erosion. Some of this land should not be tilled but kept in grassland for grazing by beef and dairy animals. A county farm agent as a resource person in the classroom showed a filmstrip on proper methods of farming land to prevent soil erosion. Pupils were greatly interested in the need to have much farm land in grass and trees together with other soil erosion prevention methods when land is tilled.

Pupils asked the county farm agent about problems that prevents wheat and grain farmers from making a good living from farming. Answers given were the following:

1. weather conditions such as drought, late cold spells in spring, too much rain, hail, tornadoes, insects, weeds, and other natural phenomenon.
2. price of commodities such as too much wheat in a nation lowers the price, governmental policies such as grain embargoes against selected nations makes for excess holdings of wheat, reserve acreage of land in which land not tilled to support conservation purposes receives payments from the federal government thus lowering total production of grain, and farmers letting land lie idle on their own. Letting land lie idle or fallow made it richer in nutrients for the next crop year. The county farm agent left numerous bulletins with the teaching team and pupils on grain farming. These had illustrations as well as related abstract print to read.

As followup activities, pupils with teacher guidance recommended visiting an implement dealer's place of business. Questions were to be obtained to ask the implement dealer prior to the visitation by class members. Rules of conduct were developed cooperatively before making the excursion. On the implement dealer's lot were new John Deere tractors with air conditioned cabs. There were also two older tractors from 1955 and 1953 that did not have any air conditioning, but did have a place for an umbrella to shade the farm operator from the hot sun. These two tractors did not have a hydraulically operated three point hitch to lift plows and other farm implements out of the ground. Pupil could then see first hand how effective and easy it is to use a modern tractor with a three point hitch, hydraulically operated. Clear in back of the lot was an old combine from the early 1950's that did not have an air conditioned cab as compared to one new combine on the lot that had this modern convenience. The implement dealer said that grain binders and thrashing machines were very hard to locate. He stated that Old Order Amish in many cases still use these implements. The implement dealer also mentioned that at old settlers' reunions antique farm machinery was exhibited in large numbers, such as in early September in Mount Pleasant, Iowa with their annual Old Settlers' Reunion. The implement dealer told of how he watched his father shovel wheat by hand from a trailer/wagon into a grain bin. The implement dealer answered the questions raised by pupils in an understandable way.

Back in the classroom, a committee of pupils volunteered to write a thank you note to the implement dealer for his excellent help in teaching pupils.

A second follow-up activity stressed each pupil bringing to class an empty container pertaining to some food item made of wheat. These were displayed in the classroom, labeled into categories such as cereal of flour and displayed for other classes to see. Later, the empty containers were taken home by the pupil who brought them initially.

Third, illustrations from the bulletin board were taken down and related content written by a committee of five volunteers. The Illustrations and content were placed into booklet form and bound with plastic spiral. Learners might then pick the bound volume to read in teams or individually.

Fourth, the teaching team took pupils on an excursion to a grain farm. Here pupils saw a two ton truck with a grain box operated with a hydraulic lift. The farmer showed how the hydraulic lift operated. He showed his large tractor with a swivel in the middle. There were dual tires on the front wheels as well as on the rear wheels of this tractor. The large tractor had an air conditioned cab and a radio. Pupils took turns and got a ride on this tractor inside the cab. The grain farmer used no till farming and discussed why this method of farming was used. He had a large grain drill that was especially designed and built for no till farming. Pupils could hardly understand that one large tractor like this cost $110,000. They realised what a large investment was needed to engage in grain farming. Learners had previously heard in the classroom from the country farm agent tell of the risks involved in farming such as hail, excessive rain or a lack of it, costs of fertilizer, weed and insect control, low prices received for grain, among others. Thus, heavy hail can wipe out a crop of wheat and other grains in a matter of seconds!

Conclusion

Pupils should have ample opportunities to perceive the relationship of the school curriculum and the community. The two should be integrated, not separate entities. Too frequently, pupils fail to see how the social studies can become useful and functional. The model presented for this social studies unit can be applied to other themes and units of study. Concrete, semiconcrete, and abstract materials of instruction need to be implemented in teaching and learning situations so that meaning, interest, and purpose in learning are in evidence.

Objectives of instruction need to be carefully chosen. Learning opportunities need to guide pupils to achieve valuable objectives. They should assist each pupil to learn as much as possible. Quality evaluation techniques should be in the offing. Approaches to evaluation need to be valid and reliable.

16

MEASUREMENT AND EVALUATION IN THE SOCIAL STUDIES

As a skeptic in Ancient Athens, Georgias was to have stated that nothing could be known. If something could be known, it could not be communicated. If it could be communicated, it would not be understood. Drawing a corollary, attempting to determine how much pupils have learned in school appears to be baffling and even doubtful if it can be done. To be sure, there are many means to ascertain pupil achievement in school such as norm referenced or standardised and criterion referenced tests, port folios, performance tests, and authentic evaluation. Then too there are numerous kinds of test items that teachers may write such as true-false, multiple choice, matching, completion, and essay items.

Teachers, administrators, supervisors, and parents eagerly desire to know how well children are doing in school. And yet, many problems stand in the way of truly reporting what pupils have achieved.

The problem is further complicated when international comparisons are made. From data obtained for test results of diverse nations on the face of the earth, selected educators state that the United States is near the bottom of all industrialised nations whereas other educators will say that the US is doing very well in educating their children when apples are compared with apples and not with oranges. Thus the US has pupils in school for a longer period of time, agewise, than most other nations; therefore pupils in the US will not do as well as others due to more of the cream of the crop of pupils being tested in nations outside the US. The more pupils being tested in any nation, of course, will lower the average for that country. There is even disagreement if Scholastic Aptitude Test (SAT) scores have gone up or down during the ensuing years when viewing the population taking that test. Again as numbers increased over the years in pupils taking the test, the lower the average score will be. An increased number of lower achieving pupils are taking the test as numbers increase for the total number of test takers.

HOW SHOULD PUPILS BE MEASURED AND EVALUATED?

There are diverse philosophies in evidence pertaining to measuring and evaluating learner progress. Ediger (1997) discussed the following philosophies of evaluation:

1. Measurement driven instruction advocates the use of precise objectives in teaching and learning situations. Alignment of learning activities and appraisal procedures with the objectives is vital. A highly structured curriculum is then in evidence. Pupil progress is measured in terms of achieving the precise ends... .
2. Problem solving methods harmonise with that which exists in society. In the societal arena, persons identify and solve problems, be they major or minor. Teacher observation emphasising quality flexible standards are necessary to evaluate learner progress in problem solving... .
3. Pupils individually making choices in school, be it problem solving or other types of activities and experiences. Quality open-ended criteria need to be utilised by the teacher to appraise decisions made by pupils. With pupil choices and decision making in the curriculum, there are no valid tests for measuring progress for all learners in a classroom... .

Standardised tests have long been used to ascertain learner progress in the US. E.L. Thorndike (1874-1949) was a pioneer in developing standardised tests at the beginning of the twentieth century. He believed that whatever existed (such as academic achievement), existed in some amount. If it exists in some amount, it can be measured. This line of thinking is quite opposite of what the skeptic Georgias in ancient Athens believed. When standardised tests were developed, educators placed much faith in their results when measuring learner achievement.

Standardised achievement tests and their use one way to measure learner progress in academic areas. Educators like to believe that objectives results are in the offing when standardised tests are used to measure pupil achievement. However, there is subjectivity and judgment involved when determining which items should go into the test. Based on these subjective items used in pilot studies as well as in measuring pupil progress, statisticians develop means, medians, modes, standard deviations, and quartile deviations, among other terms familiar in statistics, to describe learner achievement. The concepts of validity and reliability are also brought in numerically to show objectivity in testing. In some cases, one would need to use the same scoring key to come up with the same results when two or more are evaluating a single pupil's test results. The two may not agree on which answer is correct from four responses on a multiple choice test. There certainly is much to disagree with when in pilot studies, items are finally chosen to be placed on the final form of a standardised test. Thus an item on the test discriminates the right way if the person responding correctly to a test item also has the largest number of items correct for the total test. Conversely, a test item probably should be eliminated if it discriminates the wrong way, e.g. the pupil secures a correct answer on a single test item and yet does poorly on the total test (item discrimination). Test writers use this approach to secure a large range in test results such as different pupils scoring all the way from the 99th to the first percentile on the same test. One of my graduate students in ED 680 Methods of Research stated that it was not moral to write a test that contains test items in the final form which is based on who secured the right answer, or the incorrect one for that matter. Validity has always been a problem in the use of standardised tests. There are no objectives that are available for teachers to guide instruction so that what is on the standardised test has related objectives of instruction available to the teacher.

Human beings always determine which items go in to the making of a test. Objectivity then does not exist in test writing. The same can be said in writing criterion referenced tests. Criterion referenced tests do have high validity due only to their alignment with the pre-determined behaviourally stated objectives which accompany. The pre-determined objectives have been written prior to instruction and each may be announced to learners before being emphasised in a lesson taught in the curriculum. Pupils then have security in terms of knowing what is to be learned as a result of instruction. It probably is no wonder that pupils can do well on a CRT since what is taught is contained in the behaviourally stated objectives and what is tested is also based directly upon the stated objectives. The objectives, learning opportunities, and appraisal procedures are indeed carefully aligned. Since the behaviourally stated objectives are stated with precision so that little if any latitude exists pertaining to their interpretation, factual knowledge is taught rather than stressing higher levels of cognition such as critical and creative thinking, as well as problem solving.

CRT's are not written to spread pupils out from high to low with a great range of achievement such as the 99th to the first percentile. Rather CRT's stress absolute standards such as either a pupil does or does not attain an objective as a result of instruction. Hopefully pupils will be successful and achieve many objectives. However, if test results are too high, were the test items excessively easy or did good teaching occur? CRT's are generally a part of state mandated systems of instruction. The objectives then have been written and developed on the state level and made available to teachers in the different public schools. Teachers are held accountable for pupils achieving these state mandated objectives.

A few states have mandated tests which need to be passed in order for pupils to obtain a high school diploma. Items on the test and the cut off point for passing the test are strictly arbitrary. Pilot studies may even be run here to develop validity and reliability data, but the subjective factors come first in that the test items are chosen and written by human beings and subject to change in terms of possessing perceived relevance. Truth is in the eye of the beholder. Then too, clarity in written test items is of utmost importance, otherwise lower reliability enters in. All written test items may stress reliability more so than validity. Why? Consistency of results is wanted from each pupil taking a test. If a pupil should receive a ranking on the tenth percentile when taking a test the first time and a ninetieth percentile the second time the same test is taken, where does the learner then stand in terms of achievement? To secure high reliability, test writers may sacrifice validity in test items written. When teaching Ed 680 Methods of Research to graduate students, the writer has frequently stated that he can write a test in which everyone in class gets all the answers correctly, such as a simple test on addition and subtraction facts. In taking the test over again, students should receive the same score on this easy test. However, validity would be completely lacking here for a test on course content on and in Ed 680 Methods of Research. How does one harmonise the concept of validity and reliability when writing test items in any class pupils are taking or have completed? Highly factual items on a history test such as names, dates, and places that pupils need to recognise on a multiple choice test could make for high reliability. Thus the chances are good that each pupil will remember the same name, date, and/or place in a test-retest situation to determine reliability. If guessing of each item occurred the first time the test was taken, the chances are that guessing will occur the second test taking time, lowering the reliability indeed. The problem then arises on writing test items which measure higher levels of cognition pertaining to course content. Which kinds of paper-pencil test items should then be written? Most norm referenced and criterion referenced tests contain multiple choice test items. If there are four responses given for and in a multiple choice item, the test taker must select which is correct. The chances are one in four that a pupil will guess the correct answer to any multiple choice item. Recognition of the correct response is needed. If true false items are used in testing pupil achievement, the chances are 50-50 that a pupil will guess the correct answer to a test item. To hinder guessing on test item, the teacher might have pupils correct that which is incorrect in a true-false test item. If a short answer or completion test is used to measure pupil progress, a short answer is needed which is highly factual. Higher levels of cognition then are omitted. Matching tests to tend to measure factual knowledge, rather than thinking about subject matter. Essay test items have the best chances of measuring higher levels of cognition as compared to any other teacher written test item. With essay items, the teacher needs to make certain they adequately delimited, but not factual in terms of responses wanted. Critical and creative thinking can be stressed by pupils when responding to essay test items. A major problem with the use of essay tests, is the lack of reliability when different evaluators assess pupils' responses to the same test. A major lack of agreement might even result by the evaluators in terms of which letter grade or score points to give to any response to an essay test item, let alone for all the rest of the responses of pupils. There is criticism that paper pencil tests do not measure what has been learned in school that is useful in the societal arena. Thus to make functional use in the societal arena of what has been learned in school is difficult to ascertain. Should schools not emphasise that which is relevant and useful in society?

John Dewey (1859-1952) was a strong advocate of problem solving stressed in the curriculum. The problems emphasised in the curriculum should be related school and society. Thus life-like, real problems would be identified by pupils with teacher guidance. Data and information from a variety of reference sources are gathered to obtain information for the problem. A hypothesis or tentative answer to the question or problem is then developed. The hypothesis is tested in a realistic setting. As a result, the hypothesis may need revising. In Dewey's problem solving philosophy of experimentalism, the pupils can know experience only, not the real world a it truly is. Advocates of experimentalism are not as certain of their answers as are behaviourists. The former emphasises the tentativeness of solutions and answers to problems whereas the latter believes that one can know specific knowledge that is absolute. The behaviourist believes in a limited amount of change in comparison to the experimentalist who accepts rapid change as reality in society. Teacher observation is necessary to appraise learner abilities to select problems in the curriculum, securing needed information in answer to the problem, developing a hypothesis, testing the hypothesis, and making revisions of the hypothesis if necessary. Authentic assessment is then in evidence. There could be major problems in inter-observer reliability when using observation to appraise learner performance. Thus raters might have a difficult time, for example, in agreeing if a pupil is truly proficient in problem identification. But should evaluation be objective? Existentialism, as a philosophy of education, stresses the subjectivity of each person's experiences. Each person is unique and has inner feelings, beliefs, and values. Reality then differs from one person to the next. Each person to be authentic makes choices in an open environment. What is chosen might well cause anxiety, tension, and even alienation. The moral person chooses what is ethical for the self and its consequences for others. Never is the self alone to be considered in choosing and making choices. If truth then resides in the beholder, how can objective subject matter be possible? The behaviourist may well argue that measurable achievement test results are possible from pupils. He/she may also argue that there is a body of knowledge that is essential for all to learn. The existentialist, however, believes in the authentic person that must make choices from among alternatives that are not objective at all. Choices may need to be made from competing evils or from competing positive situations. To be human, choices do need to be made, even in an absurd world! Subjective decisions are then continually made.

THE PORTFOLIO APPROACH TO EVALUATION

A compromise to the complex problems of evaluating pupil achievement tends to be the portfolio approach in appraising learner progress. There are states in the US such as Vermont which by law have adopted portfolio methods of evaluating each pupil's achievement. Many workshop then have been provided by colleges and universities for public school teachers and administrators in the development and implementation of portfolios. What is a portfolio? There will not be perfect agreement by any means in terms of a definition. A portfolio can contain norm and criterion referenced test results for a pupil. But more is involved since much concern has been shown by educators that test results do not, by any means, tell the entire story of a pupil's achievement. Portfolios then can contain written products of a pupil, involving a variety of purposes in writing. Art work of the involved learner may also be an important part of the individual pupil's portfolio. Snapshots of construction work projects may be salient for the portfolio. Cassette recordings of oral reports and committee endeavours can be useful indicators of a pupil's achievement. A portfolio can be quite cumbersome in terms of what is contained therein. It should be reasonable in amount as to test results, written work, and snapshots, as well as recorded items. Whoever evaluates a portfolio will have much to appraise. If several evaluate the portfolio, one may have difficulty in securing high reliability results from the different evaluators. Interscorer reliability could be high or low, on a continuum.

There are many assumptions that test writers and publishers of tests operate under in developing their measurement instruments. Walsh and Betz (1985) listed the following:

1. It is assumed (at least to some extent) that each item on a test and all the words in that item have similar meaning for different people...
2. A second assumption is that people are able to perceive and describe their self-concepts and personalities accurately...
3. It is assumed that people will report their thoughts and feelings honestly...
4. It is assumed that an individual's test behaviour (and actual behaviour) is rather consistent over time...
5. It is assumed that the test measures what it is supposed to measure...
6. It is assumed that an individual's observed score... on a test is equal to his/her true score (true ability)... plus the error...

Thus, test writers and publishers operate under numerous assumptions that cannot be verified in an objective manner. Subjectivity is certainly in evidence in these assumptions. Ediger (1997) wrote:

The teacher must be a good evaluator of pupil progress. Quality procedures of evaluation used by the teacher make it possible to plan sequential learning activities for pupils. Thus previous achievement provides opportunities for pupils to build upon what has been learned. Wholesome attitudes might well be developed by pupils if they are successful achievers. Each goal attained provides a building block for the next level of achievement.

Conclusion

There are numerous ways available to ascertain pupil achievement. Diverse specialists in measurement and evaluation list, among others, the following:

1. criterion referenced tests
2. standardised tests, also called norm referenced tests
3. personality tests
4. teacher observation
5. teacher written tests items, such as true-false, completion, multiple choice, matching, and essay tests
6. anecdotal records
7. sociograms
8. portfolios
9. interest inventories
10. file of completed projects of students, such as written work, to make comparisons of earlier versus later endeavours to notice progress Ediger (1995).

Finding appropriate means of evaluating pupil achievement presents numerous problems. Can appropriate approaches be found whereby educators can agree, in degrees, how well any one pupil is doing in school? Continuous experimentation must be in evidence for measurement and evaluation specialists to devise better approaches to determine each pupil's progress. Presently, there is much disagreement in terms of how pupils should be evaluated effectively to determine their progress. Educators must try continuously to find improved means of evaluating learner achievement. Hopkins and Stanely (1991) in writing about the paradox of testing wrote:

... Many people are opposed to measurement and evaluation, yet at the same time favour excellence, which is facilitated by and can be identified only through measurement and evaluation.

References

Bhaskara Rao, Digumarti (2000), *Teaching of Science*. Guntur, India: Nagarjuna Publishers.

Ediger, Marlow (1997), *Teaching Reading and the Language Arts in the Elementary School*. Kirksville, Missouri: Simpson Publishing Company, page 237.

Ediger, Marlow (1995), *Philosophy in Curriculum Development* Kirksville, Missouri: Simpson Publishing Company, page 102.

Ediger, Marlow (1997), *The Modern Elementary School*. Kirksville, Missouri: Simpson Publishing Company, pages 228-229.

Hopkins, Kenneth D., and Julian C. Stanley (1991), *Educational and Psychological Measurement and Evaluation*, sixth edition. Englewood Cliffs, New Jersey, page 5.

Walsh, W. Bruce, and Nancy E. Betz (1985), *Tests and Assessment, 309309* Englewood Cliffs, New Jersey, pages 17 and 18.

SOCIAL STUDIES IN TEACHER EDUCATION

Making the connections between the graduate class and the public school is a major objective of instruction. Thus, what is emphasised in Social Science in the Elementary should have direct application in teaching pupils in the elementary school. Each student in class selected a social studies unit taught in the elementary school and develop a teaching unit which followed selected criteria.

UNIT CONSTRUCTION

If two or more teachers taught the same unit title, they could volunteer to work collaboratively on this project. Strong emphasis was placed upon being able to connect the graduate course and the public schools where the unit will be implemented in teaching-learning situations.

After choosing the title for the social studies unit, participants chose objectives for pupil attainment in terms of knowledge, skills, and attitudes. There were social studies teacher-education textbooks and periodicals available in the classroom for reference use in planing the unit of study. Audio-visual aids were also available for teacher use. The classroom was quite busy when participants gathered needed information from the different reference sources. A few teachers based their unit on the present series of adopted textbooks that were used in teaching pupils. Most wanted to develop a completely new unit. There were selected elements that were emphasised in each unit. First, participants needed to stress balance among objectives in the social studies unit being worked on. Thus all three kinds of objectives needed to be in evidence—knowledge, skills, and altitudes. Even though some kind of balance was stressed in selecting objectives of instruction, selected educators were more subject centered in their teaching and thus stressed more of concepts and generalisations for pupils to acquire. A few believed strongly in skills receiving major emphasis in an ongoing social studies unit. A third group felt that quality attitudes for learner acquisition should receive primary stress. The author and instructor of Social Science in the Elementary School next stressed that students choose learning activities so that pupils may attain the chosen ends. The activities should guide pupils to make connections among the different social science disciplines which comprise the social sciences. These social science disciplines are history, geography, political science, anthropology, sociology, and economics, as a minimum. Learning activities need to meet selected criteria. The criteria include the following:

1. pupils must perceive relationships between and among subject matter emphasised from the diverse social science disciplines.
2. pupils must perceive connections between themselves and the subject matter taught and acquired.
3. pupils must perceive connections between themselves and their environment—the societal arena.
4. pupils must attain vital concepts and generalisations that come from each social science discipline in an integrated curriculum.
5. pupils must perceive how subject matter can be used in society.
6. pupils must develop skills pertaining to critical and creative thinking as well as problem solving.
7. pupils need to be able to work effectively with others in committees and in cooperative learning.

8. pupils need to be able to use diverse media and technology in the social studies.
9. pupils need to be responsible for their actions as well as amount and quality of work performed.
10. pupils need to learn to use time wisely.

Thus with the ten above listed guidelines, university students need to choose learning activities which will guide pupils in the public schools to attain vital objectives. The learning activities must be interesting, meaningful, purposeful, as well as provide for individual differences.

Optimal achievement from each learner is a must!

EVALUATION OF PUPIL ACHIEVEMENT

We emphasise the need to use a variety of evaluation procedures to appraise pupil performance. Each evaluation technique is a check on the results of other approaches used in appraising pupil performance. We stress that standardised test results should be used as diagnostic in that what a pupil answers incorrectly may be emphasised in a teaching-learning situation, if relevant. Graduate students when implementing the social studies unit understood the strengths and weaknesses of standardised tests in that they are one way to measure global achievement and yet the test items may lack validity to measure day to day objectives emphasised in teaching-learning situations.

Graduate students also evaluated the pros and cons of using mastery learning in the social studies. Precise objectives then written prior to instruction may stress trivia in the social studies. If objectives are stated in measurable terms, elementary pupils either do or do not attain these ends as a result of instruction. The either/or here have a tendency to limit what may be taught in an ongoing unit of study, especially if the teacher follows the measurably stated objectives sequentially as written. Subjectivity is involved when standardised achievement test writers are engaged in writing and finalising test items for pupils to respond too. Subjectivity is equally inherent when measurably stated objectives are written in mastery learning. What is salient in either case to write in a test in the eye of the beholder. Careful selection of each test item in mastery learning must harmonise and align with the measurably stated objective stressed in teaching-learning situations.

Additional kinds of evaluation approaches that graduate students wrote into their units of study included teacher observation. Graduate students tended to agree this could be one of the best procedures used to appraise learner performance in a social studies unit. They realised that one needs to be a good observer and use quality criteria to do the evaluating here. Among others, the following criteria were emphasised as being relevant in unit teaching:

1. securing the attention of learners.
2. guiding pupils to understand and attach meaning to subject matter acquired.
3. assisting pupils to select and solve relevant problem areas.
4. helping pupils attain sequence in ongoing experiences.
5. perceiving relevance in the social studies.

Graduate students analysed and studied the use of anecdotal records and their implementation in teaching learners and evaluating pupil progress. Subjectivity is involved in writing each entry for pupils on a day to day base. Each evaluation entry pertaining to appraising the learner in social studies achievement is dated. Comparisons can then be made of present entry levels with earlier ones to notice progress and achievement of a pupil. A major problem in using anecdotal records is to find time to write entries for all pupils in a classroom in order that an adequate number are available for each learner so that thorough comparisons can be made. Thus, graduate students realise the importance of adjusting the number written to the time available for a single classroom teacher. Anecdotal statements are records of observations made of each pupil so that less forgetting by the teacher is involved when evaluating pupil performance. Objective writing of each anecdotal statement is a must!

Rating scales may be used to assess learner achievement. Here, the social studies teacher lists criteria of important behaviours that pupils need to achieve in ongoing lessons and units of study. Behaviors listed depend upon what the teacher is emphasising in terms of objectives. The teacher then may rate pupils on a five point scale pertaining to each behaviour stressed in teaching learning situations. The teacher appraises in terms of how well he/she perceives the attaining of behaviours by involved learners. A teacher who advocates humanism as a psychology of instruction will desire pupils to appraise themselves in terms of the stated criteria.

A slight variation of rating pupils is to use a checklist approach. Again, the behaviours listed on the checklist depend upon what the social studies teacher is teaching at a specific time in an ongoing lesson or for a longer duration of time such as in a unit of instruction. With the checklist, instead of rating on a five point scale, the teacher checks which behaviours have not been satisfactorily attained by individual pupils. For example, how well did a specific pupil do in getting along with others in a committee setting? When recording learner results on either the rating scale or the checklist, there is less chance of a teacher forgetting how a pupil is doing at a given time. A separate sheet containing the behaviours for the rating scale and the checklist should be available for each learner. The teacher might then appraise each pupil on a separate sheet which can be filed for future reference. Comparisons may then be made with later evaluations after having used the rating scale or the checklist.

Teacher written test items have always provided data on how well pupils are attaining in the social studies. There are five common kinds of teacher written test items to which pupils may respond and reveal what has been learned. Each test items must be clearly written so that pupils may respond in a meaningful manner. These are the following:

1. true-false test items. As a variation, pupils may correct that part which is incorrect in the true-false item. By using this variation, guessing on the part of learners may be minimised.
2. multiple choice test items. Generally, a stem with four responses is indicated in a multiple choice test item. The stem must be grammatically correct with each of

the four responses, one of which is correct. All four responses should be plausible or rational.

3. short answer test items such as completion tests. Here, the pupils supplies a correct answer in context within a sentence.
4. matching tests whereby a pupil matches column A with column B in a correct matching. There should be more items in one column as compared to the others so that the process of elimination cannot be used extensively.
5. essay test items provide opportunities for pupils to compose in sentence and paragraph form answers to questions on the test. Here, pupil skill in organising and sequencing ideas is salient. The teacher may also evaluate learners progress in spelling, handwriting, punctuation, paragraphing, among other items in the mechanics of writing.

The portfolio concept has been a rather recent approach to show what pupils have learned. The teacher and/or pupils may choose what goes into the portfolio. Items such as test results, written work of the pupil, tape recordings of oral reports given, illustrations drawn, and snapshot of construction items, among others, may become an inherent part of the portfolio. Any responsible, interested person may view what is in the portfolio and appraise pupil performance.

GRADUATE STUDENT TEACHER INITIATION OF UNIT OF STUDY

Each graduate student initiated their planned social studies unit in the present school year if he/she was taking my (Ediger) class in Social Science in the Elementary School during the regular school year. If the graduate student was in my class during the summer session(s) he/she may then implement the planned unit of study during the next regular school year. I provided each graduate student with a stamped self addressed envelope to indicate what they would recommend should be changed in the planned unit, after its use in classroom teaching. Here, a summative approach was stressed in evaluating the effectiveness of the planned unit. I also provided a stamped self addressed envelope for students to indicate needed revisions in the ongoing unit as far as formative evaluation is concerned. My thinking was that students as regular social studies teachers should experience the utilitarian in teacher education classes. Thus what is stressed in the university teacher education curriculum can be used in teaching-learning situations for pupils in the public schools. Graduate students as teachers need to reflect upon what has been taught and think critically and creatively about making needed revisions. I tried to impress upon students in my class that curriculum development in the social studies is continuous and ongoing. A quality teacher must always attempt to improve instruction. The social studies curriculum is dynamic, not static. New technologies, modified ways of curriculum development, revised theories of learning, and additional research results emphasise that the teacher stay abreast of trends, issues, and philosophies of teaching.

All twenty graduate students responded with formative evaluation statements after having implemented the planed unit in the classroom. Comments made by graduate students were completely open-ended. The following comments were mentioned most frequently:

1. A added additional learning activities such as having a county agent come into the classroom and talk to pupils on sheet and gully erosion. The county agent brought a filmstrip to show to pupils pertaining to the ideas expressed orally.
2. I stressed a hands on approach in learning which was not in the planned unit such as pupils constructing a model farm scene pertaining to dairy farming. Cooperative learning was emphasised here in that pupils in a committee planned, made, and evaluated the model with may assistance.
3. I added learning activities to provide readiness for pupils to read content from their basal textbooks. Seemingly, learners needed more assistance with illustrations to attach meaning to what was being read.

Major reasons given for making changes in the unit developed in the graduate class were to provide for individual differences and guide each pupil to attain more optimally.

The summative evaluation statements I received from all graduate students who were in my class were equally revealing in terms of pupil learning. The following were typical comments written:

1. pupils need more opportunities to learn in depth and thus minimise survey teaching approaches. To do this we will add an excursion in my planned unit to a nearby place of pollution so that learners not only read about and view/discuss audio-visual materials on pollution but observe realistic situations. Pupils will then brainstorm how pollution of the stream near to the school could be minimised or eliminated.
2. at the end of the unit, pupil with teacher guidance discussed how achievement in current events could be increased. The discussion centered on having a world map placed on the bulletin board with string (coloured yarn) attaching the origin of the clipping with that containing place location on the world map. Several graduate student respondents indicated more planning time for teaching was necessary. Thus this teaching suggestion, as an example, needed adding to motivate learning and increase pupil achievement in ongoing lessons and units of study.
3. pupils did well in achievement as was planned in my unit in the graduate class Social Science in the Elementary School. Basically, I will make very minimal changes in this unit for the next school year when this unit will be taught again.

Conclusion

Most graduate students in the class Social Science in the School are practicing teachers. Practical experiences on the graduate level should better prepare these professionals to guide pupils in the public schools to achieve in as optimal manner as possible. Thus as one area of the curriculum, social studies units need careful preparation in terms of objectives, learning opportunities, and evaluation procedures. Teachers need to assess thoroughly each specific part of the unit of study being developed, prior to its implementation. Hopefully, public school pupils will learn as much as possible on an individual basis. Teachers need to reflect adequately upon what has been taught so that needed modifications can be made in formative and summative evaluation.

References

Bhaskara Rao, Digumarti, ed. (1998), *Teacher Education in India*. New Delhi, India: Discovery Publishing House.

Ediger, Marlow and Digumarti Bhaskara Rao (2000), *Teaching Mathematics Successfully*. New Delhi, Discovery Publishing House.

18

Restructuring the Social Studies (A Public Debate)

Leading social studies educators are seated in front of the auditorium; each is ready to present his/her recommendations pertaining to restructuring the social studies curriculum. A large audience of approximately 500 people are eager to hear each presentation in hopes of developing a quality, new social studies curriculum for the elementary grades and hopefully make the new curriculum K-12 in sequence. The moderator has now completed introducing each distinguished social studies educator. Social studies educator #1 is ready to give a prepared report on the kind of social studies curriculum all pupils need in order to be functionally literate as well as achieve optimally in social studies.

Social studies educator #1. For pupils to do well, we need to identify the basics in social studies. Unless this is done, pupils will be wavering and not know in what direction to go in learning. Once the basics have been chosen and implemented in instruction, pupils will have key facts, concepts, and generalisations to achieve. The social studies teacher must then arrange sequentially the objectives pupils are to attain. Why have pupils done poorly in the past in social studies achievement? Little effort has been put forth in selecting goals that are vital for pupils to achieve. These goals must represent basic knowledge and skills that pupils should learn. There is too much disagreement among social studies teachers as to what should be taught. If national goals, like Education 2000, as well as state mandated objectives have been carefully selected in social studies for pupils to achieve, through instruction we can have pupils reach the top in social studies achievement internationally. The National Governor's Conference identified six lofty goals (The National Education Goals Panel 1991); Goal #4 reads as follows: 'By the Year 2000, US students will be first in the world in science and mathematics.' Why not add social studies to that list of accomplishments?

Also, there are basics locally that need to be selected in social studies for pupils to achieve. Lets have our committees busy studying which basics learners should achieve in social studies. These basics when agreed upon should provide the structure or core curriculum in social studies. For example, if pupils understand that 'society is continually changing' as a theme in historical units of study, then content can be presented by the teacher which will assist pupils to relate the new with the old in subject matter as well as achieve additional objectives emphasising the basics. If pupils in geography learn that sedimentary, igneous, and metamorphic represent three major classifications of rock, then new basic content will be that much easier to master. The new vital content is *related* to the basics which were mastered. I do not understand how any social studies teacher can teach without emphasising the basics. I think our teaching will be much more effective if the basics are identified and taught to pupils. Why waste time teaching trivia in social studies? All too frequently that is what happens when educators and others have not selected basic content for all pupils to achieve. Former President Reagan and his Secretary of Education William Bennett continually stated that pupils should learn the basics.

Teaching social studies becomes more professional once the basics have been identified. A sower (the social studies teacher) that goes out to sow will then reap not thirty nor sixty fold, but one hundred fold. Why? Time spent in teaching social studies has been spent on the basics, not upon the irrelevant.

Social studies educator #2. I agree with much that my friend here has presented, but it does no go far enough in emphasising a quality social studies curriculum. What do I disagree with? We need to state the basics in measurable terms. After instruction, we can measure if a pupil has/has not achieved each precise objective. Then too, the social studies teacher should state, prior to instruction, what is wanted from pupils in terms of learning from a lesson or unit of study. I see no reason for keeping pupils in the dark a to what they are to learn. This needs to be communicated in a clear, concise manner. Vagueness has no role to play in teaching-learning situations in social studies. Measurably stated objectives, announced clearly by the social studies teacher to pupils before learning opportunities are implemented, will assist learners to achieve as well as possible. Evaluation to determine pupil achievement needs to be aligned with the measurably stated objectives. Validity and reliability are then in evidence. Pupils achieve poorly in social studies if the evaluation techniques are not matched with the precise objectives. Pupils do not need to guess what they will be evaluated in; this was announced to pupils by the social studies teacher prior to instruction.

Measurably stated objectives on the national level (Education 2000) or the state level must be written with precision. The precise objectives emphasise what is vital and significant to learn. Never shirk in choosing objectives that are truly important in social studies. Locate evaluation techniques that measure what is stated inside each objective. It is the social studies teacher's role to teach toward the objective. Why should precision be emphasised in writing objectives in social studies? The aligned evaluation techniques with the precise objectives of instruction will then be used to ascertain pupils progress in measurable terms. Results of pupil progress in social studies can then be clearly communicated to parents. Parents do not need to guess how well their offspring is doing in social studies achievement. Numerical results must be used to report pupil progress to parents. This is what parents accept and understand. If a pupil receives an 'A grade' in social studies, this says nothing at all. Nor does it say anything about a pupil's achievement in social studies if the following categories appear on a report card—understands vital concepts, thinks creatively, solves problems, and has good attitude. These are vague areas. If letter grades are given for each category, it fails to communicate how well a pupil is doing in social studies.

With measurably stated objectives and pupil results form testing, we get numerical results from each learner. A pupil then is on a certain percentile level, a specific standard deviation above or below the mean, and/or a particular quartile deviation. Numerical results communicate very clearly to parents in terms of their offspring's achievement in social studies. Effective Schools and Classrooms (1985) research results has shown time and again how well pupils do in social studies with the approaches in teaching and learning I have indicated.

Social studies educator #3. I disagree completely with my two predecessors as to the kind of social studies curriculum any school should desire. I have heard no mention made of the learner's interests and purposes in learning in either presentation. Are they not interested in the pupil who will be taught? Social studies is more than choosing the basics for pupils to acquire. It is also more than measuring and reporting to parents what the measurement results say. Both approaches can truly emphasise the insignificant and the unimportant to the parent and the pupil in the social studies curriculum. Thus we need a child centered curriculum in social studies. It is the pupil that will do the learning (Ediger, 1998 ERIC).

The late Carl Rogers, humanist educator, told of his starting public school as a child with great interests in moths. No one including the teacher could come close to Carl Roger's knowledge and interests in moths. There were children in school who made fun of these interests. The teacher, however, showed much interest in the young Carl Rogers and his purposes in learning. The teacher assisted him to increase his interests and goals in learning. Notice, the teacher helped the pupil build on his interests. The teacher did not lecture to the pupil on the basics nor in testing for progress in social studies learning. Dr. Rogers, as we all know, became a great psychologist and writer in educational psychology. His thesis was that the interests of pupils should provide the basis for all instruction. Good social studies teachers I have observed over the years find out what pupils are interested in and bring these interests into each lesson and unit taught. Learning stations with fascinating materials set up in the classroom by pupils and the teacher guide learners to become curious and develop an inward desire to learn. Pupils may then choose sequential tasks to complete from the learning stations, omitting those not possessing perceived purpose.

Pupils are naturally curious in social studies as young learners. The curiosity seems to leave them as they move through the public school years. This lack of interest is due to teachers forcing the basics upon pupils as well as the continuous emphasis placed upon testing to find out what pupils have learned. Rather, we need to have stimulating materials in the classroom to encourage intrinsic motivation among pupils for learning in social studies. Thus a multimedia approach in teaching assists pupils to develop or remain curious in learning. But the emphasis must be upon the pupil with teacher guidance deciding upon what is of interest to the former.

If we permit much pupil input into the curriculum, learners will bring many, many items of interest to school which stresses social studies. Achievement and progress in social studies will be spontaneous and intrinsic (Ediger, 1998, ED—ED420393).

Social studies educator #4. I am shocked that all my predecessors who are supposed to be specialists in teaching social studies have left out the role of parents in developing the social studies curriculum. Research data indicates how important parents are in helping their children learn. Time and again, research indicates that if parents assist their children in learning, achievement continues to rise. Teachers, administrators, and supervisors must learn to work cooperatively with parents to increase pupil achievement. Too often, parents have been written off in being actively involved in the social studies curriculum. Why? Is it because we fear parental input into the curriculum? Or, do we feel parents have nothing to offer? This is indeed a sad situation. Parents are responsible for their children. They have been the first teachers of their offspring. Time and money has been invested by parents in their children. If parents lack parenting skills, is it not up to the schools to provide the needed knowledge and skills? Let us educate parents as needed. We need parental input into the social studies. Why? Parents need to support, be highly knowledgeable, and feel ownership in the social studies curriculum. Parents should come to visit the classroom where their children are being taught. They should have continuous contact with the teacher and school and not during the traditional parent-teacher conferences only. Coming to open house once a year does little to involve parents in the social studies curriculum of their children. Have we ever asked parents to serve as volunteers in our schools? Have parents ever been consulted as to which objectives their children should achieve in social studies? If we implement a needs assessment programme to secure input from parents, we would then be empowering parental roles in curriculum development. We as educators need to get busy and carefully design a set of objectives in social studies for all parents to respond to. Parents may then rate on a five point scale the worth of each objective to be emphasised in teaching and learning. The results form this survey secure information in terms of what parents want to have emphasised in social studies lessons and units of study. Teachers and administrators must also respond to the survey. From the needs assessment programme, we can obtain objectives that are truly worthwhile to emphasise in the classroom. When parents have input into developing the social studies curriculum, they will support their children more so in learning as well as support the goals of the school. Joyce Epstein (1995) a co-director of the Centre on Families, Communities, and Children's Learning is a leading advocate in getting parents involved in their child's education. I agree wholeheartedly with her in having parents improve in their parenting skills, communicating with the schools, volunteering their services in school, learning to teach pupils at home with teacher guidance, and assisting in decisions made pertaining to their child's education and school curriculum. Those are excellent ways of improving the social studies curriculum!

Social studies educator #5. I cannot believe what I am hearing at this debate. All we have heard is teach the basics, have precise objectives for teaching, let the pupil decide what to learn, and permit parents to determine what should be taught in social studies. My friends, let us wake up to what social studies is all about. Let us wake up to what life itself is all about. In the social studies curriculum and in society, there are problems that need to be identified and solved. What is perceived to be the basics today may become outdated tomorrow. What can be measured may not represent that which is important to learn. What the child wishes to learn may be frivolous. What parents want to have emphasised in the social studies curriculum might well represent the irrelevant. Thus we need to stimulate pupils to identify and solve problems within ongoing lessons and units of study in social studies. Cooperatively, learners with teacher assistance need to choose problems to solve which are perceived by pupils as being significant. Significant problems make for interest in learning. Interest then makes for effort that pupils put forth in learning social studies. Why do we struggle to motivate pupils by forcing them to learn? We as social studies teachers can do much better than that with problem solving procedures used in teaching. The interest factor alone propels pupils in desiring to learn. Then too, problem solving will always be important regardless of the involved subject matter used. Subject matter may become outdated due to new research findings in social studies, but problem solving is here to stay. Let us not focus so much on the subject matter of social studies, but processes which pupils are to learn.

Once pupils have adequately delimited the problem in social studies, they may select activities which will obtain information directly related to the problem. Notice, we do not minimise subject matter acquisition, rather the subject matter is instrumental and used to solve problems. The subject matter must be critically evaluated by pupils to notice its accuracy, thoroughness, as well as its relevance in solving a problem. A hypothesis results which is tentative, not absolute. Additional subject matter needs to be attained to check the hypothesis. The subject matter comes form using a variety of media, including a hands on approach to learning. Thus social studies experiments and demonstrations are very important activities for pupils to gather information and to check hypotheses. Creative thinking is needed to guide pupils in achieving new ways of solving problems in social studies. Friends, I think we are missing the boat in the teaching of social studies unless problem solving is at the heart of the curriculum. Higher levels of cognition are emphasised here with process objectives stressed in social studies teaching.

Let us not forget the late John Dewey (1916), America's foremost and widely quoted educator, who continually emphasised problem solving as being the heart of the curriculum. Literature in the field of social studies pedagogy can assist teachers in emphasising problem solving in teaching-learning situations. The National Council for the Social Studies (NCSS) publishes a monthly periodical entitled *Social Education*, among their many other publications, which contain many articles on problem solving in the social studies. Let us emphasise what is truly important in the social studies curriculum as well as what is salient in society and that is problem solving.

Social studies educator #6. I agree much what my predecessors has just said. Processes such as problem solving are significant in social studies and yet the reasons are not holistic enough in terms of work what a social scientist does. I recommend we observe what social scientists do in obtaining knowledge and then base our objectives on those observed processes. It is true that knowledge changes much and new subject matter in social studies is coming to us in astounding amounts. Thus we as social studies teachers must emphasise skills and processes in teaching that *social scientists* recommend and do in a functional situation. There have been numerous studies made of the approaches social scientists use in acquiring relevant facts, concepts, theories, principles, and generalisations. It is ridiculous for teachers to teach pupils and then use methodology that does not relate to the world of social studies and the world of social scientists. Pupils in ongoing lessons and units need to use the same methods of acquiring information as does the social scientist. Thus historians use primary and secondary sources of information. The content studied is analysed, evaluated, and synthesised to arrive at conclusions as objectively as possible. Learners in the school setting should also learn to use the methods of securing information that a professional geographer, a political scientist, an economist, a sociologist, and an anthropologist use.

Social studies educator #7. I agree with much of what my two predecessors have said. I believe that a major element is missing here and that is to set high standards for all pupils to achieve in social studies. These standards need to be elevating and challenging to all pupils. Learners need to be grouped in a heterogeneous manner, not segregated based on ability. In a heterogeneously grouped classroom, pupils can learn from each other regardless of IQ and ability levels. All pupils then, regardless of ability and achievement levels, may receive sophisticated knowledge in social studies. Too frequently in the past, the slow learner received an inferior social studies education from teachers who were not too well motivated in teaching learners. We have eliminated those situations if tracking of pupils has been omitted completely. Tracking segregates and destroys interest in learning in social studies. Little is expected of pupils in the lower tracks. So, let us place pupils of mixed achievement levels in a classroom and have high expectations for all. Research states again and again that pupils in heterogeneously grouped classrooms achieve better than in a homogeneously grouped room of pupils. Tracking is undemocratic in that we have better teachers teaching social studies in homogeneously grouped classrooms of gifted pupils as compared to those classrooms having pupils of lesser talents. We can provide additional assistance to those pupils who find it difficult to keep up with the fastest learners in social studies.

Low achievement tends to come from lower teacher expectations for some pupils as compared to others. What chances do pupils have in the future when they are placed in lower tracks of school? What chances do pupils have in the future when social studies teachers have low expectations for these learners today? Let us then move away from this negative practice of tracking pupils for instruction in social studies (Oakes, 1990).

Chairperson of the debate. I think that we can see rather wide disagreement among educators as to what makes for a quality social studies curriculum in our public schools. The following points of view were given in moving from what is to what should be in the social studies:

1. A basic approach in determining what should be taught in social studies. These essentials provide a framework for what pupils are to learn in social studies. I well remember when pursuing the Ph.D. degree in social studies education how the professor stressed the eminent William Chandler Bagley's (1934) strong emphasis upon teaching the basics in social studies as well as other curriculum areas. Advocates of the basics are very much with us as social studies educator number one indicated.

2. a measurably stated objectives approach whereby precise objectives would be chosen in social studies for pupils to attain. The late B.F. Skinner (1979), Rebert Mager (1972), and all behaviourists in psychology, advocate stating each objective in social studies in measurable terms. The teacher can then determine if pupils are/are not successful in learning after instruction has taken place.

3. pupil involvement in developing the social studies curriculum. Here, the emphasis is upon pupils individually being involved in deciding upon objectives, learning opportunities, and evaluation procedures in social studies. The individual pupil decides upon working individually or within a committee. The task selected by the learner with teacher guidance may/ may not involve problem solving. Learning content for its own sake might also be salient, based on pupil interest. This should certainly *empower* the learner in the social studies.

4. parental involvement in helping to shape the social studies curriculum. In a democracy, we should not leave out those who will be affected by the decisions made by educators. Much research has and will continue to be conducted to show what affect parents have on their child's achievement. A needs assessment procedure may involve parents rather thoroughly in developing the social studies curriculum.

5. a problem solving social studies curriculum in which processes, not subject matter, receive primary emphasis. Problem solving truly is important. I well remember the first home my wife and I bought. There were so many problems to be solved such as how to finance the buying of the house, what kind of house to buy, what size of house to purchase, and the problems went on endlessly. One of my professors stated that his major problem in life so far had been who to marry.

   When studying all the changes in social studies content that is new and replaces the old, it is truly astonishing. Wars, inventions, changes in state and national government, among other items, add to the knowledge that we have about social studies! We do live in a fascinating era where new knowledge in social studies abounds. Problem solving as a process and skill seemingly remains highly important amidst the changing knowledge base.

6. the methods of the social sciences emphasised in ongoing lessons and units in social studies. Since this debate focused upon what kind of a social studies curriculum to stress in our public schools, perhaps social studies educator #6 truly hit at the heart of our discussion. Certainly, the methods used by social scientists are central to the teaching of knowledge, skills, and attitudes.
7. high standards for pupils to attain in social studies so that optimal achievement is a goal for all. Tracking and segregating pupils need to be avoided in social studies. Certainly, we must stress democratic tenets in our classrooms. Now are there any questions from the audience?

Audience participant #1. I would like to address my question to social studies educator #3. How can pupils know what is important to learn in social studies? They have not had the training and education that teachers have had. I just cannot see how we can have pupils follow their own interests and whims in social studies.

Social studies educator #3. If you noticed in my presentation, I stated that pupils *with teacher guidance* should make decisions on what the former is to learn. I did not leave the social studies teacher out of teaching and learning situations. The teacher is there to assist, guide, and help pupils. For example, if a contract system of instruction is used, the pupil decides upon which tasks to pursue within the contract he/she agreed to fulfill. Here, the teacher encourages and enables the learner to pursue worthwhile goals in social studies. The pupil is rather heavily involved in developing the social studies curriculum because he/she will do the learning If the teacher decides what pupils are to learn, the learner will turn off and out of what is being presented by the teacher. It is no wander that pupils fail to achieve well in social studies. Arthur Combs (1972), a well known educational psychologist, advocates pupils being involved in determining the objectives, learning opportunities, and evaluation procedures in the social studies curriculum. Otherwise, the teacher is at the centre of the stage in deciding upon what pupils are to learn. Pupils lack purpose for achievement in these situations. It is the pupil, not the teacher, who is to do the learning.

Audience Participant #2. My question is directed to social studies educator #5. I am leery about pupils identifying questions and engaging in problem solving. I am a former teacher and my experiences have been that pupil attention span is too short to truly engage in the identification and solving of problems. This is a lengthy and drawn out process. I would rather have the teacher determine objectives, learning opportunities, and appraisal procedures for pupils in social studies. This goes back again to teachers being educated and trained to teach pupils in social studies. Our teachers are better educated than ever before with many possessing masters degrees and beyond in the teaching of social studies.

Social studies educator #5. It is no wonder that pupils, when adults, enter the world of work and cannot think well to meet requirements at the work place or at home if the social studies teacher teaches as you advocate. Teachers must assist pupils to engage in flexible steps of problem solving and that won't be easy. Easiest it is if the teacher lectures and spoon feeds pupils social studies facts in ongoing lessons in social studies. I cannot and will not buy that outdated approach in teaching. Lets have a learning environment, rich with materials and technology, whereby pupils become curious and start selecting problems to solve. You know as well as I that life itself consists of identifying and solving problems, be it in social studies or in the larger societal arenas. The social studies curriculum must consist of what is truly important and that is for all pupils to be good problem solvers.

Audience participant #3. My question is directed to social studies educator #1. Do you have a list of the basics in social studies that pupils should learn? It sounds good to talk about the basics in social studies, but no one knows what these are. It seems to me if you have truly selected the basics for pupils to learn, you would be famous and maybe even wealthy, as far as society are concerned. All trivia could then be avoided in teaching; only what is salient would be emphasised.

Social studies eductor #1. I detect a note of sarcasm in your question. Lets be serious in raising questions and making comments. We as teachers must always view content in social studies with the intent that what is taught is truly essential for all pupils. I do this continuously and ask myself the question, 'is what I am preparing for teaching vital for pupil learning?' If it isn't, I call that subject matter from my teaching. There is so much for pupils to learn in social studies; shouldn't teachers select what is basic for all pupils to learn? It is foolish to think otherwise.

Audience participant #4. I wish to ask a question of social studies educator #2. I feel that teaching becomes a joke when the measurably stated objectives are announced to pupils prior to teaching. We teach toward the precise objectives and then we evaluate to notice if pupils have achieved these same objectives. That certainly sounds mechanical as a method of teaching. Will pupils learn anything but specific facts under those conditions?

Social studies educator #2. I do not think that you understand basic assumptions of the measurably stated objectives movement. Clarity in stating objectives is necessary; otherwise we do not understand, as teachers, what we are teaching to pupils. Vagueness and uncertainty are there unless we state our objectives in measurable terms. We have no basis for choosing our learning activities in social studies unless the objectives are precise. How can we possibly evaluate unless teachers assess learner achievement against the stated objectives? Validity and reliability are possible in measurement if we align the measurement procedures with the stated objectives; otherwise our evaluation procedures miss the mark in deciding what pupils have learned.

Audience participant #5. I would like to direct my question to social studies educator #4. There are so many excellent statements of objectives in social studies for pupils to attain. This include the standards developed by the National Council for the Social Studies. Why should we waste time in having parents respond to a questionnaire in helping teachers determine what should be taught and what pupils should learn? Why can we not just enlist parents in helping to educate pupils as well as support the gals of education? I realise the importance of the home and school working together for the good of the offspring.

Social studies educator #4. I believe you are talking about indoctrinating parents to accept what has been worked out ahead of time for pupil learning. You need to realise the importance of democracy in the school and community setting. How can we leave an important group out of decision making in working on the social studies curriculum? There is so much research available that indicates how important parents are in their child's education. Let us then obtain the knowledge, interests, and purposes of parents in developing the best social studies curriculum possible for their children. Parents want the best for their offspring. They want their children to become proficient, knowledgeable, skillful, and possess good attitudes in social studies and in all curriculum areas. I agree here with parental input and definitely desire their assistance to guide optimal pupil achievement.

Audience participant #6. I wish to address my question to social studies educator #6. I get the impression when social scientists emphasise objectives in social studies for children to achieve that the moral, ethical, and feeling dimension of human beings is omitted. We are all human beings and hopefully we can feel with others in times of happiness as well as despair. There are so many disasters due to nature such as floods, hurricanes, cyclones, and earthquakes, among others. Unless human beings assist and aid each other we may not survive. Then too, subject matter in social studies may place heavy stress upon pupils studying mass means of destroying each other such as in weapons of war. I believe less emphasis should be placed upon pupils studying wars and military endeavours and more stress upon altruistic concerns and needs of human beings.

Social studies educator #6. I appreciate your concerns in emphasising humanitarian effort in the social studies. I recommend that adequate time be devoted in our lessons and units in social studies to themes of morality and ethics. Other curriculum areas may also stress the human dimension of individuals assisting each other in altruistic ways. However, we need to remember that pupils have many relevant content objectives to achieve in social studies. Depth learning indicates that time on task is important so that each pupil achieves as much as possible in the social studies curriculum.

Chairperson. We have time for one more question from the audience and then our time will be up for this session.

Audience participant #7. My question is addressed to the last presenter. Your entire presentation emphasised setting high standards in social studies for all pupils to achieve in a heterogeneously grouped classroom. You also emphasised that all pupils in that classroom should achieve in a similar manner so that sophisticated social studies knowledge is available to all, not just for the talented and gifted. Don't you respect individual differences in the classroom whereby learners are different in achievement in social studies? The gifted and talented need a more rigorous social studies curriculum with higher academic standards than do the slow and average achievers. We need to guide all pupils to attain optimally. Individual differences among learners exist including full inclusion of the handicapped in the classroom. With diversity in the classroom, we certainly need a multicultural social studies curriculum.

Audience participant #7. I do not agree on segregating pupils based on ability levels. Democratic tenets say that we must have all pupils obtain sophisticated knowledge in social studies so that they are not hindered in achievement as compared to those possessing increased ability levels. We have under estimated the achievement of what former were called the slow learners. They can learn along with others in a mixed ability classroom in teaching social studies. With ample opportunities in cooperative learning, pupils of different ability levels can assist each other in learning. They may also learn to work harmoniously with other pupils in cooperative learning. Therefore, let us avoid segregating pupils in the classroom.

References

Bagley, Willaim Chandler (1934), *Education and Emergent Man.* New York: Ronald Press Company.

Combs, Arthur (1972), *Educational Accountability: Beyond Behavioral Objectives.* Washington DC: ASCD.

Dewey, John (1916), *Democracy and Education.* New York: Macmillan Company.

Ediger, Marlow (1998), 'Caring and the Elementary Curriculum', ERIC—ED422168.

Ediger, Marlow (1998), 'Character Education and the Elementary Curriculum, ERIC—ED420393.

Epstein, Joyce L. (1995), School/Family/Community Partnerships. *Phi Delta Kappan*, May, 701-712.

Mager, Robert (1972), *Goal Analysis*. Belmont, California: Fearon Publishers.

National Education Goals Panel (1991), *The National Education Goals Report: Building a Nation of Learners*. Washington DC: National Eduction Goals Panel.

Oakes, J. (1990), Lost Talent: *The Underparticipation of Women. Minorities, and Disabled Persons in Social Studies*. Santa Moncia, California: The Rand Corporation.

Skinner, B.F. (1979), *Beyond Freedom and Dignity*. New York: Alfred A. Knopf.

Squires, David, and others (1985). *Effective Schools and Classrooms*: A Research-Based Perspective. Alexandria, Virginia: ASCD.

INDEX